Kant's Practical Philosophy

Kant's Practical Philosophy

From Critique to Doctrine

Gary Banham

Research Fellow in Transcendental Philosophy
Manchester Metropolitan University

First published 2003 by
PALGRAVE MACMILLAN
Houndmills, Basingstoke, Hampshire RG21 6XS and
175 Fifth Avenue, New York, N.Y. 10010
Companies and representatives throughout the world

PALGRAVE MACMILLAN is the global academic imprint of the Palgrave Macmillan division of St. Martin's Press, LLC and of Palgrave Macmillan Ltd. Macmillan® is a registered trademark in the United States, United Kingdom and other countries. Palgrave is a registered trademark in the European Union and other countries.

ISBN 0–333–99399–3 hardback

This book is printed on paper suitable for recycling and made from fully managed and sustained forest sources.

A catalogue record for this book is available from the British Library.

Library of Congress Cataloging-in-Publication Data

Banham, Gary, 1965–
    Kant's practical philosophy : from critique to doctrine / Gary Banham.
        p.   cm.
    Includes bibliographical references and index.
    ISBN 0–333–99399–3
    1. Kant, Immanuel, 1724–1804—Ethics.   2. Ethics, Modern—18th
    century.   I. Title.

B2799.E8B275 2003
170′.92—dc21
                                                                2002193091

10   9   8   7   6   5   4   3   2   1
12   11   10   09   08   07   06   05   04   03

Printed and bound in Great Britain by
Antony Rowe Ltd, Chippenham and Eastbourne

For All My Polish Friends
with Gratitude

Contents

Acknowledgements ix

Introduction 1

1. Kant's 'Pre-Critical' Ethics 8

2. Freedom and the Ends of Reason 37

3. The Supreme Principle of Morality 64

4. The 'Fact' of Reason and the *Summum Bonum* 93

5. Radical Evil and Moral Redemption 118

6. Possession, Property and Contract 152

7. The Ends of Virtue 181

8. The Final Ends of Practical Philosophy 212

Notes 239

Bibliography 259

Index 265

Acknowledgements

The thoughts underlying this work have been gestating for some time and versions of the general conception or parts thereof have been presented to a conference on Ethics and Time at Lancaster University, the Summer Seminar Series at Manchester Metropolitan University, the students of Parrs Wood Adult Education Centre, the Philosophy Seminar at Bolton Institute and the exchange programme between Manchester Metropolitan University and the Institute for Philosophy and Sociology at the Polish Academy of Sciences. I would like to thank participants on these occasions for helpful comments on certain points especially Rachel Jones, Adel El-Beik, Suzanne Stern-Gillet, Jim Urpeth and Agata Bielik-Robson. The writing of the work has been helped by my appointment as a Research Fellow in Transcendental Philosophy at Manchester Metropolitan University and I would like to thank my colleagues for providing me with a supportive environment for research. My thanks should also go to Howard Caygill for judicious advice and general inspiration, to John Protevi for encouragement and useful comments, to Heather Gibson for her support for this project, Joe Whelan and Mary Naughton for supererogatory hospitality and to Anastatazja Dwulit and Kasia Nowak who showed me something of the other side of the rainbow. My greatest debt continues to be to Don Milligan, whose support is constant and who steers me through.

Introduction

The study of Kant's account of ethics has attracted the attention of a great number of philosophers, and there has tended to form, over many years, a broad consensus about the scope and range of Kant's views on this area. This consensus could broadly be summarized in the view that Kant's ethics are primarily formalist, that they support a deontological rather than a teleological account of the nature of ethical claims, that Kant has virtually no room for an account of moral feeling and that his position is one that is scarcely tenable.[1]

There have been works that have objected to this general picture of Kant's ethics, occasionally because it has been argued that his account is only an analysis and not intended to guide action at all.[2] Such a 'defence' of Kant has the clear problem that it seems to make his account of absolutely no relevance to situations of ethical deliberation. As opposed to this line of 'defence' there have been accounts that focus on providing a rationale for a deontological ethics within the broad purview of intuitionism, to which it has been suggested that Kant belongs.[3] Apart from the many difficulties of this position, its alignment of Kant with intuitionism has appeared less appealing as this overall view of ethics has declined in popularity.

The difficulty with the generally accepted consensus view is not merely that it renders Kant's ethics untenable. If it is true that his position is untenable, this merely has to be accepted, though it is worth inquiry as to whether it can really be as untenable as is commonly presented given the general agreement about the high standing accorded to Kant's theoretical philosophy. The more important problem with this view, however, is that it is presented in relative ignorance of the full range of Kant's ethical writings and it is the intention of this book to present for consideration an overview of all Kant's major writings on practical philosophy as the corrective to a very partial focus in the majority of treatments.[4]

The fact that the received view of Kant's ethics is based on a partial response to his writings is evident since the philosophical responses broadly reflect the bias exhibited in undergraduate (and even postgraduate) courses on Kant. Such treatments are based primarily on a study of Kant's first critical work on ethics, the *Groundwork of the Metaphysics of Morals* with occasional attention paid to the *Critique of Practical Reason*.[5] This focus has some justification. After all, if the account given within the *Groundwork* is misunderstood, then it is likely that the full view of ethics that Kant wishes to provide in later works will be also one that is not grasped clearly. This focus has also had extremely damaging consequences, however, for the understanding of Kant's practical philosophy. Due to this concentration, the development of Kant's views has been rarely studied, the attention provided by him to problems of political and religious thinking has been marginalized and, perhaps most importantly of all, scant cognisance has been developed of the nature of his account of virtue, and this last point has perhaps led to the striking and very odd choice suggested to exist between Kant and Aristotle.[6] In presenting an alternative to this concentration I will set out in this introduction some of the key reasons for resisting this general view and connect this book to recent treatments of Kant that also tilt away from this view.

The development of Kant's ethics

There has been a traditional avoidance of considerations of the history and development of Kant's positions in Anglo-American treatments.[7] This general avoidance has resulted in failure to articulate the types of position that Kant is engaged in developing his response to, and concomitant failure to recognize the motivations that would have led Kant to develop certain strands of moral thinking rather than others. Whilst there are works devoted specifically to treating Kant's 'pre-critical' works on ethics there is as yet little consensus in the understanding of the works that are discussed under this heading.[8] Attention to the background of Kant's works shows that he is responding to a German rationalist tradition as well as the British school of 'common-sense' philosophy, but there has been little agreement about the relative weight that Kant attached to these positions prior to articulating his critical work.

It is with regard to an evaluation of these works that my treatment will begin. I will here set out initially my contention that Kant's concern in practical philosophy was to set out a form of perfectionism, a perfectionism that is based squarely upon a teleological response to ethics that becomes in its full articulation a type of ethical eschatology. This view will be controversial though there is precedent for it within serious treatments of Kant.[9] In considering Kant's lectures on ethics alongside the early works and giving also here a rationale for reading some of Kant's more popular lecture courses such as those on education and anthropology alongside these other works I will be suggesting that Kant began by attempting to integrate an understanding of human purposes with a decisive and definite commitment to a perfectionist standard of morality. This treatment of Kant's 'pre-critical' works will also enable a new vantage to be given to the works that are usually presented as if they contained the major statements of importance Kant made on ethical matters, the *Groundwork* and the Second Critique.

The discussion of Kant's critique of ethics needs to begin from an account of the First Critique as it is here that Kant performs the 'critical turn' and this turn involves him in addressing the problem of freedom. Whilst the Third Antinomy is a much visited part of the First Critique the description of the antinomy is often cast in terms that do not connect it to the broad horizon of Kant's Dialectic. My treatment discusses it in relation to the notion of Ideas and clarifies this notion in terms that help to make sense of how Kant's work moves beyond the horizon of the 'pre-critical' works. The Third Antinomy has been claimed to conflict with statements made within the Canon of Pure Reason and in my account of the First Critique I investigate the reasons for this claim and present an account of why I take it that there is no such conflict. Making the case for the treatment of practical philosophy in the First Critique allows the interpretation of the *Groundwork* and the Second Critique to be given its critical setting.

There have been persistent problems involved with the interpretation of these works, the works on which the majority of treatments of Kant's practical philosophy have focused. There has been the persistent suggestion that in writing the Second Critique Kant departed from a central position of the *Groundwork* and there has been in addition serious confusion about the treatment of the status of transcendental deductions in Kant's practical philosophy. I will respond to both of these problems in this work by suggesting, in contrast to the vast majority of commentators, that there is broad continuity between these two works, that it is not the case that Kant comes to reject a central argument of the *Groundwork* and that the transcendental deduction presented within the *Groundwork* does not conflict with the one given in the Second Critique.

The status of concepts in practical philosophy will also be given treatment. There is a distinction between purely moral concepts and theoretical concepts that serve a practical need that should be recognized and the nature of this distinction needs to be traced in order that the long-running dispute over the nature of the *summum bonum* can be responded to, a dispute that it is easier to resolve after having reviewed the early appearance of this notion in Kant's pre-critical works. The discussion of the *summum bonum* is also essential in coming to view the place of *Religion within the Limits of Reason Alone* within Kant's practical philosophy. This work is almost invariably treated in isolation from Kant's practical philosophy as if it was part of some independent 'philosophy of religion' of little evident import for those concerned with ethics.[10] In connecting this work with the Second Critique's treatment of the postulates of practical reason I intend to recover it as a work of importance for understanding Kant's moral psychology in addition to discussing the account of moral history provided here, an account that presents one of the fullest forms of eschatological response to history in Kant's work.[11]

The most serious problem with existing treatments of Kant's practical philosophy is revealed in the consistent failure to mark the distinction between his 'critical' treatments and his 'doctrinal' works. Attendant upon this failure is a decisive gap in the account of Kant's practical philosophy in the general lack of attention to the doctrinal works. This is the major deficit that this study seeks to remedy.

Practical philosophy: From critique to doctrine

Kant's most studied contributions to the consideration of the philosophical treatment of practical reason are intended and self-consciously presented by him as propaeduetics. This is the reason why the *Groundwork to a Metaphysics of Morals* has its title, it is intended to 'lay the ground' for what is truly needed, a full metaphysics of morals. Similarly, the *Critique of Practical Reason* is written to present a reason for thinking that there is a pure element in practical reason, not to provide a detailed account of the manner in which this pure element operates in moral judgment or to relate it to an understanding of political thought. These tasks are reserved for the major work that Kant wrote on practical philosophy, the *Metaphysics of Morals*. This latter work presents Kant's ethical 'doctrine' as opposed to his 'critique' or delimitation of the scope of moral claims. This distinction would appear to be largely forgotten as it is very rarely mentioned in contemporary philosophical work on Kant.

Dick Howard provides an exception to this and he explains the terms 'critique' and 'doctrine' in the following way:

> Critique is the method which asks for the conditions of the possibility of a given lawful relation. But these conditions of possibility do not explain why the empirical manifold is receptive to the a priori categories of the understanding or to the exercise of free-rational will. Doctrine determines *which* particulars are in fact susceptible to incorporation within the lawful philosophical universe. Critique and doctrine are mutually necessary if a theoretical position is to claim to be both complete and rational. Critique alone cannot be assured that the object whose conditions of possibility it determines is not simply accidental. Doctrine alone cannot be certain that the rational particularity whose necessity it demonstrates can in fact be realized in the empirical world. Critique shows the possibility of a lawfully universal realm at the risk of losing particularity. Doctrine preserves particularity within the context of the universal whose necessity can only be demonstrated by a critique.[12]

As this is one of the few attempts given in the contemporary literature to describe this distinction it is worth serious consideration. There is one serious problem with it though, which is that Howard bases this distinction upon the text of the Third Critique, effectively treating the Third Critique as a 'post-critical' work whereas the introduction of this book presents the work as the conclusion of Kant's critical treatment (Ak. 5:170), a view hard to square with the notion that it is a doctrinal work. If the *Critique of Judgment* is to be treated, as its title would give further reason for thinking it should be, as a critical work, it is unlikely that the distinction presented within it between reflective and determinative judgment can be said to accord, as Howard's statement would suggest, with that between critique and doctrine.

Whilst Howard's treatment of the distinction has a clear problem it is the case that it captures something of the importance of the distinction in terms of the different types of procedure. In Kant's critical works on practical philosophy there is an enquiry conducted into the nature of the principles of moral philosophy. The search for and discovery of these principles does not lead to a description of how they should be applied, although *Religion within the Limits of Reason Alone* does provide an extensive account of moral psychology.

Hence it would appear that if the principles of moral philosophy are provided within the critical works, it is the province of the doctrinal works to describe the method of their application.[13] But Howard's way of demarcating this does not allow for a clear understanding of the way in which this application is presented by Kant in terms of any detailed treatment of the relationship between critical and doctrinal works as he gives only a general account of this relationship. It is part of the ambition of this book to set out the manner of the application of moral principles within the *Metaphysics of Morals*, an application that will require investigation of the relationship between the principle of autonomy and the supreme principles of right and virtue, in addition to requiring discreet treatments of the principles of application of right and the practice of moral casuistry in the treatment of virtue.

Recent work on Kant's practical philosophy

In recent years there have been consistent attempts within work on Kant's practical philosophy to emend the consensus view of his treatment that I described in opening. These attempts have included works on Kant's treatment of political thinking. In response to the odd and unconvincing attempt of Hannah Arendt to confine Kant's political thinking to the horizons of the Third Critique, there have been produced works on Kant's political thought that include reflection on his treatment of history.[14] Such works have provided access to the broader horizons of Kant's practical philosophy, though they have not attempted to integrate such treatments with a new account of the areas traditionally privileged.

In addition to this new focus on Kant's political thinking, a focus long overdue, there has also come a rejection of many of the details of the treatment of the *Groundwork* that were provided by previous generations of interpreters.[15] This work has included much that has been new and important and has exposed the assumptions of the traditional consensus reading of Kant's ethics to critical interrogation, not least with regard to the notion that Kant is to be viewed as a deontological theorist. Whilst it is undoubtedly true that the work produced by commentators such as Paul Guyer has allowed a quite new response to Kant's ethics however the focus of concentration of this work has remained consistently narrower than Kant's own.[16] The concentration on Kant's ethics that has emerged in the main in recent years has in fact been prompted primarily by students of John Rawls, a fact that has ensured that it remains the case that the main concern of many recent works has been to provide an account of the 'categorical imperative procedure' rather than a systematic investigation of Kant's view of the nature and scope of practical philosophy.[17]

There is much good new work that, as already suggested, challenges and presents important alternatives to aspects of, the received image of Kant's practical philosophy and this book is certainly a product of reflections produced by this work. It is however noticeably the case that a systematic and sustained account of the range of Kant's enquiries in practical philosophy is as yet lacking and in the absence of such an account the force of the received image of Kant is unlikely to be diminished. Hence it is the import of this work to systematically present a contrary image of Kant's ethics to that prevalent. The image that this work will present of Kant will be one that involves presenting his ethics as not merely formalist, but requiring a matter for ethical judgment to take place, as not opposed to feeling *per se* but rather as requiring an account of pure feeling, as based not only on the categorical imperative but including in addition principles of application, as intimately concerned with ends and purposes not opposed to them. In accord with the account I provided in *Kant and the Ends of Aesthetics*, Kant will be revealed as a thinker of ends and a defender of a metaphysical approach to ethics.

The re-description of Kant's practical philosophy that accords it the range that Kant wished for it and allows justice to be done to the extent of his enquiries in this area is one that has been for a long time required in order for a fuller assessment of Kant's views to be possible. It is not my view, as a patient reader will discover, that Kant's system is one that is entirely defensible but approaching it otherwise than as a system as has been traditional has resulted in a distorted and partial understanding of his positions. For the sake of a fuller and more balanced engagement with Kant on the terrain of practical philosophy to be possible the vision of his overall endeavour is required. It is my hope that I provide that vision in this work and that on the basis of it there can be better informed and more comprehensive discussions of his legacy than has been common.

1
Kant's 'Pre-Critical' Ethics

In this chapter I will investigate the nature of Kant's early writings on ethics, but the designation 'pre-critical' does not mean that only writings prior to 1770 or 1781 will be discussed. There is a case for utilizing the term 'pre-critical' in a conceptual rather than a chronological sense as referring to writings of Kant's, that do not conduct a *critique* of moral claims. If a critique is taken to mean an investigation of the limits and status of claims made about an area from within the area in question hence as an immanent questioning, then the writings of Kant's which do not carry out such a style of investigation must be regarded as 'pre-critical'. In this conceptual sense of the term Kant's *Anthropology from a Pragmatic Point of View* is a 'pre-critical' work despite being published in 1798, as are his posthumously published lectures on education. Where there is a true borderline, however, is in relation to Kant's lectures on ethics, lectures which whilst originating as an exposition of Baumgarten's 'universal practical philosophy' culminate in important statements about the nature of virtue which are returned to in Kant's doctrinal work *The Metaphysics of Morals*.

The number of Kant's 'pre-critical' writings on practical philosophy is smaller than his 'pre-critical' works on theoretical philosophy but is still large enough to evade summary in one chapter. I will therefore focus only on giving a selective interpretation of these writings with the purpose of elucidating Kant's early writings initially and subsequently indicating how he developed the notion of a critical approach to practical philosophy. The investigation in this chapter will culminate in considering the relations between *Anthropology from a Pragmatic Point of View* and the lectures on ethics.

Kant's early writings

Kant's first discussion of practical philosophy is in the context of his 1755 treatise, the *New Elucidation of the First Principles of Metaphysical Cognition*.[1] In this work Kant sets out to present a response to the impasse that prevailed at this point in German philosophy between the system of Christian Wolff and the work of Christian August Crusius. The debate between them turned on the traditional metaphysical problem of free will versus determinism. Wolff favoured a determinist solution, which turned the principle of sufficient reason into a key argument for assuming that each occurrence depended on a set of others with a culmination in the divine reason. Wolff's system was fundamentally an interpretation of Leibniz which was the basis of academic philosophy at the time Kant was writing. By contrast, Crusius attempted a new justification of faith by appealing to immediacy and in response to Wolff pointed to an equivocation between logical and real grounds in the latter's argument.[2]

Whilst the dispute between Wolff and Crusius can be seen to occupy a traditional place in metaphysics, it also at this point established a demarcation between academic philosophy and fideist intellectuals who attempted to present free action as a *causa sui*. Kant in this essay stated the positions of both parties and attempted to mediate between them. But as his description of 'free judgment' as arising from 'conscious impulses' indicates (Ak. 1:404) Kant at this point can do little more than restate the notion of freedom and is not capable of present-ing a defence of it which really responds to the Wolffian position except by restating the Crusian objection of a conflation between real and logical grounds.

Whilst the discussion in the *New Elucidation* is philosophically unsat-isfactory two points are made clearer by being reminded of it. First, Kant's initial interest can be seen to be primarily theoretical in character rather than practical. Second, Kant's first response to philosophy was to articulate the standpoints that he found established in tradition and to consider his orientation in regard to the competing positions he found there. The move from a primarily theoretical interest in philosophy to a practical one will turn on a reconsideration of the problem of freedom that makes possible critique. The response to philosophical tradition by contrast will be revealed to be consistently important for Kant.

Kant's next work on practical philosophy emerged as a response to the setting of a question by the Berlin Academy of Sciences in 1761 on whether metaphysical truths and particularly the first principles of natural theology and morality are capable of the same proof as geometrical truths. The essay deadline was 1 January 1763 and in May of the latter year the academy awarded first prize to Moses Mendelssohn and second prize to Kant. The two essays were published together in 1764. The question set by the Academy indicates a concern with a Cartesian notion of certainty and Mendelssohn's essay defends the claim that our knowledge of moral truths corresponds essentially to that given in Wolff.[3] Whilst the theoretical element of Kant's essay involves an early form of constructionism about mathematics, this essay does not connect such a position with an account of the ultimate basis of such construction in the manner which will be provided in the Transcendental Aesthetic. In metaphysical terms Kant again reiterates Crusian objections to the Wolffian notion of *Grund* but he nonetheless still avoids committing himself to the ultimate voluntarism of this outlook.

Unlike in the *New Exposition*, however, Kant does here consider some aspects of practical philosophy in a manner that begins to build away from just seeing these questions as subordinate to problems of a theoretical type. In considering the notion of obligation Kant distinguishes between types of obligation which relate to means from those which relate to ends and then describes the latter as necessarily referring us to the notion of an end in itself (Ak. 2:298). Whilst this repeats the Wolffian claim that necessity must point us to a supreme principle, this argument does not take a cosmological form concerned with causes but rather points to a difference between types of purposes, distinguishing relative from ultimate purposes in a form which will later be restated in the *Critique of Teleological Judgment* (Ak. 5:449). The notion of ultimate purposes as utilised in this early essay is related to the Wolffian notion of the 'total greatest perfection' which determines the understanding of the will of God (Ak. 2:298).

The relation of the greatest perfection to an understanding of ultimate purposes is furthered by Kant's presentation in this essay of the fundamental principles of morality. In this essay Kant suggests that there are two fundamental principles, a formal ground which is stated positively as 'Do the most perfect thing which is possible for you' and negatively as 'Omit that which would hinder the greatest perfection possible through you' (Ak. 2:299). The reason why Kant states the perfectionist principle in both positive and negative forms appears to be because of a commitment to a theory of truth as necessarily including negative and positive propositions. Whilst this eccentric position gives two principles instead of one it also ensures that there are resources within Kant's position for dealing with the problem of acts of omission as morally significant. Even more importantly however, these formal grounds of obligation are not the full account of ethics for Kant as he contrasts them with *material* grounds of obligation which include information about what types of thing will in fact relate to the possibility of acting in a manner which fits the perfectionist criteria. Kant is clear that 'no particular determinate obligation flows from these two rules of the good if indemonstrable principles of practical cognition are not connected to them' (Ak. 2:299). Since the formal principles require material grounds to be added in order for duties to be specifiable it follows that the formal principles taken alone cannot supply us with the sufficient basis for ethics. In response to the Cartesian framing given to the essay by the Academy's formulation Kant distinguishes the formal principle from the material grounds of obligation by describing the latter as 'indemonstrable' which in the context of this work means that they are not derivable from concepts. But whilst the material grounds of obligation are not based on conceptual grounds they do have a basis that can be pointed to: feeling. This feeling is immediately pleasurable and Kant refers in this connection to the work of Francis Hutcheson (Ak. 2:300).[4]

The Prize Essay marks a considerable advance on the position of the *New Elucidation*. Whilst the framing of the Prize Essay is still given by theoretical philosophy the consideration of practical philosophy is much deeper here than in the *New Elucidation*. The presentation of supreme principles anticipates the fundamental problem which animates the *Groundwork*: 'seeking out and establishing the supreme principle of morality' (Ak. 4:392). The description of the need to add material grounds of obligation to formal principles will also be shown subsequently to be fundamental to Kant's mature conception of ethics. Finally, whilst the distinction of types of certainty as related to a difference between concepts and feeling is here dealt with rather summarily it indicates a concern with the aesthetic basis of morality which we will see later to be of considerable importance in Kant's practical philosophy as he conceives of it after the critical turn.

The same year that the Prize Essay was published by the Academy Kant also published his entertaining essay *Observations on the Feeling of the Beautiful and the Sublime*.[5] Since the Prize Essay described the basis of material principles of obligation to be feelings of pleasure this essay's concern with feeling brings it closer to Kant's practical concerns at this period than is often noticed. Kant here relates the distinction between pleasure and displeasure to the relation between external things and inner disposition. This leads Kant to a form of anthropological description that is related to a theory of humours (Ak. 2:218). The notion of 'true virtue' introduced here is distinguished however from a mere 'good-naturedness' in a manner which already anticipates Kant's later rejection of sentimentalist theories of morals but which here involves an assimilation of agreeableness to beauty in a manner later rejected in the *Critique of Aesthetic Judgment* (Ak. 5:206–7). Practical principles are here closely attached to aesthetic grounds when Kant declares such 'true virtue' to be 'sublime' (Ak. 2:214–17). The theory of humours is also developed here in an original fashion when Kant describes the melancholic as having a deep sense of the dignity of humanity and as hating dissemblance (Ak. 2:221). Whilst the relation of beauty to mere agreeableness allows Kant here to align beauty with femininity and declare women to be incapable of principles, he does go on to add that men are rarely capable of principles either. Furthermore, he suggests that acting on principle is often a cause of very undesirable outcomes. This essay involves Kant in a largely empirical or, as he will later term it, 'pragmatic' enquiry, which however does not prevent it from developing a richer account of the aesthetic basis of morals than he has been capable of providing thus far. Subsequent marginal emendations to the essay also reveal real disquiet about the nature of Rousseau's moral philosophy at this point with which he was both deeply impressed whilst also profoundly disturbed by some of its consequences.[6]

Observations on the Feeling of the Beautiful and the Sublime reveals a continuing engagement with philosophical tradition which is now, following the lead of the Prize Essay's conclusion about feeling, expanded to include investigations of rich detail given by more empirically oriented enquirers. What is gained in richness is lost in precision however and whilst this work has always been one of the more popular of Kant's writings for general readers it has gained little favour from philosophers. *Dreams of A Spirit-Seer Elucidated by Dreams of Metaphysics* (1766) by contrast, has never much appealed to either audience.[7] Conceived as an investigation of the mystical claims of Swedenborg this work conflates, in passages which shocked Kant's contemporaries, this visionary writer with the philosophers Crusius and Wolff. This conflation damaged Kant's claim that the work was intended as a serious contribution to metaphysics, but the motivations of this claim and the result of it in the shape of the work that was produced make this book of signal interest.

The motivation Kant had for conflating Swedenborg with Wolff and Crusius was to do with the investigations into other worlds which the mystic claimed to have made and which Kant was now claiming had a clear analogue in the speculations of the philosophical tradition: 'the dreamland of Wolff built with only a few blocks of experience but with plenty of dodgy concepts, or that of Crusius produced from nothing by the magical power of a few spells about what is thinkable and unthinkable' (Ak. 2:342). The nature of the problem with both the philosophers in question and the mystic visionary who gave Kant the ostensible occasion for writing this work is that they lack an orientation for judging the claims they are making, the reason being that they have left behind them all earthly terrain and are journeying in the supersensible. The basic problem with the thinkers castigated can be reduced to a primary heading of what Kant will later term a 'transcendental topic' (A269/B325), the heading of 'inner and outer'. The 'dreamers' Kant is here assessing confuse the imagination with its objects and delude themselves that their fancies are realities. The Cartesian echoes of the charge are vivid in a passage that clearly evokes Descartes' *Meditations*: 'They read, even when awake, and often with the greatest vivacity of perception, certain objects as if they were placed among the things that they really perceive around them' (Ak. 2:343). The reason for the disorientation of the mystic is that perception of the senses, real or apparent, precedes the judgment of the understanding and has an evidential form not susceptible to rational persuasion (Ak. 2:347). This claim indicates that Kant is still at the time of writing this essay committed to the notion that the fundamental claims of sensibility are indemonstrable and also practically determinative. However, more importantly, he attacks the metaphysicians not for committing the same error as the mystic but an analogous one of attempting to discover 'hidden properties' through reason instead of asking the question what relation metaphysical concepts have to 'the concepts of experience' (Ak. 2:367–8). Whilst *Dreams of A Spirit-Seer* adds nothing to Kant's positive notion of practical philosophy it does indicate the practical results of theoretically misconceived investigations and its alliance of mystical enthusiasm with the stalemates derived from philosophical tradition will prove to have a long life in Kant's development influencing the *Critique of Pure Reason* itself and receiving clear later statements in *What Is Orientation In Thinking?* (1786), *Religion Within the Limits of Reason Alone* (1793) and *The Conflict of the Faculties* (1795).

After the writing of *Dreams of A Spirit-Seer* Kant was becoming ready to explicitly announce the need for philosophy to become critique and in many respects this work is already guided by a notion of critique which however it is not as yet ready to clearly enunciate as such. Four years after writing it Kant wrote his inaugural dissertation as a professor at the university of Königsberg: *On the Form and Principles of the Sensible and Intelligible World.*[8] The inability of 'dreamers' to establish the placing of thought is now related to the fundamental transcendental difference between sensible and intelligible and with this statement critical philosophy as a theoretical project is begun. It is possible now to understand that Wolff was misled here and that his prime fault in philosophy was to confuse logical distinction not just with real distinction but, even more importantly, with transcendental distinction. The fundamental basis of the First Critique is now stated and the key thoughts of the Transcendental Aesthetic are traced within the pages of this dissertation. In practical terms there is less development in this work on earlier writings.[9] The agenda of understanding a necessary perfectionism within practical philosophy is returned to with the discernment of a practical *perfectio noumenon* which corresponds to the theoretical form which belongs to God and practical thought is understood to belong to the 'real' use of the intellect as opposed to its merely logical use (Ak. 2:392–6). Otherwise, there is little of practical interest in the dissertation.

The 'early writings' show a developing interest in the material grounds of practical philosophy that are related to feeling and understood to be the source of being able to state something determinate practically. But the oscillation between anthropological description and the perfectionist agenda of ultimate principles is not clearly brought to any satisfactory statement and none of these works takes practical philosophy as its principal concern. The developing response to tradition becoming the ante-chamber to the enunciation of a critical turn can however be discerned and is repeated in the manuscripts of a more strictly practical kind to which I will now turn.

Kant on education

In turning from Kant's early writings to an investigation of other 'pre-critical' texts it will be necessary to depart from strict chronology, not least because the publication dates of the texts which will now be addressed are not a guide to the thoughts expressed in them. Whilst it would be plausible to discuss many sets of lectures and reflections I will here focus on only two published works and some of the lectures on ethics.[10] The published works I will discuss are *On Education* and *Anthropology From A Pragmatic Point of View*. The former of these works was initially published in 1803 and based on a selection of notes from Kant's lectures on the subject whilst the latter was published in 1798 on the basis of Kant's own selection of material from lectures. Both these works are therefore instructive of the type of teacher Kant was, as are the lectures on ethics which we possess in a number of different forms and which were published posthumously. The reason for concentration on these materials in the rest of the chapter is that, unlike other lecture series of Kant's which we possess, such as the lectures on anthropology, they either exist in a published form which Kant was at least partially responsible for or they are of fundamental practical importance (such as the lectures on ethics).

Kant's *On Education* is unlikely ever to become one of his more visited works. It is based on a response to manuals of education current at the time Kant was lecturing and includes the rudiments of a theory of education as divisible between physical, mental and practical elements of which only the last is of real interest here. The account of moral development which guides the work is quite different from that of Rousseau as Kant's inclination towards children is guided both by his conviction that the type of solitary education recommended in *Emile* is inefficient and by an understanding of children as governed primarily by an appetitive psychology which needs to be restrained and that this disciplinary operation is the prime requirement of preparation for maturity. The reason why Kant was concerned with education is however ultimately practical:

> children ought to be educated, not for the present, but for a possibly improved condition of man in the future; that is, in a manner which is adapted to the *idea of humanity* and the whole destiny of man.[11]

This fundamental practical goal of education is what both parents and legislators primarily overlook as the former adopt principles of prudential adaptation and the latter conceive of their subjects instrumentally. Hence, of the four objects Kant discerns education to have, the most important is neglected (the other three being discipline, culture and refinement). This is what leads Kant to see that the indictment of Rousseau against civilization has some justification.

Due to the state's interest in obedient and instrumentally useful subjects Kant also proposes the establishment of experimental schools to concern themselves with the chief aim of education. The moral possibilities of public education are also more clearly esteemed by him than a private education with a personal tutor due to the mutual moral education of the children. Whilst physical education is treated by Kant in an expanded manner to include even an education in permissible crying and is directed by a moral aim of forming character this aspect of his theory is intended as primarily negative and does not even include a discussion of physical exercises which latter are left for his account of *Bildung*. When Kant turns to this latter discussion however we are given a litany of the uses of games that are conceived of wholly instrumentally by Kant.

When dealing with cultivation of the mind Kant discusses exercises, which enable the development of the memory, the learning of languages and the importance of learning through doing. In discussing moral culture however a marked change occurs in the work and Kant's real interest begins to be displayed. It is noticeable instantly in his casting aside the aspect of education which earlier he described as central for children: discipline.

> Moral culture must be based upon 'maxims', not upon discipline; the one prevents evil habits, the other trains the mind to think. We must see, then, that the child should accustom himself to act in accordance with 'maxims', and not from certain ever-changing springs of action. Through discipline we form certain habits, moreover, the force of which becomes lessened in the course of years. The child should learn to act according to 'maxims', the reasonableness of which he is able to see for himself. (Churton, p. 83)

The contrast between a 'maxim' and living according to a discipline imposed on one is clearly set out as being based on the difference between self-regulation and the outward conformity which arises from mechanical rote. This difference illustrates that whilst Kant understood physical habits and even much of mental life as requiring a form of drill moral matters are different in kind in requiring self-legislation.

The learning of right behaviour requires a departure from mere coercion as dependence on this reduces conduct to agreeable or disagreeable prudential arrangements.

> Morality is something so sacred and sublime that we must not degrade it by placing it in the same rank as discipline. The first endeavour in moral education is the formation of character. Character consists in readiness to act in accordance with 'maxims'. (Churton, p. 84)

If the prime task of moral education is to form a moral personality, then it is necessary to enquire what the prime characteristic of such a personality is and this Kant comprehends as the ability to set rules for oneself which rules are what he understands by 'maxims'. Despite this commitment to the formation of self-legislating persons as the end of education Kant has considerable trouble indicating how to separate the giving of a rule to oneself from the following of rules that are imposed outwardly. This problem, which we will discover to be of some importance in *The Metaphysics of Morals*, concerns the fact that for a maxim to conform to a rule for which there is not inclination requires a process of conformation extremely intricate and difficult to execute without the threat of punishment. Kant understands the necessity of punishment even though it would appear to threaten the possibility of self-legislation. But he divides punishment into two kinds: physical and moral. Moral punishment is preferable and its prime instrument is humiliation: 'for instance, if a child tells a lie, a look of contempt is punishment enough, and punishment of a most appropriate kind' (Churton, p. 88). Physical punishment, which consists in denying a desired object, is also regarded as a type of moral punishment and contrasted with the direct infliction of pain that is taken to be a last resort by Kant. This scale of punishments does not entirely resolve the dilemma, which is expressed by the relation of outward rule and inward consent. Whilst moral punishment has its effect entirely on personality the physical punishment that is analogous to it is a form of disallowance of the agreeable and has the difficulties associated that Kant has already conceded. Physical punishment through the administration of pain by contrast is based only on power and the legitimacy of this power is precisely what is called into question through its exertion in this form.

In turning to practical education as a project in itself Kant states the Stoic maxim *sustine et abstine* (endure and abstain). This involves learning to manage without whatever we lack and renouncing whatever is not attainable. The purpose of this maxim is not as grim as this sounds as its ultimate point is to sharpen us into a person capable of adopting steadfast purposes and the person who can hold to a purpose to the extent of accomplishing ends they set for themselves has the basis of good character, Kant declares. How can this sharpening be developed? Through setting before children duties. These duties are of two kinds: duties of the child towards itself and duties of the child towards others. Kant initially states the duties towards oneself in negative form (training of inclinations) but the principle of them is positive:

> they consist in his being conscious that man possesses a certain dignity, which ennobles him above all other creatures, and that it is his duty so to act as not to violate in his own person this dignity of mankind. (Churton, p. 101)

The principle underlying the child's duties to itself is hence the same idea as should underlie education in general, the idea of humanity. This principle is hence emerging as the material ground of obligation that gives us the sense of education. The principal vice which is to be regarded as most opposed to the dignity of humanity is lying which is 'a means of robbing' one of respect for oneself.

The child's duties to others turn on respect for them. Kant suggests that one way of teaching the commonality of respect is through a moral catechism (an idea repeated in the Doctrine of Virtue: Ak. 6:480–4). The basis of such a catechism, as of any other part of practical education, still has to be the formation of self-legislation and the principal means of this remains the instillation of feelings of justified humiliation which arise by comparing oneself with a perfectionist ideal:

> humility is really nothing else than the comparing of our own worth with the standard of moral perfection. Thus, for instance, the Christian religion makes people humble, not by preaching humility, but by teaching them to compare themselves with the highest pattern of perfection. (Churton, p. 105)

Here we can see a connection between *On Education* and the practical aspects of the inaugural dissertation in the perfectionist notion of morality being analogically based on the relation of humanity to God.

The basis of this perfect standard is illuminated by a typological classification of cravings, vices and virtues which Kant provides. Under the heading of cravings we find two types of desire given: formal and material. Under the former heading we have cravings for freedom and power, under the latter cravings for certain types of object. Cravings are distinguished here by Kant from vices which are also of three types: vices of malice, vices of baseness and vices of narrow-mindedness. Malice includes envy, baseness, dissoluteness (squandering), narrow-mindedness and idleness. Finally virtue, by contrast with vice, is of three kinds: virtues of merit, virtues of obligation and virtues of innocence. Under the heading of merit falls benevolence, under obligation honesty and under innocence modesty. What this typology illustrates is the difference between inclinations and maxims of a good or bad kind. The cravings are inclinations that arise spontaneously and are in principle morally neutral but can become harmful. The vices are exemplified in patterns of deliberate conduct based on lack of respect for others or for oneself. The virtues by contrast are patterns of conduct based on good maxims that express respect for others or oneself. Hence the perfectionist basis of Kant's account of moral education is respect for the moral status of oneself or others.

The comparison of moral perfection with the notion presented to us in the Christian religion of an exemplar of virtue is returned to in a discussion of religious education. Kant here describes what he takes religion to be:

> Religion is the law in us, in so far as it derives emphasis from a Law-giver and a Judge above us. It is morality applied to the idea of God. (Churton, p. 111)

This notion of religion emphasizes the judgment that is applied by the moral personality to itself. This judgment is presented analogically in an idea of perfection, which we term God. This makes the effect of conscience sensuously comprehensible.

These remarks on religion are followed by a reminder of the Stoic maxim that underlies the whole pattern of Kant's notion of practical education and the work concludes with statements about how to establish patterns of behaviour, which will reinforce this maxim. Whilst the work as a whole is pitched at a popular level and lacks philosophical sophistication it does relate to the early works that we have just been examining and builds substantially upon their pattern. As with the early works the ultimate basis of Kant's practical approach here is shown to be perfectionist and this perfectionism is connected to both the idea of God and the idea of humanity. Whilst the idea of humanity points us in the direction of understanding the notion of moral personality as involving respect for the dignity of others the idea of God enables us to comprehend the self-legislation of morality as commensurate with a perfect standard of a supersensible type. The idea of God as uniting self-legislation with the imposition from without of law also helps us to come to a comprehension of the necessity of giving oneself the law. The notion of practical faith is thereby given in outline and will form the central nexus of *Religion Within the Limits of Reason Alone*.

Kant's pragmatic anthropology

Kant lectured on anthropology from 1772 onwards and, since the notion of a pragmatic anthropology developed from his earlier lectures on physical geography, it is plausible to argue that it was his most continuous subject as a teacher. These lectures were extremely popular and the digest of them that Kant selected and published has also enjoyed fair popularity. Philosophical readings of the latter work have been rare however because the work seems to rest largely on anecdote and to lack the systematization found elsewhere in Kant's work. The book Kant published is divided into two parts: an Anthropological Didactic and an Anthropological Characterization. In the Didactic we find a further tripartite division corresponding to that provided in the three critiques with part one focusing on cognition, part two the feeling of pleasure and displeasure and part three giving an account of what Kant terms 'desire'. The section headed 'desire' relates to practical philosophy and will be the main focus of my attention. The Characterization is divided into discussions of personality, sexuality, nationality, racial types and the notion of the species. Whilst some aspects of the Characterization are of interest (such as the discussions of personality and the species) much of the rest amounts to little more than scattered remarks of a personal nature. If we combine the discussion of 'desire' with some of the parts of the Charaterization, however, we will be able to expand our account of Kant's 'pre-critical' ethics whilst the notion of anthropology itself will subsequently be demonstrated to undergo a decisive alteration from the standpoint of critical and doctrinal thought.

In the 'Introduction' to the *Anthropology* Kant sets out a grand vision:

> All cultural progress, which represents the education of man, aims at putting acquired knowledge and skill to use in the world. The most important object of culture, to whom such knowledge and skill can be applied, is Man because he is his own ultimate purpose. To recognize him, according to his species, as an earthly creature endowed with reason deserves to be called *knowledge of the world*, even though he is only one of all the creatures on earth. (Ak. 7:119)[12]

Whilst *On Education* restricted its account of education primarily to the correct principles for rearing children, the *Anthropology* immediately adopts a much larger notion of education as the self-instruction of humanity. The notion that humanity's self-instruction is equivalent to knowledge of the world as such is based upon the understanding of humanity as an end in itself. This follows from the rudimentary comprehension of the notions of 'respect' and 'dignity' which we have derived from *On Education*.

The education that is involved in 'pragmatic anthropology' involves 'Man as a citizen of the world' (Ak. 7:120). That this is of practical import can be seen from the subtitle of the Didactic: 'On the Art of Knowing the Interior as Well as the Exterior of Man'. Since the confusion of inner and outer is what led both the metaphysicians and the mystic into raving it would seem practically beneficial to comprehend on the basis of this investigation what seems to belong to each of these headings in order to determine the basis of practical obligation. But the progress of the Didactic does not strictly follow the publication priorities indicated by the succession of the three critiques. Rather than discussing practical philosophy after theoretical philosophy Kant places it third after his account of the feeling of pleasure and displeasure. Since we have seen from the early writings that Kant did in fact publish a work on taste well before a work devoted entirely to practical philosophy this arrangement perhaps refers to the order of Kant's early works rather than that of the three critiques. The discernment of the terrain correctly belonging to practical philosophy would need to be separated both from theoretical questions of a metaphysical nature and enquiries into sensibility of a more empirical temper. Since this separation requires on the one hand confronting the prejudices of the schools and on the other setting to rights the standpoint of 'common sense' it would perhaps be the most precarious and difficult to perform.

When we turn to the third part of the Didactic we learn quickly the nature of the difficulties involved in an anthropological investigation into practical questions. At the opening of this part Kant indicates why he is classifying this part of his enquiry as an investigation into the faculty of desire by giving a definition of desire:

> Desire (*appetitio*) is the self-definition of the power of a subject to imagine something in the future as an effect of such imagination. (Ak. 7:251)

If 'desire' is the relation of a person to the future as material to be shaped through the indication of what means are necessary to make changes take place then it is fundamentally equivalent to the possession of purposive direction. Within this general notion of 'desire' we will include a particular relation to sensibility as given in the Latin *appetitio*. A desire which is habitual in its sensuous intentionality is described by Kant as inclination (*Triebfeder*). It now becomes clearer how the account of practical principles relates to the preceding investigation of the feeling of pleasure and displeasure as, if inclination is a particularly insistent form of desire, then it may also be the prime matter that needs to be shaped for moral character to be formed.

This suspicion will be strengthened by Kant's definition of passion as an inclination which 'can hardly, or not at all' (Ak. 7:251) be controlled by reason. If passion is a particularly violent and ungovernable form of inclination it remains true that 'both emotion and passion' (Ak. 7:251) challenge the order of the mind in threatening the sovereignty of reason. There is therefore a need for a 'physician of souls' (Ak. 7:251). For this physician to be able to safeguard the order essential to mental health the comprehension of the desiring forces that threaten anarchy is necessary. Whilst emotion and passion both threaten mental balance it is the latter which is clearly the greater danger. Emotion occurs through sensations interrupting mental composure and is opposed by a positive force of 'apathy', understood as self-possession. Given that emotions are precipitate storms, if the mind affected by them can maintain composure for a sufficient length of time the pressure of sensation will gradually lessen and eventually cease. It is a different story with passion which is deep in effect. However whilst these remarks suggest an entirely negative understanding of feeling there is given a different type of account when Kant considers the limits of apathy:

> For the purpose of enlivening us Nature has done so by adding to the moral motives for the Good those motives of pathological (sensuous) inducement as a temporary surrogate of reason. (Ak. 7:253)

With the exception of this connection between the moral motive and a sensuous inclination the broad typology that is given of emotion divides into strong and weak effects of sensation on the mind and discussions of degree of feeling. This also fades into broad-brush descriptions of characterizations of nationalities and gendered oppositions. These purely empirical (and particularly partial) generalizations include both trite and contentious observations enlivened by the occasional sagacious insight into psychology. There are also points of characterization which are intriguing as when resentment is described as 'a grieving over not having responded to insult with proper means' (Ak. 7:260), an observation weakened by the failure to enquire whether this grievance can develop into passion. It is in discussing passion rather than emotion that Kant discovers his real interest in this area as passion is the form of feeling that presents the real moral problems.

Kant describes a passion as an inclination which hinders the use of reason 'to compare, at a particular moment of choice, a specific inclination against the sum of all inclinations' (Ak. 7:265). This means that passion is an intense emotion that has the effect of undermining mental balance by preventing the reflection that enables a person to keep matters in proportion. This is why Kant links passion with 'enchantment' and mania. But because acting on the basis of passion is equivalent to the tendency of a person to formulate maxims of action under the guidance of the strength of an inclination it is requisite that reason be involved in its mode of operation, albeit subordinated to its power. This is why passion is the property of a rational being. Kant classifies passions into two kinds: passions for natural properties and passions for cultural acquisitions. Under the former head is included the passions for freedom and sex, under the latter ambition, lust for power and avarice. The second type of passion is the more substantially interesting as it involves the intensification of maxims into fixed patterns of behaviour that thwart the purposes for which they are formulated rather than simply being the impression on the mind of strong sensations.

The passion for freedom is exemplified in the reluctance to accept constraint and the impulse to rebel against law. The 'naturalness' of this passion consists simply in its presence in the early history of humanity and the repeated difficulty in establishing ordered conduct through the construction of states and civilizations. Whilst this passion is merely negative the passion for revenge which arises on grounds analogous to those which enable the construction of systems of justice departs from this ground in its lack of measure. But the passion for power is the one that is closest of all to the ground of practical reason itself. With this passion a person labours to exert influence over others, an influence akin in its effects to that gained by the rational activity of ruling and governing according to the requirements of rational intercourse. However, its self-destructive nature consists in the fact that precisely what imparts strength to the passion is also what renders the person gripped by its effects vulnerable:

> Ambition is a weakness of people, which allows them to be influenced through their opinions; lust of authority allows them to be influenced through their fear; and avarice allows them to be influenced through their own interest. Servile submission will always result when a person has been seized by someone who has the faculty to use that person's inclinations for his own purposes. (Ak. 7:272)

Thus one who is ambitious for a good opinion not earned by his moral qualities can easily be undermined by flatterers, the one who lusts for power makes others suspicious and the avaricious person turns against themselves the means which they have made into an end. In all cases of passion delusion is at work and Kant rounds off the discussion of passion with an account of delusion as based on the fantasy that something subjectively desirable is an objective (unearned) fact.

Whilst the passions promote unreason in the fixation of the mind on an object not worthy of a person's singular attention, the effects of the emotions on the passions can be to weaken the latter in a manner which is beneficial to humanity:

> If cowardice did not have pity on man, then belligerent bloodthirst would soon annihilate him; and if there were no deceit (for among the many scoundrels united through conspiracy, for example, in a regiment, there will always be one to betray it), then, because of the inborn wickedness of man, whole states would soon be overthrown. (Ak. 7:276)

Hence there is a cunning attached to the feelings that promotes a self-destruction of vice by its own means.

By contrast with the tendencies that promote vice the nature of goodness can be discerned as consisting for each one of us in two distinct aspects, the combination of which forms the central problem of the Dialectic of the Second Critique. Physically, happiness is the greatest good, whilst virtue is the goodness of action that follows from the formulation of good maxims. The combination of virtue with happiness would create the highest good, a combination of the physically good with the habit of mind best conducive to morality. However: 'inclination to pleasurable living and inclination to virtue are in conflict with each other' (Ak. 7:277) so that there is a problem in achieving their combination.

The combination of virtue with physical happiness is indicated by Kant to reside in the possession of 'humaneness' or the propensity to balance good physical arrangements with the cast of mind that promotes the moral. What 'humaneness' consists in is the seasoning of pleasure with the orientation towards moral ends. Hence, sociability promotes concord and harmony, which are ends to be considered as practically desirable and attainable by the provision of occasions of mutual enjoyment such as dinner parties. But such events in themselves can also give licence to licentiousness, squandering and divisive competition so that the practical success of them requires that the physical comfort provided by them be tempered by the moral end for which they are conducted. (This gives Kant the occasion to discuss the role of amusements by contrast with conversation: Ak. 7:277–8.)

The next area of interest in the *Anthropology* for an understanding of the development of Kant's practical philosophy is his account of the character of the person in the Characterization. Kant here presents moral character as consisting in the possession of principles. Whilst the treatment of temperament given here draws on the theory of the humours the basic notion of moral character is pinpointed with decisiveness as 'absolute unity of the inner principle of conduct' (Ak. 7:295). This consists in adopting as the maxim which is basic and must govern all others 'uninhibited internal truthfulness towards oneself' (Ak. 7:295). This basic maxim of moral character is what enables there to be rational personality at all and is the basis of dignity in conduct.

In treating the character of the species as such there is again an admixture of empirical observation and rational insight. The basic orientation of the species, which corresponds to the maxim of the individual towards self-understanding and inner truth, is the Idea of a cosmopolitan society as the inner goal of development. This also indicates the real basis in practical terms for constructing an anthropology at all as such a condition cannot be reached 'by the free consent of individuals, but only through progressive organization of the citizens of the earth within and toward the species as a system' (Ak. 7:333). This suggests that whilst there is a great deal to say about individual conduct and the nature of the types of maxims which should guide it the ultimate horizon of practical reflection should rather be with the circumstances in which such reflection takes place.

Whilst the *Anthropology* is fundamentally akin to the early writings the horizon it promotes is wider than that given in them. Whilst *On Education* outlined conditions for viewing children as parts of a moral world the *Anthropology* makes clear the need for thinking conditions of historical and social development as integral to the perfectionist horizon of practical thought.

Kant's *Lectures on Ethics*

Whilst Kant himself published the *Anthropology* and was involved in the publication of *On Education* the lectures on ethics were published posthumously and on the basis of student transcriptions. They are thus less reliable philologically than the works already discussed but the material offered in them is of much greater interest philosophically. There are four basic sets of notes available: Herder's notes from the 1760s, notes from Georg Ludwig Collins from 1784, notes from Mrongovius dating from 1785 and notes from Vigilantius dating from 1793.[13] The notes from Collins are much the most extensive and will form the basis of my treatment but I will briefly touch on Herder's notes and provide an account of what is distinctive in Mrongovius' notes. Vigilantius' notes are not, I will suggest, appropriate for discussion here as they are on the subject of the metaphysics of morals and hence need to be consulted by comparison with Kant's book of that title as preliminary to the full doctrinal treatment of practical philosophy.

Herder's notes are dated to the period 1762–4 and hence are from the same period as the Prize Essay and *Observations on the Feeling of the Beautiful and the Sublime*. Whilst the reliability of these notes has been questioned[14] they confirm many of the features of Kant's early writings. They open with the question of whether it can truly be said that we possess a disinterested feeling of concern for others. This is answered in the affirmative and 'the greater it is, the more it is felt as a perfection' (Ak. 27:3). Furthermore, it is stated that God gave us a self-interest in our own perfection and 'a disinterested concern for the perfection of others' (Ak. 27:3). The concern for the perfection of others is the real end since the concern for our own perfection is in fact a means for the former. This assertion is used here to justify a criticism of Hobbes and moralities based on self-interest.

After venturing to present logical grounds for placing pleasure in the perfection of others ahead of pleasure in our own egoistic desires Kant turns to assessing the characteristics of good actions. He suggests that actions are good by virtue of two aspects: a) physically, in terms of consequences; b) morally, in terms of intentions. This division, which replicates the difference between consequentialist and deontological ethics, conveys the clear sense that Kant includes reference to consequences within his assessment of the good of actions but does not regard it as the ultimate basis of the goodness of the act. Pleasure in an act is moral when directed to the intention that actuated it and this pleasure is called 'moral feeling' (Ak. 27:4). The connection of these lectures to the *Observations on the Feeling of the Beautiful and the Sublime* is clearly stated:

> The feeling inspired by morality (without profit) is beautiful or sublime; my joy at the perfected in myself (feeling of self-esteem, of one's own worth) is noble; my joy at satisfaction (feeling of goodwill) is beautiful. (Ak. 27:5)

Whilst these connections are in accord with what we have garnered from Kant's early writings the development of the notes is in some respects surprising. Kant denies here the perfectionism that he has asserted earlier when he states that in moral terms perfection is 'never the transcendental' (Ak. 27:6) as, however good I am, I could always be better. This peculiar argument is then accompanied by a statement of what he now takes the supreme law to be, namely: 'act according to your moral nature' (Ak. 27:6). This supreme law is supported by reference to an expanded notion of moral feeling:

> My reason can err; my moral feeling, only when I uphold custom before natural feeling; but in that case it is merely implicit reason; and my final yardstick still remains moral feeling, not true and false; just as the capacity for true and false is the final yardstick of the understanding, and both are universal. (Ak. 27:6)

The difference between feeling and the understanding consists in the latter's fundamental guide being the distinction between true and false, the former's between good and bad. At this point Kant's commitment to giving attention to feeling against the rationalism of Wolff leads him to a reliance on the naturalism of Rousseau, a reliance not stated so boldly in anything Kant *published* in the 1760s.

After a digression on the relation between God and morality Kant returns to the notion of perfection and now affirms again that it is 'the end' not the means of moral action. He also affirms the distinction between ethics and law that guides the doctrinal work on practical philosophy when describing ethics as concerning 'inner duties' and law outward actions. Since, however, even angels could be conceived of as ethical if this merely meant the disposition towards inner maxims the notion of it is made coterminous with virtue by stating that it involves a consciousness of inner struggle. These considerations also prompt Kant to favour a particular understanding of ethical maxims: 'The greater the moral perfection of an action is to be, the greater must be the obstacles, and the struggle, and hence the more needful, in that case, is the *strict* ethic' (Ak. 27:14).

Kant is in these lectures, as in the later versions we have, expounding the ethics of Baumgarten as part of the task of teaching the subject in view. But he is also attempting, under the guise of this exposition, to present a critical response which will permit him to convey to his students a sense of what is the real basis of ethical thought. Hence he reports here that Baumgarten's perfectionist ethics consists in two major rules: perfect yourself as to the end and perfect yourself as to the means of your action. Taken as supreme rules they present serious difficulties:

> By this perfection is meant either moral perfection, and in that case the latter is already presupposed, so that this rule is not a basic one,

for it presupposes a ground; or else by this perfection is meant something undetermined, e.g., health, etc., and is again not a basic rule, on account of its instability. If I am to seek perfection as a rule, this amounts to saying: Desire all perfections, a proposition quite certain, indeed, subjectively speaking, whereby we always act; but objectively speaking an empty proposition, since it is wholly identical. The sole moral rule, therefore, is this: Act according to *your moral feeling!* (Ak. 27:16)

Here Kant's earlier distinction between physical and moral goodness is brought back into play as Baumgarten's maxims may well promote the former but not the latter. Like Wolff, of whom Baumgarten was the disciple, the notion of perfection is related merely to relations of cause and effect and hence ultimately based on grounds of aversion as produced by relations between objects.

As opposed to the subtle confusion between types of perfection produced by the Wolffian school and repeated in the text Kant is expounding there is counterposed time and again in the Herder notes the natural virtue praised by Rousseau. In discussing the peculiarity of modern child-drearing Kant points to the fact that it was customary amongst the Spartans to allow girls up to the age of nine and boys to the age of thirteen to be routinely naked and suggests that the progress of chaste physical arrangements has gone hand in hand with the decline of chaste minds. This leads Kant to a set of sentimental reflections on the nature of marriage, which unsurprisingly have a patriarchal cast (Ak. 27:50). The difficulties of this position are however already discussed by Kant as when he maintains that the effect of the progress of civilization must be to destroy a natural basis for feeling hence creating the consequence that love now is merely 'a yearning of the fancy' (Ak. 27:65). Following Rousseau Kant here espouses an egalitarianism based on natural equality and an extended attack on intolerance.

Herder's notes are instructive in indicating a greater confusion than is presented in Kant's published writings from the 1760s. Within them we note both perfectionist and anti-perfectionist elements and a general tendency (as with *Observations on the Feeling of the Beautiful and the Sublime*) to follow Rousseau's guidance and to promote a sentimentalist morality.

Whilst Herder's notes are short and difficult to grasp in terms of the fundamental standpoint articulated, the major notes of Collins are very extensive and bring us to the brink of Kant's account in the *Groundwork*. These notes date from the winter semester 1784–5 and hence from the period just after Kant composed the *Groundwork* and immediately prior to its publication. Unlike in the *Groundwork* however we find here a rich treatment of many themes which will be revisited in *The Metaphysics of Morals*. These lectures are still an exposition and criticism of Baumgarten and are divided into three main parts corresponding to the articulation of the idea of a universal practical philosophy, the understanding of religion and the elements of morality (including the subdivision into duties towards oneself and duties towards others). I will here mainly look at the account of universal practical philosophy as the basic conception which Kant inherits from Baumgarten, subjects to rigorous criticism and, in a fundamental sense, reformulates into the systematic treatment of the mature works.

At the beginning of the Collins notes Kant defines what is meant by 'practical philosophy':

> Practical philosophy is practical not by form, but by the object, and this object is free acts and free behaviour. The theoretical is knowing, and the practical is behaving. If I abstract from the particular matter in hand, the philosophy of behaviour is that which gives a rule for the proper use of freedom, and this is the object of practical philosophy, without regard to particulars. So practical philosophy treats of the use of free choice, not in regard to particulars, but independently of all of them. (Ak. 27:243)

Practical philosophy is thus made equivalent to the treatment of free actions at the level of highest generality. This permits formulations that apply not to man only (as with pragmatic anthropology) but to rational beings in general. However: 'morality cannot exist without anthropology, for one must first know of the agent whether he is also in a position to accomplish what is required from him that he should do' (Ak. 27:244). This implies that whilst the general content of practical philosophy has to be formulated in a manner that does not include an understanding of the nature of particular moral beings that there are in fact circumstances, which do need to be treated in the concrete appraisal of action that involve recourse to the understanding of who is being appraised.

Having indicated the broadest understanding of what practical philosophy consists in Kant now turns to what practical rules are like. Three separate types of practical rule are distinguished: rules of prudence, rules of skill and rules of morality. From these rules three types of imperative arise. Sciences are governed by rules of skill and such rules instruct us 'hypothetically' since we must first have an end in view before consulting such rules as means. Practical philosophy hence does not concern itself with rules of skill but only with rules of prudence and rules of morality. Rules of prudence relate to conditions of happiness and imperatives of prudence are subjectively necessary. Moral imperatives by contrast are objectively necessary and unconditional.

The distinction between prudential and moral presupposes a rejection of the notion that there is a single highest good or *summum bonum*, a rejection we have also noted in the *Anthropology*. In support of this position Kant distinguishes the ethical systems of antiquity. The purpose of this discussion is to demonstrate the variety of ways of dealing with the question of what the *summum bonum* consists in. Kant separates here the Cynical school from the Epicurean and both from the Stoic. The Cynical notion of the *summum bonum* is stated to be 'innocence' or simplicity in contrast to the Epicurean valuation of prudence and the Stoic prizing of wisdom. This typological treatment allows the Kant of 1784 to identify the system of Rousseau with the Cynical notion of innocence. The opposition to this by the Epicureans is in accord with the problems we already noted Kant to have discerned in the Herder notes: 'Epicurus said that even if we have no vice by nature, we do have an inclination to it, so that innocence and simplicity are not assured ...' (Ak. 27:249). If corruption is possible for us this must be part of our nature and hence appeal to simple circumstances is faulty because the opportunities for vice in such circumstances may simply be limited.

The distinction between physical goodness and moral goodness is at stake in attempting to think the nature of the *summum bonum* as a unity of disparate elements. But if the Cynical notion is problematic in its false portrayal of our nature, the Epicurean valuation of happiness or pleasure makes morality itself into a means to something else and achieves the unity of disparate elements by subordination without clear justification. The Stoic notion of wisdom by contrast in promoting the notion of a sage neglects to note the fact that satisfaction is not entirely derived from virtue alone but requires other elements. Kant contrasts all these systems with the Christian notion of perfection and states that this notion is purer than any given in antiquity.

Whilst this suggests that Kant is deriving from this survey a conclusion favouring perfectionism he does not turn to setting out maxims of the kind rejected in the lectures from the 1760s but instead begins to inquire into the nature of moral goodness as an extended preliminary to presenting his own solution of the problem posed by the notion of the *summum bonum*. But he does not even address this question directly but through a critical discussion of the various systems of determining the nature of moral goodness. Kant states:

> The theoretical conception of morality (which does not specify a theory, but only a concept from which a theory can be constructed) consists in this, that morality rests either on empirical or intellectual grounds, and must be derived from either empirical or intellectual principles. (Ak. 27:252)

We can now see that this type of conception is one that Kant has again and again discussed and that the early works, in their critical treatment of the notion of intellectual grounds tended towards a conception based on empirical ones (feeling). However, Kant's commitment to thinking that the notion of perfection was of some importance in thinking about the ultimate nature of morality also tended to give him grounds for favouring an ultimate intellectual basis to morality. This oscillation is precisely what has constituted his debate with tradition up to this point.

Empirical grounds for morality are sensuous grounds; intellectual grounds are based on reason. Sensuous grounds include egoistic systems, altruistic systems and thoughts based on moral feeling. Other empirical systems are plausible which appeal to sensuousness not as primary grounds but as basic in combination with something external such as education, government or society. Systems that are relativistic in description of customs are of this type as are decisionist accounts of sovereignty. Intellectualist systems by contrast are based on purely *a priori* grounds. Such systems are not contingent in nature like the empirical ones but have complete necessity built into the nature of moral principles. There are two forms of intellectualist system: those grounded on the inner nature of the action and those based on something external to the action. The latter types of intellectualism are theological and are rejected immediately by Kant.

The inner practical necessity recommended by the intellectualist of a non-theological type is discerned by Kant as requisite for a description of moral imperatives. Imperatives express necessity and since empirical occurrences are of their nature non-necessary there cannot be in principle an empirical ground for them. Hence it is necessary to consider the moral motive purely, in separation from sensuous conditions. So the problem with perfectionism is that it indicates a general basis for comprehending practical necessitation without however indicating what aspect of the moral agent is to be made perfect. In contrast to

Baumgarten's principles (which are given again in these lectures) Kant states: 'moral goodness consists in the perfection of the will' (Ak. 27:266) but since the will to be effective requires the development of capacity to act the inner nature of the will must itself be classed as moral and require a relation to means. Hence, perfection is in fact convertible into an imperative of self-cultivation (which is expressed as a duty in the *Groundwork*, Ak. 4:423).

In stating that an imperative contains in itself a reference to necessity Kant indicates his understanding that morality is a system of constraints. However, the moral agent is not restrained from without in acting in accordance with a moral rule. Rather, they freely act in conformity with a rule and hence: 'The more a man can be morally compelled, the freer he is' (Ak. 27:268). This follows from the separation of moral goodness from conditions of physical goodness. If moral goodness is different from physical goodness in arising from a pure motive then the one who acts according to a moral rule is under no outward compulsion so to do but is purely inwardly conforming to a rule, an action which requires separation of oneself from any constraint other than that given by oneself. But whilst this may suggest an absolute separation between head and heart things are not so simple as it is still necessary to distinguish between the principle which states that something is good and the motive which impels to act in accordance with this principle. As Kant puts it:

> The supreme principle of all moral judgment lies in the understanding; the supreme principle of the moral impulse to do this thing lies in the heart. This motive is the moral feeling. Such a principle of motive cannot be confused with the principle of judgment. The latter is the norm, and the principle of impulsion is the motive. (Ak. 27:274–5)

The relation between the principle of judgment and the motive of action is what has been systematically obscured by tradition. Whilst intellectualist systems assimilate the motive to the principle, empirical systems assimilate the principle to the motive (which explains the young Kant's suspicions about principles). Without a motive to act morally we have a bad will, without a principle as to what it is to act wrongly a poor understanding. The former is a moral failing, the latter a theoretical failing.

The intellectualist answer Kant has given about the principle of morality does not entail an intellectualist answer about the motive to moral action. An intellectualist account of moral motivation would entail that there are feelings of an intellectual kind and Kant rejects this as absurd (Ak. 27:275). Kant also treats the notion that the principle of morality could be based on empirical grounds to scorn. Kant expounds the principle of morality positively as 'the conformity of the action to a universally valid law of free choice' (Ak. 27:1426).[15] This is used here to examine the maxims underlying certain actions and to determine whether they are in principle permissible. This universal principle gives us a form of judging the morality of action. But the connection of this to the motive actuating action is here frankly stated by Kant to be a mighty problem:

> Nobody can or ever will comprehend how the understanding should have a motivating power; it can admittedly judge, but to give this judgment power so that it becomes a motive able to impel the will to performance of an action – to understand this is the philosophers' stone. (Ak. 27:1428)

Whilst this problem repeats the tremendous difficulty of the relation of pure morality to anthropology Kant does at least now resolve the problem in what immorality consists. The understanding can be taught to accept the principle of moral action but this does not entail that the mind, which has learnt the moral principle, will be part of a moral personality who performs good action. Hence the basis of immorality is not cognitive, it is grounded in the will. The nature of the difficulty presented as a 'philosopher's stone' is now restated:

> It is quite impossible to bring a man to the point of feeling the abhorrence of vice, for I can only tell him what my understanding perceives, and I do indeed bring him to the point of perceiving it; but that he should feel the abhorrence, if his senses are not susceptible to it, is impossible. Such a thing cannot be produced, for man has no such secret organization, that he could be moved by objective grounds. Yet we can indeed produce a *habitus*, which is not natural, though it replaces nature, and becomes habitual through imitation and frequent exercise. (Ak. 27:1429)

In illustration of this need for a *habitus* Kant returns to the difficult problem of punishment which we noted his treatment of in *On Education*. As with *On Education* the example is the moral education of a child. The pure moral education would consist in bringing the child to seeing a bad action as bad in itself and hence the use of physical punishment is problematical as a response to actions of a type not in accordance with the moral principle as it promotes action which is not purely motivated. But in neglect of punishment to instil feelings of self-actuation which promote responses of shame and remorse, bad conscience and an inward disposition to the good on the grounds of a repeated exposure to pure example is still to envisage a situation not present as the education to which a moral actor will be exposed will not be so continuous and harmonious. This solution therefore is ideal and itself would be the product of the situation it wishes to bring about. As Kant goes on to state, the purpose of punishment on the whole is pragmatic, to bring about outward conformity of action in response to an external law. This promotes 'Jesuitical cunning' (Ak. 27:287) but without the conformity of virtue to law the *habitus* produced will always of necessity be imperfect.

The problem here raised is pursued in Kant's discussion of conscience. Conscience is described here by Kant as an 'instinct' because it has a 'driving force' to make us judge ourselves in ways we would prefer not to. It is distinct from judgments of prudence that we often use to reproach ourselves with for having committed actions whose bad consequences *for ourselves* we did not foresee as it is rather a judgment upon ourselves that we committed an action, which is bad *in itself*. Since there may be some who are never moved by such a conviction it follows that some do not have a conscience and hence that the 'instinct' in question is an odd one since it can fail to operate! Kant is at pains however to insist on this point since if conscience were entirely an effect of education and instruction it would follow that the ignorant would lack it and hence could not be blamed for having failed to follow its promptings. The loss of its prompt is however itself due to a *habitus* albeit one towards vice and in fact this can also occur through a micrological attention eventually wearying one entirely (Ak. 27:357).

A central difficulty of Kant's treatment is now visible: how to connect the formal commands of moral principles with the motive to action. The conscience is one way and it is pure because inward. The *habitus* inculcated by education is another and takes its purity from resort to practices of reproach replacing physical punishments. But the former can wither under the impact of a *habitus* to vice and the latter is never presented alone and is merely an ideal condition. This difficulty is connected to the question of the relationship between pure morality and anthropology, a difficulty continuously stated in Kant's references in these lectures to our nature.

The notes from Mrongovius overlap those of Collins and date from the same period, winter semester 1784–5 and are again based on a critical exposition of Baumgarten. Here we find a different account of the nature of practical philosophy:

> Practical philosophy and morals are not identical. General practical philosophy is related to morals as logic is to metaphysics. Logic abstracts from content, and treats of the laws whereby the understanding operates. Metaphysic deals with the pure use of reason. General practical philosophy exhibits the rules whereby the will is determined *a posteriori*; morals, the *a priori* rules whereby I ought to determine the will. (Ak. 29:597)

General practical philosophy therefore wishes to show us the ways in which the will is in fact empirically determined whilst morals shows us how it should be determined. The relation between the two is intimate but again seems to require an intermediary element which will show how what ought to be the case can become the case.

This leads Kant again towards the problem of the *summum bonum* as the two elements that would be combined therein are related to the difficulty of how to bring the inward disposition in accord with the moral principle through the nature of resistance to this union residing in the problem of how to make moral action sensuously agreeable. Kant recasts his earlier statement that moral perfection consists in the possession of a moral will in the following form: 'a good will is simply good without restriction, for itself alone, in every respect and under all circumstances' (Ak. 27:599). But whilst a good will is good unconditionally the problem of the *summum bonum* can be expressed concisely in the statement that the good will is not completely good. It does not comprise the whole of goodness.

> The greatest worth of one's state is happiness. So virtue combined with happiness is the highest good. Virtue is the condition under which I am worthy of happiness, but that is not yet the highest good ... (Ak. 29:600)

The combination of the two elements of happiness and a good will in one notion as the highest good is now stated by Kant only to be possible under the supposition of the existence of God. This concept allows for the combination of the two elements to be an object of hope (as a request made to a benevolent being) but cannot give it actual force in any existing circumstance and hence is, like the *habitus* of morality, an ideal condition and, as Kant himself states: 'All ideals are fictions' (Ak. 29:605).

Since the maxims of a good will cannot be based in their purity upon anything other than the moral principle then the motive that might actuate action (the hope of achieving a *summum bonum*) is not itself the basis for judging an action right or wrong. This is rather from the universal ground of formulating a law. In these notes we see Kant formulating the moral imperative clearly: 'Act so that you can will that the nature of your will becomes a general rule. If my will can become a general rule, then it agrees with itself in all circumstances, and is an intrinsically good will' (Ak. 29:610). The form of the moral law thus gives the content of a good will. The moral law is also stated by Kant to be the basis of two kinds of duties, perfect and imperfect. Perfect duties are those that strictly accord with the principle of the moral law and whose opposites rest on strict conceptual incoherence in terms of universal conditions whilst imperfect duties command something whose opposite is possible but which I could not will to be possible.

With the statement of the moral law as based on a principle of universality and the uncovering of the problem of the *summum bonum* as the difficulty of reconciling the necessity of the moral law with the urgent inclination towards happiness Kant has here reached the very edge of a critical treatment of morality. The nature of this critical treatment can here be discerned. It will be necessary to demonstrate that the universal principle of moral judgment is a possible basis for motivation and it will be necessary to show that the principle of the *summum bonum* can in some respect be saved from being merely a fictional resolution. Both will pose formidable difficulties for Kant.

2
Freedom and the Ends of Reason

Having reached a statement of the fundamental problems of Kant's practical philosophy from considering the *Lectures on Ethics* it is now time to set out the considerations of practical import that are presented in the *Critique of Pure Reason*. This is necessary due to the fact that the consideration of freedom within the First Critique adds a further element of difficulty in the comprehension of Kant's practical philosophy, an element that will guide the consideration of the relationship between the *Groundwork* and the Second Critique. It is within the pages of the First Critique that Kant sets out a distinction between two types of freedom: practical freedom and transcendental freedom. It will be necessary in this chapter to attend to the question of how Kant understands these types of freedom to be related and to give a description of the characterizations he provides of each.

The relationship between these two types of freedom is connected also to Kant's detailing in the First Critique of a distinction between two types of character: empirical character and intelligible character. This distinction, like that between the two types of freedom, follows from the Critical revolution in philosophy brought about by the First Critique. Both these distinctions require to be understood as involving a consideration of the unity of the First Critique as some have suggested that the treatments provided of these distinctions within the Transcendental Dialectic do not match those given in the Transcendental Doctrine of Method.

In addition to questions concerning the unity of the First Critique it will also be necessary to review here the suggestion that the resolution of the Third Antinomy is problematic given the treatment of the Antinomy of Teleological Judgment. Hence it will be necessary to consider what the resolution of these two antinomies consists in and whether there is, as has been suggested, an 'antinomy of antinomies' between them.

Finally, rarely discussed within the treatment of the First Critique is a section entitled 'the ideal of pure reason'. I will suggest that this section is of importance in understanding the Critical revolution in practical philosophy.

In this chapter, therefore, I will proceed in the following manner. I will first discuss the motivation of the Third Antinomy, and then state what the antinomy consists in and give its resolution. Next I will discuss the suggestion that the resolution of this antinomy does not admit of unification with the resolution of the antinomy of teleological judgment. Having treated these questions I will next turn to the interlocked problems of the relationship between practical freedom and transcendental freedom and empirical and intelligible character. These considerations will lead me to consider the suggestion that the treatment of practical questions in the Dialectic is not consonant with that given in the Doctrine of Method. Finally, I will provide an account of the place of the 'ideal of pure reason' within the practical philosophy, indicating its connection with the Fourth Antinomy.

The motivation of the Third Antinomy

We saw in the previous chapter that Kant's first consideration of the question of freedom in the *New Elucidation of the First Principles of Metaphysical Cognition* emerged as a response to a conflict between the philosophies of Wolff and Crusius. This context is also of import for understanding the fact that the antinomy is included within a consideration of 'cosmological ideas' which frames the setting of the antinomies in the First Critique. In describing what these ideas consist in Kant relies on the treatment of the pure concepts of the understanding provided in the Transcendental Analytic:

> Now in order to be able to enumerate these ideas with systematic precision according to a principle, we must *first* note that it is only from the understanding that pure and transcendental concepts can arise, that reason really cannot generate any concept at all, but can at most *free* a *concept of the understanding* from the unavoidable limitations of a possible experience, and thus seek to extend it beyond the boundaries of the empirical, though still in connection with it. This happens when for a given conditioned reason demands an absolute totality on the side of the conditions (under which the understanding subjects all appearances to synthetic unity), thereby making the category into a transcendental idea, in order to give

absolute completeness to the empirical synthesis through its progress toward the unconditioned (which is never met with in experience, but only in the idea). Reason demands this in accordance with the principle: *If the conditioned is given, then the whole sum of conditions, and hence the absolutely unconditioned, is also given,* through which alone the conditioned was possible. Thus *first,* the transcendental ideas will really be nothing except categories extended to the unconditioned ... . *Second,* however, not all categories will work here, but only those in which the synthesis constitutes a *series,* and indeed a series of conditions subordinated (not coordinated) one to another for any conditioned. (A409–10/B435–6)

So the cosmological ideas arise from the extension of a category beyond the limits of possible experience in accord with a demand for totality (which demand is of the essence of reason). The only categories, which get treated in this manner by reason, are those that concern a regressive synthesis and hence we are only concerned here with the categories of quantity, reality, causality and contingency. The first two types of category are mathematical and thus concern the conditions of worldhood or 'the mathematical whole of all appearances and the totality of their synthesis in the great as well as the small' whilst the latter two types of category are dynamical and concern nature or 'the unity in the *existence* of appearances' (A418–19/B446–7). The latter two categories when given the extension of 'freedom' give rise to the thoughts of the Supreme Being (contingency) and freedom as 'the unconditioned causality of the cause in appearance' (A419/B447). Hence the object of the Third Antinomy is a problem with causality and since causality is also treated in the Transcendental Analytic under the heading of the Second Analogy we would expect the account provided there to be of some significance in grasping the nature of this antinomy.

The treatment of the antinomies requires, states Kant, a 'sceptical method' which 'aims at certainty' (A424/B451). The treatment of the antinomies will thus indicate the basis of the claims of both parties to the dispute and the reasons why the dispute is irresolvable unless a step is taken which goes beyond the claims of both whilst satisfying what is legitimate in their claims.

What the Third Antinomy consists in

In stating the Third Antinomy to concern the extension of the category of causality beyond the conditions of possible experience we reveal the reason why freedom is first encountered as a problem of theoretical philosophy. The basis of the arguments for the two claimants within the dispute will have to be treated in relation to the 'remarks' Kant makes about the arguments of each in order to test the nature of the argument. The position of the thesis is given as follows:

> Causality in accordance with laws of nature is not the only one from which all the appearances of the world can be derived. It is also necessary to assume another causality through freedom in order to explain them. (A444/B472)

The thesis thus emerges from reason's extension of the category of causality beyond the limits of possible experience. The argument for this extension is given in a *reductio* argument. The argument in its favour is given in seven steps that I would summarize as follows:

1. Assume there is no other causality than nature.
2. Everything that happens presupposes a previous occurrence in accord with a rule.
3. Each previous occurrence must itself have arisen.
4. Thus the causality through which something has happened presupposes a previous state which brought it about.
5. If everything happens in accord with the causality of nature there are only relative but no first beginnings.
6. The law of nature is that nothing happens without a cause.
7. So if the law of nature is taken in 'unlimited universality' (A446/B474) then it contradicts itself.

When we break the argument down we can see that the crucial step is point six in the argument, which however is no more than a restatement of point three. The reason for the difficulty which here is taken to undermine the notion that there is only one type of causality is the typical rationalist construal of the principle of sufficient reason as containing both logical and real grounds (precisely the supposition which in fact Crusius objects to in Wolff's determinism and Wolff's argument is replicated in the argument in favour of the thesis of the Fourth Antinomy). This indicates the basis of objection to the argument of the thesis but does not touch the problem that underlies the argument as its motivation, a problem that connects what is essentially a version of the cosmological argument for the existence of God to the problem of the freedom of moral agents:

that in the question of freedom of the will which has always put speculative reason into such embarrassment is really only *transcendental*, and it concerns only whether a faculty of beginning a series of successive things or states *from itself* is to be assumed . . . . We have really established this necessity of a first beginning of a series of appearances from freedom only to the extent that this is required to make comprehensible an origin of the world, since one can take all the subsequent states to be a result of mere natural laws. But because the faculty of beginning a series in time entirely on its own is thereby proved (though no insight into it is achieved), now we are permitted also to allow that in the course of the world different series may begin on their own as far as their causality is concerned, and to ascribe to the substances in those series the faculty of acting from freedom. (A448–9/B477–8)

The problem is that of a *causa sui* or a first beginning in regard not to time but to causality (A450/B478). If a causal series can start *ex nihilo* then this beginning of causality could take place within the appearances as well as outside them so that establishing it as a thought opens out the possibility that rational agency includes freedom, just as divine agency does on the argument of the thesis.

The fact that the argument of the thesis is thus open to an easy objection given the rationalist construal of the principle of sufficient reason does not in itself indicate that the motivation behind the proof is as worthy of rejection as the proof itself as the notion of such a *causa sui* does seem to be involved in the description of rational agency (even to the basic notion of self-movement). This point is made in Kant's remark on the thesis and it gives a clear reason for arguing in its favour. This is part of the sceptical method with which Kant is treating the antinomies; as we will see that the argument of the antithesis, though also presented in a manner, which is clearly inadequate, will nonetheless, likewise possess a clear motivation.

The antithesis is given in the following manner:

There is no freedom, but everything in the world happens solely in accordance with laws of nature. (A445/B473)

As with the argument for the thesis this is a *reductio* proof, which can be given, in the following five steps:

1. Suppose there is transcendental freedom, that is, a special kind of causality that absolutely begins a state.

2. The beginning of this causality will thus have no preceding determination.
3. But every beginning of action presupposes a state preceding it.
4. Hence transcendental freedom is contrary to the principle of causality itself.
5. If freedom had laws guiding its causality it would simply be the same as nature.

The argument in favour of the antithesis hence turns on step three which indicates that the thought of a causality of freedom contradicts the conception of causality established by the Second Analogy. Due to this, the argument of the antithesis rests on the results of the Transcendental Analytic, a fact that gives the antithesis the appearance of an advantage. As we shall shortly see this appearance is deceptive, as whilst resting on the results of the Analytic, the argument of the antithesis also flouts the rule of the Analytic in ruling out *in conception* something that can only be ruled out as a *possible experience*. This conflation mirrors the double meaning given to the principle of sufficient reason in the thesis and reveals both arguments to be sophistical.

Whilst the argument of the antithesis thus steps beyond its own guiding rule in not placing the conception of transcendental freedom within the realm of possibilities that logically are conceivable so long as they do not pretend to be included within the notion of a possible experience the basic motivation behind the argument of the antithesis can be defended. Kant's 'remark' on the argument of the antithesis indicates that one in favour of it will tend to assimilate the dynamical antinomies to the mathematical antinomies and assure themselves of the unity of experience through conflating nature with worldhood. Whilst this 'remark' accentuates the difficulty with the argument of the antithesis it also points to its clear rational motivation as being to give an account of experience which permits us to cognise it as unified, a notion which is clearly regarded by Kant himself as necessary.

Thus whilst both the claimants in the dispute have rational motivation for their positions neither argument in fact is convincing although the argument of the antithesis does rest on a prime condition of the possibility of experience. In stating the Third Antinomy and comprehending the motives behind the arguments of both sides we have disclosed how the cosmological problem leads to a question about rational agency and a question about the unity of experience. Whilst the resolution of the antinomy that Kant presents will give us new understandings of these conjoined topics it will also raise new questions about them both.

Preparing the resolution of the Third Antinomy

Before turning to Kant's account of the resolution of the antinomy it is worth looking at the lengthy sections of the chapter on the antinomy of pure reason that are presented between the statements of the four antinomies and the treatment of their resolution. In these sections Kant prepares us for the solution of the antinomies by treating further the motivations for arguing in favour of the positions of thesis and antithesis. The position of the antithesis is understood to be 'a principle of pure *empiricism*' (A466/B494) whilst that of the thesis has an empiricist view of the series of appearances but a intellectualist starting point and so is characterized by Kant as 'the *dogmatism* of pure reason' (A466/B494).

After stating the positions of both claimants and adding his comment indicating the motivation behind the respective positions Kant goes on to discuss what 'interest' reason has in the conflicts exhibited in the antinomies. With regard to the position of the thesis Kant discerns three distinct interests: a *practical interest* is indicated as primary and as based on the fact that the notion that the self is free is a 'cornerstone of morality and religion' (A466/B494). Second, there is a *speculative interest* in the thesis as it follows the demand of reason for totality. Thirdly, there is the interest of *popularity* in the thesis as the common understanding can grasp the demand of reason for totality. By contrast there is no practical interest in the argument of the antithesis as if we are not free then '*moral* ideas and principles lose all validity' (A468/B496). There is however a speculative interest on the side of the antithesis as the principle of empiricism ensures that 'the understanding is at every time on its own proper ground, namely the field solely of possible experiences' (A468/B496). It is not the case, however, that the principle of empiricism is popular as this principle prevents the common understanding from taking its ease by being eloquent about matters no one knows anything about which is a negative reason for its lack of popularity whilst the positive reason is that for the common understanding 'every speculative interest vanishes before practical interest' (B501/A473).

This indicates that if we are considering the arguments not in terms of their truth but in terms of the reasons we might have to believe them to be necessary then the argument of the thesis has got more to support it than the argument of the antithesis. The argument of the thesis gives support to morality, realizes reason's demand for totality and also has the common understanding in its favour. The antithesis has as its sole recommendation by contrast the mere fact that there is a speculative interest in preventing dogmatic flights of thinking, an interest which is of necessity not popular and has nothing here presented in its practical favour (although elsewhere, in *Dreams of A Spirit-Seer,* we have seen some practical interests to be manifested on the side of empiricism).

The next question which Kant raises concerns what we must be able to claim is capable of solution within the antinomies and here he states that:

> One must be able to know what is *just* or *unjust* in all possible cases in accordance with a rule, because our obligations are at stake, and we cannot have any obligation to do what *we cannot know.* (A476/B504)

If we have obligations then it must be possible for us to know of them, a fact which connects an elementary practical experience to a transcendental condition of that experience. The basis of this condition and the reasons we have for supposing it to be justified are what have to treated in a transcendental practical philosophy.

With regard to the cosmological ideas however it seems that there is a problem inherent in the statement of the antinomies concerning them, which touches upon 'the way the object of these ideas is given to us' (A490/B518). This is what leads Kant to restate the position of transcendental idealism as the key to resolving the antinomies. Since this position is based centrally on the ideality of space and time the results of the Transcendental Aesthetic are cardinal for the whole of the First Critique and are repeated here.[1] After this reminder Kant draws from it the appropriate consequences in relation to the arguments of the antinomies. First, the regress of conditions demanded by reason is a problem but it is nonetheless a 'logical postulate of reason' (A498/B526). Second, within appearances this postulate ensures that there 'could not fail to be conditions given through this regress' as appearances are 'nothing other than an empirical synthesis (in space and time) and thus are given only *in this synthesis*' (A499/B527). The consequence of these points that follow from the transcendental ideality of space and time is a new understanding of the nature of the principles underlying the antinomies:

> it is clear that the major premise of the cosmological syllogism takes the conditioned in the transcendental signification of a pure category, while the minor premise takes it in the empirical signification of a concept of the understanding applied to mere appearances; consequently there is present in it that dialectical deception that is called a *sophisma figurae dictionis.* (A499–500/B527–8)

The antinomies, as already noted, trade on equivocation. This equivocation, which in the argument of the thesis concerned the use of the principle of sufficient reason and in the argument of the antithesis the principle of causality itself, concerned the relationship of the pure category to the appearances but whilst this equivocation vitiates the arguments in favour of both thesis and antithesis and already points us to the nature of Kant's resolution of the antinomies it does not remove the motivations which underlay the arguments, motivations which indicate that the dialectic of the Third Antinomy is 'natural' to reason.

The reminder of the ideality of space and time presents us with a new description of the demand of reason for totality as being 'only a *rule*' and not a principle of the possibility of experience but rather should be understood as a '*regulative* principle of reason' which cannot point us towards knowledge but only to how '*empirical regress is to be instituted*' (A510/B538). Since the notion of reason's demand has already been stated to be a postulate the presentation of it as regulative is not surprising since Kant clearly stated in his discussion of the Analogies of Experience that postulates are regulative and not constitutive principles and clearly marked the difference between the former and the latter as being that the former are dynamical, the latter mathematical (A181/B223). This distinction is the key to how Kant understands how the antinomies will be resolved. With the mathematical antinomies we should cease to apply to nature the concepts which only describe world-hood whilst with the dynamical antinomies we should come to see that nature itself has be considered in relation to principles which are not the basis of a possible experience but do provide us with a rule that enables us to make sense of the experiences we do have.

The resolution of the Third Antinomy

The mathematical antinomies contain arguments for propositions both of which are false, as both arguments traded entirely on attempting to treat the sensible as if it were intelligible and hence ended with an impossible result. With the dynamical antinomies by contrast, the situation is quite different, as here we begin from conditions of sensibility and try to regress to intelligible conclusions. Because of this difference the arguments of both thesis and antithesis of the Third Antinomy could both be true once they have been adjusted in light of the reminder of the ideality of space and time that underlies transcendental idealism. In applying this result to the resolution of the Third Antinomy Kant reminds us that freedom, in a cosmological sense, is a *causa sui* and in this signification is 'a pure transcendental idea' which is not borrowed from any experience and cannot be given in any experience as the principle of causality (given in the Second Analogy) requires that every cause in turn has a cause. This reminder tilts us in the direction of the antithesis' speculative interest and to balance this Kant reminds us of the thesis' practical interest:

> It is especially noteworthy that it is this *transcendental* idea of *freedom* on which the practical concept of freedom is grounded, and the former constitutes the real moment of the difficulties in the latter, which have long surrounded the question of its possibility. (A533/B561)

The reason for this claim is that practical freedom involves action not necessitated by sensibility but arising from a 'faculty of determining oneself from oneself' or, in other words, being a *causa sui*. If there were only causality of a natural type there would only be causality arising from sensibility and hence all actions would become necessary leading us to 'the abolition of transcendental freedom' which would simultaneously 'eliminate practical freedom' (A534/B562).

Practical freedom consists in the notion that there is not acting on the rational agent any force so overwhelming as to make his capacity of choice inoperative and hence requires that this capacity was open to the assertion that something *ought* to be done which is capable of being asserted as a capacity independent of sensible impulse and hence points us to the *causa sui*. The point, which makes possible the thought of transcendental freedom, is the ideality of space and time.

> If ... appearances do not count for any more than they are in fact, namely, not for things in themselves but only for mere representations connected in accordance with empirical laws, then they themselves must have grounds that are not appearances. Such an intelligible cause, however, will not be determined in its causality by appearances, even though its effects appear and so can be determined through other appearances. (A537/B565)

This double aspect of actions is rendered thinkable by the notion that if appearances are underlain by the thought of the transcendental object = x, then this thought of the transcendental object = x, whilst not an object of knowledge for us, is nonetheless an object we can think. All presentation of action in accordance with the conditions of possible experience has to follow the rule of the Second Analogy but the thought of action which involves rational content can be presented as motivated by a rule which derives from the basic principle of practical freedom and hence grounded in a capacity we can call that of transcendental freedom.

This thinking in accord with a 'double aspect' (A538/B566) allows these two types of freedom to be presented in accordance with two types of character, an empirical character describable by conditions of sensibility and an intelligible character describable as the self in itself or the self as transcendental object = x. Since the conditions of appearances are temporal, the intelligible character would not be presented under the conditions of time.

Within the appearances themselves there is no possibility of finding a *causa sui* and thus if we are speaking merely of the conditions of the concepts by which appearances are cognised then the argument of the antithesis can be granted. It will continue to be necessary to comprehend all actions under the rule of necessity so long as we are thinking of actions as appearances. At this level 'we need not worry about what sort of ground is thought for these appearances and their connection in the transcendental subject' (A545/B573). Human beings, considered purely as appearances, can hence be grasped as necessitated in their action. However since we are aware of ourselves not merely through sensibility but also through 'pure apperception' then we are aware of ourselves also according to ideas, ideas expressible in the form of the 'ought'.

> Now this 'ought' expresses a possible action, the ground of which is nothing other than a mere concept, whereas the ground of a merely natural action must always be an appearance. Now of course the action must be possible under natural conditions if the ought is directed to it; but these natural conditions do not concern the determination of the power of choice itself, but only its effect and result in appearance. (A548/B576)

The influence of sensibility can never provide us with the thought of an action which is motivated intelligibly and stimuli cannot produce an 'ought'. The thought of this 'ought' relates us to a world of ideas. The nature of reason's causality is given in the thought of a *causa sui*, a thought through which the opening of a series is given and it is given so completely that we cannot ask why a particular decision is made when we are considering it intelligibly but can only assert that it is made (and even here there are some limitations: A551/B579n).

Whilst this resolution of the antinomy points us to a fundamental basis for maintaining the notion of transcendental freedom it does not prove that freedom is a reality or even a possibility but only shows us that it is 'a transcendental idea' and that 'nature at least *does not conflict with* causality through freedom' (A558/B586). As we shall go on to see, even this is disputed by some philosophers and the question of the connection of the resolution of the third antinomy to the principle of the Second Analogy has been thought to place in jeopardy the unity of the Critical Philosophy because of the fact that this resolution has been suggested not to be consonant with the resolution of the antinomy of teleological judgment. These problems will be turned to after a preliminary survey, on the data provided of the resolution of the Third Antinomy, of Kant's two types of freedom and his two types of character.

Two types of freedom and two forms of character

Before turning to the problems that have been raised concerning the unity of the Critical Philosophy and the relationship between the Third Antinomy and the Canon of Pure Reason it is worth pausing to gather together the data provided within the resolution of the Third Antinomy about Kant's crucial but intricate distinctions between two types of freedom and two types of character. The distinction between two types of freedom is first suggested at A534/B562 where transcendental freedom is described as the capacity to initiate a new causal series which capacity allows us to consider rational agents as *causa sui* whilst practical freedom is indicated to merely reside in 'the independence of the power of choice from *necessitation* by impulses of sensibility' (A534/B562). Since practical freedom includes the attribution of praise and blame it includes the reference to the thought of 'ought'. Practical freedom here appears as merely a negative concept describing the power to act without the impress of sense whilst transcendental freedom is that which enables such action to take place by allowing the thought of a different self to that given in the stream of appearances.

This contrast between two types of freedom is what permits the distinction within the subject between an empirical character and an intelligible character. Character is understood by Kant to mean 'a law of causality' so this description of two types of character is a description of the distinction between a natural causality and a causality of freedom. The empirical character hence is the person considered only as a member of 'a single series of the natural order' (A539/B567) whilst the intelligible character is not subject to the law of time-determination and is hence not available to be known, even by the individual to whom it belongs.

Just as transcendental freedom is made clear only by the resolution of the antinomy to be at least not contradictory to nature so also intelligible character is the thought of the causality of reason as *causa sui* which we are licensed to think because of the possibility of thinking transcendental freedom but which we can know nothing of, even in our own case. Practical freedom is described simply and negatively as the capacity for non-sensible motivation and empirical character is the self considered purely as the effect of sensible impulses, which is the self as it is encountered in the stream of appearances.

Difficulties with the resolution of the antinomy

Lewis White Beck raises a difficulty about the 'double aspect' account Kant has given in his resolution of the third antinomy and this difficulty effectively reintroduces the problem, which this resolution was intended to resolve. As Beck puts it:

> If the possession of noumenal freedom makes a difference to the uniformity of nature, then there is no uniformity; if it does not, to call it 'freedom' is a vain pretension.[2]

However, part of the difficulty here is that Beck takes it to be the case that Kant is committed to the reality of 'two worlds' rather than 'two aspects' and this view of Beck's, then makes the notion of dual characters and dual freedom's more mysterious than it need be. It is also the case that whilst noumenal freedom is not cognised as a natural object it is not a 'vain pretension' to describe it as freedom merely on these grounds and only one who denied the transcendental ideality of space and time would think so.

That Beck supposes a real difficulty here and that this difficulty should be confronted need not be denied simply because it has been poorly stated. Beck suggests that the Third Antinomy's resolution should have gone along the lines of the resolution of the antinomy of teleological judgment in which the 'complete mechanical determination of nature' is regarded as 'a regulative Idea even in respect to nature' (Beck, *op. cit.*, p. 192). This solution would, states Beck, require the giving up of the sharp distinction between 'constitutive category and regulative Idea' and that the Analogies be interpreted as 'regulative in the full sense of the Dialectic' which he takes to be different from that use of regulative given when the Analogies are in fact introduced (Beck, *op. cit.*, p. 193).

The difficulty thus which Beck feels to exist in the resolution of the Third Antinomy can be said to reside in his view that the determinism of nature represented in the understanding of the Second Analogy is too strong to permit us to envisage freedom as a real practical fact unless we revise our understanding of the antinomy and consider its resolution to reside in declaring that both the principles of freedom and of natural causality should be viewed as regulative and not constitutive.[3] In responding to Beck it will be necessary to turn to the antinomy of teleological judgment to ascertain how this is stated to take place and then it will be requisite, in order to respond to another suggestion of incompatibility between the resolutions of the Third Antinomy and the antinomy of teleological judgment, to turn again to stating the basis of the resolution of the Third Antinomy.

Beck's suggestion that the Third Antinomy should have followed the pattern of the resolution of the antinomy of teleological judgment turns on his use of §70 of the *Critique of Judgment*. This section in fact *presents* the antinomy of teleological judgment and does *not* resolve it. The presentation of the antinomy is set out as a conflict between two regulative maxims, which antinomy is stated to be an antinomy of judgment not of reason as 'we cannot have a determinative a priori principle for the possibility of things in terms of merely empirical laws of nature' (Ak. 5:387). The fact that the statement of the principles of teleology and mechanism as regulative maxims is the *basis* of the antinomy and *not* its resolution suggests that if we merely took the two principles of natural causality and a causality of freedom as equivalently regulative principles this would not be sufficient to resolve the antinomy between them but would merely render it an antinomy of judgment rather than of pure reason.

Beck would have been on safer ground if he had suggested that the statement of the resolution of the antinomy took place in §71 with the distinction between a 'principle of reflective judgment with one of determinative judgment' which enables the principle of teleology to be seen as holding merely 'for our use of reason regarding the particular empirical laws' whilst the principle of mechanism is seen to conform to the laws of understanding (Ak. 5:391).[4] Even this solution to the antinomy is problematic however as this section is described by Kant as 'preliminary' to the solution of the antinomy and the solution is not provided until §78 where Kant tells us that 'it is just as necessary for reason to think a special kind of causality that cannot be found in nature, as it is necessary for the mechanism of natural causes to have its own causality' (Ak. 5:411). This causality of reason 'has spontaneity' and the question of the resolution of this causality with that of nature is then stated to require a further principle which principle is 'the *supersensible'* (Ak. 5:412), a transcendent principle which holds reflectively and can be figured in the form of a supreme understanding.[5]

If we contrast this resolution with that of the Third Antinomy we can see that whilst in the Third Antinomy the thought of a *causa sui* leads us from the supreme being to rational freedom of finite beings, in the antinomy of teleological judgment the connection between teleological and mechanistic principles is thought through the notion of a supreme understanding. Essentially, therefore, the principles of the resolution of one antinomy have a great deal in common with the other and there does not appear to be the failure of fit that Beck suggests. Before turning to examining the relationship between the Third Antinomy and the Second Analogy it will first be necessary to address a different argument concerning the incompatibility of the resolution of the Third Antinomy with that of the antinomy of teleological judgment.

Werner Pluhar, in his 'Translator's Introduction' to his translation of the *Critique of Judgment* also raises a problem about the relationship between the antinomy of teleological judgment and the Third Antinomy and refers to Beck for precedent in so doing.[6] Pluhar presents essentially the same problem as Beck albeit in a different formulation:

> If the necessity in nature is strict enough for the antinomy of teleological judgment to arise at all, and if our freedom with its contingency can be reconciled ... with that strict necessity despite having to manifest itself in that nature as appearance with its necessity, why should the antinomy of teleological judgment require a solution that is so different? Why could we not solve it by thinking, not a supersensible understanding that is intuitive and hence removes the contingency in the particular, but a supersensible understanding that determines things only practically and hence leaves the contingency intact? (Pluhar, *op. cit.*, p. cv)

The antinomy of teleological judgment is resolved, according to Pluhar, by reference to the notion of a supersensible intuitive understanding that enables us to think the relation between necessity and contingency under a condition that is not available for knowledge. Pluhar's suggestion is that if this is a plausible solution to the antinomy of teleological judgment then surely it should also form the type of resolution of the

Third Antinomy? The problem with this claim of Pluhar's is that it does not seem to include sufficient attention to the nature of the Third Antinomy. The structure of the Third Antinomy as arising from cosmological ideas in fact points us to the Supreme Being as the original *causa sui* and rational freedom in general is interpreted on the pattern of this original. Due to this the possibility of such freedom has be considered in relation to the original *causa sui* whose type we are considering ourselves in accordance with. Hence, the nature of the resolution of the Third Antinomy as pointing us to what can be thought because of the ideality of space and time, leads us to the notion of something which does not contradict the causality of nature and which the thesis in the argument of this antinomy takes to be the ultimate ground of this nature.

Thus whilst the basis of the resolution of the Third Antinomy is the cardinal principle of transcendental idealism that space and time are ideal (which principle is also at work in the resolution of the antinomy of teleological judgment) the allowance which is made possible by this principle is the thought of a type of causality which we are able to think on the basis of thinking the Supreme Being itself. This is why the Third Antinomy points us towards the Fourth Antinomy, a topic that will be further considered below. It is the causality of the Supreme Being that is at issue in the Third Antinomy and hence we cannot simply resolve it by appealing to the existence of this being but what the principle of the ideality of space and time renders thinkable is the notion of such a causality having operation *in addition to* the causality of nature. The resolution of the antinomy of teleological judgment by contrast, as the resolution of an antinomy of judgment, not of reason points us, by use of the principle of the transcendental ideality of space and time, to the thought of an understanding that is not divided between intuitions and concepts. This notion of such an understanding is rendered thinkable by the notion of the transcendental ideality of space and time, an ideality that we are persuaded of due to the division within our thought of a distinction between intuition and concepts. The principles of both aspects of the antinomy of teleological judgment are reflective and hence what the resolution of this antinomy has to show is that there is a way of maintaining two reflective judgments that apply to the same forms of nature. This is possible due to thinking the type of understanding that would not make reference to the division within our thought that creates the problem. But the Third Antinomy was not considering the same problem as with it we have an antinomy that arises from reason's demand for the unconditioned in conflict with the understanding's demand for unity of cognition. This antinomy is rendered resolvable merely by pointing to the possibility of viewing matters from two aspects and this possibility enables us to think ourselves after the manner of the Supreme Being.

The real basis of both Beck's and Pluhar's objection to the idea that the resolution of these two antinomies can be thought to result in a harmony is due to their understanding of the problem of causality that is at the root of the Third Antinomy and which is manifested anew in the antinomy of teleological judgment in the notion of mechanism. The distinction between the Third Antinomy as an antinomy of causality that leads to the problem of determinism and the antinomy of teleological judgment as an antinomy of different modes of reflection that leads us to the thought of mechanism now needs to be set out clearly and the status of the Second Analogy revisited in order to lay to rest this long-standing objection.[7]

Causality, freedom and the Second Analogy

The statement of the Third Antinomy as an antinomy of reason and the antinomy of teleological judgment as an antinomy of judgment is not precise as both in fact involve judgment but do so in different ways. Comprehending the difference between them will require revisiting the problem of the status of the Second Analogy.[8] The Third Antinomy as an antinomy of causality points us back to the Second Analogy and the principle of the Second Analogy is referred to explicitly twice in the argument for the antithesis. The effect of Beck's and Pluhar's accounts is effectively to support the suspicion mooted in the antithesis and should be seen as arising from the same motive, the attempt to safeguard the unity of experience and maintain a vigilant defence of the results of the Transcendental Analytic.

Since this is the motive of Beck's and Pluhar's readings it is worth reverting to the Second Analogy in order to make clear how its principle should be understood and thus how the antinomy concerning it arises in order then to contrast this with the motivation underlying the antinomy of teleological judgment. The category of causality falls under the heading of relation and is schematised as 'the succession of the manifold insofar as it is subject to a rule' (A144/B183). Each group of categories has its corresponding group of principles or judgments 'that the understanding actually brings about *a priori*' (A148/B187). If such judgments are synthetic *a priori* then the 'supreme principle' of all synthetic judgments applies to them which is that: 'Every object stands under the necessary conditions of the synthetic unity of the manifold of intuition in a possible experience' (A158/B197). The dynamic principles or judgments involve reference to the '*existence* of an appearance in general' (A160/B199) and thus carry with them *a priori* necessity but only under the 'condition of empirical thinking in an experience' (A160/B199). Under this heading fall the Analogies of Experience, which place the schematised categories of relation under this condition by showing how things appear to be related in time.

> The three *modi* of time are *persistence, succession,* and *simultaneity.* Hence three rules of all temporal relations of appearances, in accordance with which the existence of each can be determined with regard to the unity of time, precede all experience and first make it possible. (A177/B220)

So the point of the Analogies is to show that the relations between appearances are governed by these modes and that each mode yields a particular rule for relating appearances to each other. In considering the status of the Second Analogy we need to grasp the status of the Analogies as a whole in contrast to that of the Axioms of Intuition and the Anticipations of Perception. Whilst the two latter are 'mathematical' principles which justify applying mathematics to appearances and teach how one can 'construct' appearances and are thus 'constitutive' (A178–9/B221), the former concern existence which cannot be constructed but whose relations can be discerned and so they are 'merely *regulative* principles' (A179/B222). Kant explains the difference between these types of principles or judgments:

> Here therefore neither axioms nor intuitions are to be thought of; rather, if a perception is given to us in a temporal relation to others (even though indeterminate), it cannot be said *a priori which* and *how great* this other perception is, but only how it is necessarily combined with the first, as regards its existence, in this *modus* of time. (A179/B222)

Thus whilst the axioms allow us to construct the forms of intuition the analogies do not concern the construction of what will follow in accordance with a rule (thus do not construct the nature of the objects) but rather the basis of the rule under which they will follow (thus *regulating* them).[9] The Second Analogy sets out the principle that temporal sequences follow irreversible patterns, that succession is the principle of cognition of appearances.

The principle underlying the antinomies of pure reason was the cosmological principle of totality, the principle of searching always for the conditioned which makes possible all conditions and this principle is presented by Kant in his resolution of the antinomies as being 'only a *rule*' (A509/B537) or as a '*regulative* principle of reason' (A509/B537) which regulates what we ought to postulate but can provide us with no object of cognition, *just as the Second Analogy cannot*. The basis of the Third Antinomy can now be disclosed: the supporters of the antithesis take this principle to be constitutive which is why they convert the rule which indicates the manner in which appearances must be presented into a principle of sufficient reason which latter has thus to be taken in both a real and a logical sense. The supporters of the thesis, despite spotting the problem inherent in the antithesis, have no other argument to give than to attempt to extend the rule of temporal succession into a constitutive principle and thus present the absurd spectacle of trying to give an *a posteriori* argument for a necessary being. But both parties to the dispute have made the error of taking a regulative judgment for a constitutive one, which is why the reminder of the principle of the ideality of space and time is required in order to undermine the standpoint of both parties and render thinkable the notion of a causality of freedom.

If the Third Antinomy can be set out as resolvable, once the notion of causality has been demonstrated to be regulative and not constitutive in its application to appearances then it is worth pointing out that by contrast the antinomy of teleological judgment cannot be resolved by arguing that the dispute between mechanical and teleological notions of causality is decided by declaring both to be regulative as it is between them as two understandings of the regulative principle of causality that Kant sets the antinomy of teleological judgment out when he states that the maxims of mechanism and teleology are 'regulative principles for our investigation' (Ak. 5:387). Hence the resolution of this antinomy cannot reside in the same move as the resolution of the Third Antinomy as the latter concerned a problem that arose from taking the principle of causal succession constitutively whilst the former concerns two regulative views of this principle. The resolution of the antinomy of teleological judgment thus has to show that the two regulative interpretations of the principle of causal succession can in principle be both held to apply to the same *judged objects* whilst the resolution of the Third Antinomy had to demonstrate that the two ways of grasping causal connection were at fault in making a regulative principle constitutive. The same object can be judged according to teleological and mechanistic presentations of the causal principle once we remember the ideality of space and time which notion is built upon the division of our cognition into intuitions and concepts, a division which prompts for us the problem of conceiving purposiveness. The thought of our own action can be seen to be either free or necessitated once we recall the merely regulative status of the principle of causality, a status which enables us to conceive of a different type of causality *which is not temporal* by conceiving of ourselves in intelligible aspect after the type of a *causa sui*. Both antinomies point us to the thought of a transcendent notion which we cannot claim to experience but the thought of which is rendered possible for us by the principle of the ideality of space and time.

Beck's and Pluhar's mistake therefore is not to have understood the regulative status of the Second Analogy, a mistake compounded in Pluhar's case by not having grasped the basis of the different antinomies, a failure which leads him to suppose that there is an 'antinomy of antinomies'. In reminding ourselves once again of this status of the Second Analogy it is hoped that loose talk of the constitutive nature 'of the categories' will cease and the nature of the way the schematised categories are given experiential demonstration will instead be attended to.[10]

In summary, therefore, the antinomy of teleological judgment concerned two different ways of construing the regulative rule of temporal succession both of which were applied to the same objects whilst the Third Antinomy concerned two different ways of viewing the principle of causal connection as if it did not concern temporal succession but rather was applicable as a category to the construction of objects. Thus whilst both antinomies concerned causality they did not do so in the same manner and this is why whilst one concerned the question of mechanism (judgment by efficient causes) the other concerned the question of determinism (ultimate claim of impossibility of freedom). Disentangling the problems posed by the two antinomies and thus disclosing the motive of them as distinct enables us to avoid seeing them as conflicting in their respective resolutions.

Difficulties with the unity of the First Critique

In addition to dissatisfaction with the Third Antinomy on the grounds that its resolution does not fit with the resolution of the antinomy of teleological judgment there is also dissatisfaction with the account of the relationship between transcendental freedom and practical freedom in the Antinomy. The suggestion that the concept of practical freedom requires the transcendental idea of freedom (A533/B561), a suggestion which motivates the practical interest in the argument of the thesis is thought by some to be not of a piece with the treatment of practical freedom given in the Canon of Pure Reason. Bernard Carnois presents the difficulty in the following manner:

> In the Doctrine of Method the fact of practical freedom reveals nothing about the reality of transcendental freedom. This should be no cause for surprise, since the two concepts were radically independent of one another. But it is no longer so in the Dialectic: from now on practical freedom includes transcendental freedom as its ground.[11]

The reason why Carnois takes it that there is a lack of fit between the treatment of the relationship between transcendental freedom and practical freedom in these two sections of the First Critique is that whereas the treatment in the discussion of the antinomy suggests the aforementioned dependence the treatment in the discussion of the Canon of Pure Reason is stated here to concern only practical questions and the question whether freedom is transcendental is set aside as of no practical concern (A803/B831). But if the transcendental idea of freedom is no practical concern why earlier did Kant suggest that the elimination of the former would lead to the elimination of the latter? Carnois falls back on a 'patchwork theory' to explain this and thus concurs in the suggestion that there is a fundamental problem here which compromises the unity of the First Critique. In responding to this suggestion I will be led to set out the nature of Kant's treatment of practical philosophy in the Canon and will conclude by relating this treatment to his discussion of the ideal of pure reason, a discussion which will permit some comprehension of the connection between the Third Antinomy and the Fourth Antinomy.

The Canon of Pure Reason

In responding to Carnois' suggestion of a problem we will be led not just to reject his account of the relationship between the Antinomy of Pure Reason and the Canon of Pure Reason but, more importantly, to assessing how Kant presents the prospects of practical philosophy itself in the First Critique. In opening the discussion of the Canon Kant reverts back to the problem with which the discussion of the antinomies was concerned, namely the tendency of reason to 'venture to the outermost bounds of all cognition by means of ideas in pure use' (A797/B825). Kant now asks whether this tendency of reason is grounded merely in its speculative interest or 'rather uniquely and solely in its practical interest' (A797/B825). In responding to this question Kant now sets out to describe what the ultimate end of the pure use of reason is.

> The final aim to which in the end the speculation of reason in its transcendental use is directed concerns three objects: the freedom of the will, the immortality of the soul, and the existence of God. With regard to all three the merely speculative interest of reason is very small, and with respect to this an exhausting labour of transcendental research, hampered with unceasing hindrances, would be undertaken only with difficulty, since one would not be able to make any use of the discoveries that might be made which would prove its utility *in concreto*, i.e., in the investigation of nature. (A798/B826)

If the 'final aim' of speculative reason is concerned with these three objects this aim conflicts with the 'interest' of speculative reason as the interest of speculative reason concerns the investigation of nature. This is one of the passages from the Canon that might seem to support Carnois' suggestion of a conflict between its treatment and that given in the discussion of the Third Antinomy. However, in setting out the 'interests' involved in the antinomies of pure reason Kant described the 'interest' of the antithesis as purely speculative as the motivation underlying the antithesis was that 'the understanding is at every time on its own proper ground, namely the field of possible experiences' (A468/B496). Hence, left to itself without reference to a practical interest and standing on the ground achieved in the Transcendental Analytic the 'interest' of reason would appear to be met whilst the 'interest' of speculation on the side of the thesis is in fact given only in the notion of a 'final aim' which involves giving 'answers to questions about the conditions of ... synthesis that do not leave something out' (A467/B495). Thus the description that the merely speculative interest of reason in these questions was small by comparison with the 'final aim' of reason being precisely a grasp of these questions states a point which mirrors the account given in the preparation to the solution of the antinomies of pure reason.

With regard to the investigation of nature the argument of the antithesis is effectively upheld in each case. It is this that gives such strong grounds for the antithesis. The objects that Kant points to as concerning the 'final aim' of reason are 'not at all necessary for our *knowing*' (A799/B828) and always remain 'transcendent for speculative reason' (A799/B827). So the concern of reason with them 'must really concern only the *practical'* (A800/B828). We noted above that the strong practical interest of reason in supporting the thesis of the Third Antinomy met with no correlate on the side of the antithesis. The basis of practical concerns by contrast, as revealed in the notion of practical freedom, is what is possible through freedom.

> Pure practical laws ... whose end is given by reason completely *a priori*, and which do not command under empirical conditions but absolutely, would be products of pure reason. Of this sort, however, are the *moral* laws. (A800/B828)

The notion of practical freedom thus includes a concern with these moral laws and since these laws abstract from conditions of sensibility these laws must be considered purely. They therefore concern, as Kant puts it, *'what is to be done'* (A800/B828) should it be the case that we have free wills, that there is a God or that there is a future world. In considering these questions it is not now necessary to rehearse the problem of transcendental freedom as this problem has, states Kant, 'been dealt with above' (A801/B829). Hence if we leave aside questions concerning it this is not because we no longer believe it to be the basis on which we can assure ourselves of the truth of practical freedom but rather because we have already established a response to its thought.

> We thus cognise practical freedom through experience, as one of the natural causes, namely a causality of reason in the determination of the will, whereas transcendental freedom requires an independence of this reason itself (with regard to its causality for initiating a series of appearances) from all determining causes of the world of the senses, and to this extent seems to be contrary to the law of nature, thus to all possible experience, and so remains a problem. Yet this problem does not belong to reason in its practical use, so in a canon of pure reason we are only concerned with two questions that pertain to the practical interest of pure reason, and with regard to which a canon of its use must be possible, namely, Is there a God? Is there a future life? The question about transcendental freedom concerns merely speculative knowledge, which we can set aside as quite indifferent if we are concerned with what is practical, and about which there is already sufficient discussion in the Antinomy of Pure Reason. (A803–4/B831–2)

If we look merely at the data of experience we discern our ability to act against the allurements of sense and in accord with fixed principles.

This is all that is requisite for us to claim freedom in a practical sense. The notion of transcendental freedom cannot be derived from it and is not capable of support purely on the basis of it. This does not prevent it from being the case that the problematic concept of transcendental freedom may possess a real correlate but the comprehension of our ability to grasp this thought can merely be treated by speculative reason, despite its comparative lack of interest in it. Hence, despite the real interest in the thought of transcendental freedom being practical the basis of treatment of it is only possible through speculative reason. Practical reason by contrast has to concern itself with what must be done and on this basis the questions it does have to address refer us to the other two parts of the 'final aim' of pure reason, the questions about God and the immortality of the soul.

Practically speaking, reason has interests which lead to the thought of practical laws and this fact is what prompts us to question whether 'from the point of view of its practical interest reason may not be able to guarantee that which in regard to its speculative interest it entirely refuses to us' (A804/B832). Whilst the solution to the question what I should do is not answerable within the pages of a work that presents a critique of the claims of speculative interest the question of what I might hope, construed as following from the answer to the question what I should do is 'simultaneously practical and theoretical' which ensures that 'the practical leads like a clue to the reply to the theoretical question, and in its highest form, the speculative question' (A805/B833). The theoretical question concerned what it is possible to be able to claim to know and the basic answer to it is given in the Transcendental Analytic but this answer led us to the problem posed by the demand of reason for the unconditioned, a demand which could not be met with within the boundaries of possible experience.

> For all *hope* concerns happiness, and with respect to the practical and the moral law it is the very same as what knowledge and the natural law is with regard to theoretical cognition of things. The former finally comes down to the inference that something *is* (which determines the ultimate final end) *because something ought to happen*; the latter, that something *is* (which acts as the supreme cause) *because something does happen*. (A805–6/B833–4)

Theoretical cognition leads us in the direction of a supreme cause as ultimate explanation of the fact that things take place at all in the direction of its demand for an ultimate resolution of the problem of condition and conditioned whereas the thoughts we are led to in considering morality lead us to think a ultimate final end in relation to that which ought to be. Theoretical and practical thought thus have the same terminal point, the 'highest form' of question. If we consider practical questions as of two types, those which concern what we would do if we are prudent, and those which we should do if we are moral, then we discover that each concerns a type of good, a good which is in accord with our wish for happiness and a good which is moral. There is no way of connecting these types of goodness on natural principles alone so that if we were to think of the highest felicity as combination of these two it requires us to think of a 'highest reason' (A810/B838) as their ground of combination. This highest reason thus gives us a ground for thinking the ideal of the highest good or *summum bonum*.

Since, however, the condition of felicity which we can think as possible in accordance with the purposes of a Supreme Being is not conceivable on the grounds of nature it would further require including within its remit the thought of a future life. These thoughts are the highest that reason can aim at and the necessity of them is given within the discussion of the canon as the basis of thinking what practically can be regarded as pure, a consideration that leads Kant to formulate here a reply to the question what I should do in the form of a hypothetical imperative: *'Do that through which you will become worthy to be happy'* (A809–10/B836–7).

Within the limits of a critique of speculative reason the Canon instructs us that there is a possibility of pure practical reason and delimits for us the ultimate horizon of such a reason thus allowing the formulation of an ultimate hypothetical imperative which carries with it *'promises* and *threats'* (A811/B839). That this account mirrors much of what we have discovered within the *Lectures on Ethics* should be clear. That the Canon does not directly contradict the considerations presented within the account of the Antinomy of Pure Reason as suggested by Carnois should also be clear. Further consideration of the horizon of pure reason considered from the highest standpoint we are led to by the Canon should finally enable us to assure ourselves once more of Kant's continued commitment to an ultimate perfectionist horizon for practical philosophy.

The ideal of pure reason and the Fourth Antinomy

The Fourth Antinomy discusses the question of the existence of a necessary being with the argument of the thesis arguing in favour of it, the argument of the antithesis against. Since the argument of the thesis attempts to show that the necessary being exists within time then it falls foul of the principle of the ideality of space and time and the argument of the antithesis likewise assumes that the necessary being would have to be a part of the temporal causal series it also must fall because of the principle of the ideality of space and time. The resolution of the Fourth Antinomy after reminding us of the principle of the ideality of space and time can consist in nothing else than the suggestion that 'the necessary being would have to be thought of as entirely outside the series of the world of sense' (A561/B589). Since the necessary being is thus rendered a problematic concept on the same basis as transcendental freedom we have no grounds for claiming knowledge of its existence or even of its possibility but merely for suggesting that it is at least not contradictory with the appearances of contingency that there exist a necessary being.[12]

Since the idea of a transcendental necessary being is a merely problematic thought of a general condition which contingencies require it is remote in principle from what normally goes under the name of God. What brings the thought of it closer to the popular conception is Kant's subsequent discussion of the ideal of pure reason. In the account of the antinomies of pure reason it was ideas that were in question and Kant now introduces the contrastive term ideal by which is meant 'the idea not merely *in individuo*, i.e., as an individual thing which is determinable, or even determined, by the idea alone' (A568/B596). This gives a representation of an idea through the figure of a singular image for example in the notion of a sage 'who is fully congruent with the idea of wisdom' (A569/B597). These ideals are thus thoughts of a practical kind which ground 'the possibility of the perfection of certain *actions*' (A569/B597).

There is also open to pure reason to think of the sum total of all possibilities under the condition of totalization as that to which everything must be traced back. We determined this from the Fourth Antinomy as the thought of the necessary being, but placing it under the condition of ideals we can think of this being not in the merely general form we derive from the Fourth Antinomy but as an individual being, hence as God 'thought in a transcendental sense' (A580/B608). This thought of an ultimate perfection is what is subsequently given the basis of a practical demonstration in the treatment of the Canon after the rest of the discussion of the transcendental ideal of pure reason has culminated in the rejection of all speculative proofs for its existence.

What the notion of the ideal of pure reason introduces and is given as sustained by the thought that the ultimate hypothetical imperative of moral thought leads us to is a perfectionist horizon for moral thinking. That this horizon was recurrent in Kant's pre-critical ethics was shown in Chapter 1. That this horizon also is based upon thinking the ultimate ends of reason and thus on a teleological conception of pure reason which eventually culminates in an eschatology is also clear from the examination of the First Critique presented here.

It should, however, be clear that the treatments of practical questions within the boundaries of the critique of speculative reason is necessarily narrow. The discovery of the methodology of critique has here illuminated the basis of treatment of practical philosophy however and given us grounds for thinking that theoretical philosophy cannot in principle rule out the thoughts moral reasoning might be thought to require. This negative demonstration when connected to the investigation of the need of reason itself to reach for an horizon which only seems attainable by practical consideration of a pure type is sufficient to make open to us a new investigation of practical philosophy from the perspective of the critique of the claims of tradition, a critique as extensive in its scope and decisive in its desirable outcome as that provided within the pages of the First Critique to theoretical philosophy.

3
The Supreme Principle of Morality

Since the nature of the limits of theoretical philosophy has been revealed in its problems with the notion of freedom it is fitting now to turn to Kant's first decisive contribution in his critical period to practical philosophy, the *Groundwork for a Metaphysics of Morals*.[1] This work, the most widely read of Kant's contributions to practical philosophy, is one whose significance is often misunderstood. The fact that this work is set for reading by undergraduates has tended to give it the status for many students of philosophy of being Kant's major contribution to moral philosophy. The fact is, however, that Kant very clearly did not intend this work be read in this manner. As the title of the work indicates, it is intended as preparatory to a consideration of the key questions of moral philosophy. Its task is also defined by Kant in a very clear and narrow manner when he writes that it intended to encompass 'nothing more than the search for and establishment of the *supreme principle of morality*, which constitutes a business that in its purpose is complete and to be kept apart from every other moral investigation' (Ak. 4:392).[2]

It will be my purpose in this chapter to investigate the nature of this supreme principle through accounting for Kant's discussion of 'metaphysics of morals' in the second part of the work and the manner of his justification of it through a 'critique of pure practical reason' in the third part of the work. This double agenda must involve a response to two types of problems that have been set out in the secondary literature on the *Groundwork*, a consideration of the 'multiple formulations' of the supreme principle said to constitute a problem in terms of extensionality of meaning in the second part of the work and an account of the 'deduction' of the supreme principle given in the third part of the work. This second problem is the one of greater import for moral philosophy since it is often claimed that the argument Kant gives here is obscure, that it fails, and that Kant subsequently came to reject it when writing the Second Critique. I will postpone consideration of this last claim until the next chapter but will in this chapter attempt to demonstrate that the argument of the third part of the *Groundwork* is relatively clear and that it succeeds.

The Preface to the *Groundwork*

In order to locate the *Groundwork* within the response to tradition that we have discussed in previous chapters it is necessary to pay some attention to the statements of intent Kant gives in the preface. Having described the nature of the division of philosophy into ethics, physics and logic Kant states that he 'limits the question proposed only to this: is it not thought to be of the utmost necessity to work out for once a pure moral philosophy, completely cleansed of everything that may be only empirical and that belongs to anthropology?' (Ak. 4:389). This attempt to think of a pure moral philosophy clearly involves the necessity that must be attached to obligation and, connected with this necessity, a formulation of what must be universal in obligation. The two criteria of the *a priori* are hence given, as we would expect in a pure inquiry. Such a pure inquiry is stated to be quite different from the 'universal practical philosophy' attempted by Wolff and to which Kant's *Lectures on Ethics* provide such a detailed response. Kant compares Wolff's type of practical philosophy to a general logic, which abstracts from all conditions of formulation and gives utterly general accounts of entailment. Just as such general logic tells one nothing of the distinction between pure categories and empirical ones so Wolff's type of practical philosophy cannot distinguish between the conditions of pure volition and empirical volition. By contrast a correctly metaphysical inquiry into morals would have to 'examine the idea and the principles of a possible "pure" will' (Ak. 4: 390). The transcendental distinction between pure and empirical not being available to Wolff, he must of necessity fail to grasp the basis of moral principles. But whilst Kant here initially suggests that he will be providing a 'metaphysics of morals' he almost immediately indicates that this is not the status of the work he is presenting. By contrast, he is providing only a groundwork. 'Indeed there is really no other foundation for a metaphysics of morals than the critique of a *pure practical reason*, just as metaphysics is the critique of pure speculative reason ... ' (Ak. 4: 391). Whilst suggesting that the critique of pure practical reason is less necessary than the critique of pure speculative reason as the commonest understanding can understand a great deal about morals, Kant also suggests a deeper reason for not having presented such a critique of pure practical reason when he writes that it would require an account of 'the unity of practical with speculative reason in a common principle, since there can, in the end, be only one and the same reason' (Ak. 4:391). Since this could not here be demonstrated without bringing in a great mass of complications Kant has preferred to leave the work on a preliminary level.

This level is, as already stated, given its task in the attempt to discover and establish the supreme principle of morality. In order to perform this task the methodology of the work is described as involving proceeding analytically from common understanding to the discovery of its supreme principle 'and in turn synthetically from the examination of this principle and its sources back to the common cognition in which we find it used' (Ak. 4:392). The key part of this inquiry hence must be taken to be that in which the synthetic examination of this principle and its sources is provided, that is, part three of the work.

Before proceeding with an account of the work, let us first clarify some key points of terminology. Kant has indicated that a critique of pure practical reason, if completely carried through, would be the true foundation for a 'metaphysics of morals'. This complete critique of pure practical reason would demonstrate the unity of theoretical and practical reason, but this cannot be included in the work presented. By contrast, however, a more limited critique of pure practical reason is to be included in the concluding section of the work. Since we have discovered that the purpose of a critique is provide a limitation of the true possibilities of a metaphysical inquiry we would expect this critique of pure practical reason to include an account of the limits of pure practical reason and it is noteworthy that the penultimate section of the third part of the work concerns the 'extreme boundary of all practical philosophy' (Ak. 4:455). This description of the limit of practical philosophy must be key to the argument of the third section of the work and an interpretation of the 'deduction' which we shall discover presented there cannot be convincing if it does not connect this 'deduction' with the description of this limit.

Second, the 'metaphysics of morals' itself, whilst not given here is indicated to have its basis described here in the account of the supreme principle of morality. Hence the description of a metaphysics of morals that we are promised in the second part of the work should not be taken to be anything other than a description of the most general part of such a part of metaphysics, a general part which functions in something like the same way the Transcendental Analytic of the First Critique does in relation to the outlines of a theoretical metaphysics with the difference, for reasons we shall have to discuss in the next chapter, that these outlines need to be supplemented with the considerations given in the 'analytic of pure practical reason' of the Second Critique.

Since the point of the first section of the *Groundwork* is to provide an analytical argument, which demonstrates to common consciousness the implicit reference of ordinary morality to a universal principle, it is not of great concern for our enquiries to present a discussion of it. Suffice it to say that the notion of 'good will' introduced within it can scarcely be understood except by combination with the notion of an imperative formulation, which it is the function of the second section to give. What I will now turn to is the manner in which this formulation is given there.

The 'Metaphysics of Morals' and the categorical imperative

In opening the second section of the *Groundwork* Kant reiterates the point that moral principles cannot be derived from experience, in the process presenting a rejoinder to the 'moral sense' theorists in addition to the riposte to Wolff presented in the preface. In setting out this rejection of empiricist accounts of morality Kant also firmly states that moral principles cannot be derived from examples, not even pious examples. 'But whence have we the concept of God as the highest good? Solely from the *idea* of moral perfection that reason frames a priori and connects inseparably with concept of a free will' (Ak. 4: 408–9). This warning, whilst important again in indicating a type of perfectionism that Kant will want to defend, is also key in indicating the role of the examples that Kant in fact uses in this section of the work. The notion of morality has first, as he puts it, to be '*grounded* on metaphysics' and only if established in this manner can it be subsequently given access to popular exposition by means of examples. Hence the examples used within the treatment of moral principles in this section of the work should not be the subject of enquiry until the arguments for the principle have been thoroughly investigated, and only then in order to corroborate this principle and not to give it an additional basis. Since these are Kant's clear instructions I will not enter into the discussion of these examples at all in my account of the second section of the *Groundwork*.

In rejecting empiricist theories of morality and any foundational claim for examples Kant naturally asserts that moral concepts 'have their seat and origin completely a priori in reason' (Ak. 4:411). Reason involves the cognition of laws into a totality so it is no surprise that

Kant identifies the will discussed in *Groundwork* I with practical reason (Ak. 4:412). If there are beings who are not determined entirely by reason, then the presentation in such beings of practical laws must have the form of a necessitation, the formulation of which is described as imperatival. There are two types of imperative broadly construed: those that involve the technical description of what is required for an antecedently provided purpose to be met and those that represent something necessary in itself without reference to 'another end' (Ak. 4:414). The former are hypothetical imperatives, the latter a categorical imperative. Whilst both involve reference to purposes the latter is distinguished from the former in not involving reference to an antecedently provided purpose but as rather requiring a comprehension of the structure of a purpose, which is not dependent upon a means–end relationship. Hence it is not that the categorical imperative is not purposive but that it provides us with an ultimate purpose.[3]

Kant interprets hypothetical imperatives as being directed in the main to the antecedently provided end of happiness. This notion, which we will see subsequently to be capable of more than one understanding by Kant, is here presented by him in this context as an ideal not of reason but of imagination and hence as resting merely on empirical grounds (Ak. 4:418). Since Kant has already rejected the notion that moral principles could be provided empirically as this would give us no notion of the element of necessitation present in them he must necessarily reject such eudemonistic systems. By contrast with such empiricist systems Kant's notion of a categorical imperative is a synthetic *a priori* and since this notion is one which occasions the whole critical inquiry it is evidently of some difficulty to render acceptable but also of crucial importance to securing a philosophically justifiable notion of moral principles.

Before we turn to the 'metaphysics of morals' provided in this second section of the *Groundwork* it is worth pausing a moment to see how Kant attempts to show that the mere concept of a categorical imperative provides 'its formula containing the proposition which alone can be a categorical imperative' (Ak. 4: 420). This is provided through the contrast between the concept of a categorical imperative and that of a hypothetical imperative. Hypothetical imperatives require an end to be antecedently provided and cannot be specified in any instance until that end has been provided. Thus, although we know that the hypothetical imperative will always be of the form 'do X if you want Y' there may be a number of subordinate conditions in any instance which need to be added for successful completion of the task and (hopeful) attainment of the end. The situation with the categorical imperative is quite different:

> For, since the imperative contains, beyond the law, only the necessity that the maxim be in conformity with this law, while the law contains no condition to which it could be limited, nothing is left with which the maxim is to conform but the universality of a law as such; and this conformity alone is what the imperative properly represents as necessary.
>
> There is, therefore, only a single categorical imperative and it is this: *act only in accordance with that maxim through which you can at the same time will that it become a universal law*. (Ak. 4:421)

Whilst the notion of a 'maxim' introduced here has to paraphrased as indicating the subjective principle adopted by the agent, there is otherwise nothing surprising in this statement given what has been said to this point. Indeed, this statement of the categorical imperative is an analytical consequence of the considerations thus far adduced.

Since section two of the *Groundwork* is still part of the analytical aspect of the work it cannot in itself provide reasons to motivate one to adopt the principle given here. All that can be suggested is that the system of duties (which we have visited above in the account of the commentary on Baumgarten in Kant's *Lectures on Ethics*) can be justified in accordance with this principle and Kant undertakes to do this through the provision of examples. Before setting out the examples, however, he first provides an alternative formulation of the imperative under the guise of accounting analytically for what is involved in the notion of law. Since a universal law by which things occur is what we understand (following the demonstrations of the First Critique) as nature we can also present the imperative as stating: '*act as if the maxim of your action were to become by your will a* **universal law of nature**' (Ak. 4:421). The 'as if' nature of this formulation marks it as presenting a moral world by analogy with the physical world, an analogical procedure necessary if the condition of moral statements is to be presented as related to the solution of the Third Antinomy.

The 'canon of moral appraisal' is given in the test of universality (Ak. 4:424). It is presented in two forms: 'Some actions are so constituted that their maxim cannot even be *thought* without contradiction as a universal law of nature, far less could one *will* that it *should* become such. In the case of others that inner impossibility is indeed not to be found, but it is still impossible to *will* that their maxim be raised to the universality of a law of nature because such a will would contradict itself' (Ak. 4:424). The maxims, which involve a self-refutation or contradiction in conception, are ruled out by strict decree whilst the ones that violate a condition of coherent willing are rather infringements of imperfect duty. This distinction will be important in Kant's account of duties in the Doctrine of Virtue.

The principle of duties is hence derived from setting the categorical imperative forth in a form that exploits the notion of law to provide us, by analogy with nature, with the notion of a moral world. Whilst this is set out in the second section of the *Groundwork* Kant has not yet stated that we are within the province of 'metaphysics of morals', as this is considered in the terms of the *Groundwork* itself. It is after the setting out of the categorical imperative and its reformulation in such a manner as to give the principle of duties that Kant makes the transition to 'metaphysics of morals'. This is done through raising a question:

> The question is therefore this: is it a necessary law *for all rational beings* to appraise their actions in accordance with such maxims as they themselves could will to serve as universal laws? If there is such a law, then it must already be connected (completely a priori) with the concept of the will of a rational being as such. But in order to discover this connection we must, however reluctantly, step forth, namely into metaphysics, although into a domain of it that is distinct from speculative philosophy, namely into metaphysics of morals. (Ak. 4:426–7)

The discussion thus far has given us grounds for comprehending what the imperatival nature of morality must be presented like and how we can derive from it a principle of duties. What has not been presented is any reason however for rational beings *qua* agents to adopt any such imperative or principle of duties. Hence what the 'metaphysics of morals' as understood within the purview of this work is for is to give us a completely *a priori* connection between the imperative and the concept of the will of a rational being. Just as the formula of the categorical imperative was set out analytically from its mere concept so the connection of this formula and the rational being *qua* rational agent is to be given through a merely analytical discussion of the will of such a being.

This purely analytical demonstration is hence undertaken through the connection between a set of definitions. Just as a will has to be thought of as a capacity of self-determination so this capacity necessarily has to be thought of as governed by rules and the self-representation of these rules. In determining oneself to act, then one requires the representation of an end. If the end by which the rational being acts is based purely on its own rationality, then this end would be universally applicable to the actions of all rational beings. This type of end would thus be objective and is termed by Kant a *motive* in contrast to the *triebfeder* at work in merely subjective forms of end setting. Finally, Kant distinguishes between formal principles, which abstract from all merely subjective ends from material principles, which are based upon merely subjective ends. Since the latter are evidently the grounds of hypothetical imperatives the former are grounds of categorical imperatives as these are the only types of imperative Kant has given. But what enables the latter to be the basis of something, which is not merely hypothetical is, as we have already discussed, the fact that it involves a reference to something whose status is distinctive in being an end-in-itself. We can now connect this notion of an end-in-itself to the very concept of rational nature:

> Now I say that the human being and in general every rational being *exists* as an end in itself, *not merely as a means* to be used by this or that will at its discretion; instead he must in all his actions, whether directed to himself or also to other rational beings, always be regarded *at the same time as an end.* (Ak. 4:428)

With this formulation we have a statement about the nature of rational being *qua* rational agent. Such a being has a peculiar ontological status. It is not a being that can be viewed merely as a means to an antecedently set end. This formulation is very careful as it indicates that it is possible to take oneself or another rational being as a means to an end but that there is a condition through which this should be done: namely, also through regarding oneself or the other as an end-in-itself. Taking a rational being as a means to an end is hence not forbidden *per se*, but the limits of such a relationship to the rational being are set. At this point in the work, the grounds of taking rational being to be an end-in-itself are not given and it is presented by Kant purely as a postulate that one adopt this way of viewing rational being *qua* rational agent (Ak. 4:429n). Since humans are, also without grounds yet being given by Kant, taken to be rational beings we are led to the formulation that humanity, whether in oneself or another, should not be used merely as a means but also be viewed at the same time as an end (Ak. 4:429), a formulation in which the identification of humanity with rationality has to be assumed.

Whilst the presentation of the categorical imperative under an analogical condition consequent upon exploiting the notion of law gave us a principle of duty this formulation gives us 'the supreme limiting condition' of action and is hence the principle of agency (Ak. 4:431). It is set out as such in relation to the same examples Kant used in relation to the principle of duty. This principle of agency sharpens the understanding of the second type of duty, the imperfect kind. For if all imperfect duties are those the concept of which is in contradiction to conditions of willing they must all violate this formulation. If, however, it is the case that I regard myself *qua* rational agent as an end-in-itself then this way of viewing myself must involve me in a self-attitude where the laws of willing are connected to the nature of my own use of my agency. In other words, if I am an end-in-itself then I must myself formulate from my own rational nature the law of rational action and hence be entirely self-directed when acting rationally. When acting rationally I am not acting in accordance with interests since my will is then determined by nothing that is presented to my sensibility. Therefore this notion of auto-affection is precisely what is involved analytically in grasping the notion of myself as an end-in-itself and thus in grasping myself as such I see myself as autonomous.

From an analogical extension which follows the pattern of the representation of law as tied to the concept of a nature I now can represent the moral world I have given myself previously as a world of ends in which all ends are related to each other in principle through the very conception of rational ends. This systematic union of rational beings would be the ideal of reason in terms of the relationship between agents. 'Morality consists, then, in the reference of all action to the lawgiving by which alone a kingdom of ends is possible' (Ak. 4:434).

It will be necessary in a moment to review the problems that have been raised in the extensive literature on the *Groundwork* about the formulas given in this second section. Before turning to this discussion, however, it is worth concluding this initial interpretation of the second section of the work by looking at Kant's suggestion that he has provided only three formulas which he claims are only formulas of the same law and that any one of them unites the other two in itself. The reason given for these assertions is merely implicit and occurs in the way Kant analytically discusses the notion of a maxim. Kant claims all maxims have three aspects to them: a form (which we have to understand as universal if it is to be accepted as a moral maxim), a matter (which is to be appreciated as belonging to all maxims, including moral, and which we understand to be given in the end, morally, the end-in-itself) and finally in a complete determination or totalization which is the condition of the harmonization of maxims together after a demand of reason in the form of the notion of a realm of ends. As Kant puts it: 'A progression takes place here, as through the categories of the *unity* of the form of the will (its universality), the *plurality* of the matter (of objects, i.e., of ends), and the *allness* or totality of the system of these' (Ak. 4:436).[4] Has Kant here reduced the number of formulations he has earlier given in order to make them fit some pre-arranged plan? No, as the unity of the will expresses both the notion of universality and the analogical display of it as presenting a moral world. The notion of autonomy has also not been set out in imperatival form and is given as implicit in the analogical extension that is the realm of ends. Hence, if the realm of ends and the moral law given as if it were a law of nature involve analogical extensions of the principles of autonomy and universality then there were only three independent formulas given through the universal notion of law, the notion of rational nature as an end-in-itself and the ideal condition of rational agency.

Kant concludes this second section by restating his contentions and setting out the basis of misunderstanding the ground of morals. *Autonomy of the will is the supreme principle of morality that was sought* and the principle of autonomy can be stated as 'to choose only in such a way that the maxims of your choice are also included as universal law in the same volition' (Ak. 4:440). That there exists a rational nature, which can be shown to be bound through its rational agency to this principle, is a synthetic claim and is hence not given any justification in this section of the *Groundwork*. But this principle of autonomy can be stated analytically to be the ground of morals and opposed in principle to all heteronomous principles of willing which latter must ground morals on something other than the agency of the moral actor. The demonstration that this principle applies to those of reading of it requires a synthetic account to be set out and this would need a critique to be given which is what the third section will do. Before turning to an account of this section however I will now examine critical discussion of the second section.

The problem of 'multiple formulations'

H. J. Paton, in his influential book *The Categorical Imperative*, first set out what I will now briefly discuss as the source of most critical attention given to the argument of the second section of the *Groundwork*.[5] This is the problem, if problem it be, of 'multiple formulations' in this second section. The 'problem' can be stated briefly as being that Kant sets out a number of formulations, all said to be equivalent, of the same supreme principle of morality and, in the course thereof, according to some commentators, miscounts the number of formulations he has himself given. There is an enormous quantity of writing on this topic, despite the fact that if there is a problem here at all it is a problem which does not strictly speaking belong within the purview of moral philosophy but must be regarded as part of the philosophical inquiry into the nature of synonymous statements if synonymous statements exist and hence as part of the philosophy of meaning. Given the overwhelmingly epistemological bias of the type of philosophy predominant in the Anglo-American world it is perhaps not surprising that this 'problem' has occupied so much attention. Since the literature on this 'problem' is vast I wish here to summarize only briefly some of the leading variants thus far presented and indicate a summary response both to them and to this concentration.

Paton, in his classic discussion, counts five formulations of the categorical imperative and distinguishes them as the formula of universal law (Formula I), the formula of the law of nature (Ia), the formula of the end in itself (II), the formula of autonomy (III) and the formula of the kingdom of ends (IIIa). Whilst Paton's numbering indicates his view that the law of nature formula and the kingdom of ends formula are really subordinate formulas, he nonetheless raises the problem of why Kant speaks as if there are only three formulas when he has given us five. Paton views the law of nature, formula as operating by analogy with teleological conceptions of nature; not merely the laws therefore that are operative within the coherent ordering of nature but rather those totalizing ones that bring them together. Whilst this conception would seem clearly to have an analogical notion in relation to the realm of ends where Kant even indicates this connection in a footnote (Ak. 4:437n) Paton applies it to the law of nature formula where there is no textual reference in support. The formula of autonomy is not discussed by Kant *as* a formula until after the tripartite account of the elements of a maxim being patterned on the category of quantity has been given. It is curious that those who think Kant miscounts his numbering of the formulas do not note this. Despite the fact that Paton is the classical authority for discussion of this 'problem' most of his discussion of the formulas concerns the arguments Kant gives for each one rather than being mainly an account of the problem of whether these formulas have extensional equivalence.

By contrast with Paton's inclusive discussion, which examines the arguments for each formula, and despite subordinating the law of nature formula and the kingdom of ends formula, does tend to suggest that all five are formulations of the categorical imperative, Philip Stratton-Lake argues that there are only three formulas.[6] Stratton-Lake takes these formulas to be Paton's Formula I, Formula II and Formula IIIa. The law of nature formulation is correctly identified by Stratton-Lake as just an analogical extension of the formula of universality whilst for some reason he does not see that this can also be said of the kingdom of ends formulation in relation to the formula of autonomy. Paul Guyer plausibly identifies the formulas as specifying the conditions of rational willing and in doing so defends them all as necessary except for the law of nature formula, which is correct given his focus.[7]

John Rawls has provided perhaps the most interesting attempt at discussing the relationship between the formulas and has further distinguished the categorical imperative from the moral law by suggesting that the latter only appears under the guise of the former for those who are necessitated to act morally, whilst for the holy will it does not so appear.[8] Rawls takes it that the categorical imperative requires a procedure to be applied in deliberation and identifies this procedure with the law of nature formulation but suggests that the point of the different formulations can be captured in relating them to moral points of view. The universal law formulation involves addressing a situation from the agent's point of view whilst the end-in-itself formulation involves a relationship between others and ourselves and the formula of autonomy grasps the notion of law giving. (Rawls, *op. cit.*, p. 183).

The variety of other accounts is, as already indicated, vast and I do not propose to consider all the varieties here.[9] The strengths and weaknesses of the various approaches bear a great deal in common with that of the ones about to be addressed. It is rare for a commentator to discuss the main problem of the second section as being a display of the supreme principle in relation to a 'metaphysics of morals'. Paul Guyer does recognize this and his account of the rationality of the moral agent being progressively revealed in the exposition of separate formulas is convergent with the view adopted here. It is noteworthy, however, that Guyer treats all the formulas as stating the categorical imperative rather than there being as Kant states only one such, namely the formula of universal law. The identity of the formula of universal law with the principle of autonomy is clearly stated when Kant gives the latter so there is no difficulty concerning their relationship and if the analogical status of the law of nature formula is remembered it can only be taken as a basis for regulating the system of duties in accordance with the categorical imperative. The formula of the realm of ends arises from the demand of reason to totalize and is the distributive figurative extension of the notion of autonomy. The end-in-itself formula, as Guyer rightly states, gives the conditions of agency, conditions specified in positive form in the notion of autonomy.

Rawls' distinction of points of view is a good account of a difference between the formulas but his notion that the law of nature gives the procedure of application of the categorical imperative to situations seems based only on the fact that it applies to examples which is also the case with the end-in-itself formula and, as will be seen, the latter is the basis of the system of duties in the Doctrine of Virtue. The discussion of the 'problem' in Paton and Stratton-Lake indicates that the former does not concern himself greatly with the notion of meaning as a difficulty whilst the latter's ordering of the formula does not bring out that the principle of autonomy is taken by Kant to distinguish his view of morality most clearly from that of others.

These various interpretations do all have strengths but the concentration on this 'problem' detracts from the key difficulties of the *Groundwork* as it ensures that the nature of the relationship between the notions of a 'metaphysics of morals' and a 'critique of pure practical reason' are not the main focus of the treatments given. In the interpretation defended here only the formulation of universal law is taken to be a formulation of the categorical imperative. There is, states Kant, only one categorical imperative and this is it. The notion of an end-in-itself is set out to make clear how the categorical imperative is connected to the nature of rational agency *per se*. The law of nature formula is a basis for organizing the system of duties and is hence described as a principle of duty. The principle of autonomy restates the universal law formula in the light of the end-in-itself formula. The notion of a realm of ends is the expansion of the moral world after the pattern of a harmonious world and thus is the real teleological law Paton thought to discover in the law of nature formula. The connections between the formulas after the law of nature formula are based on the notion of a 'metaphysics of morals' that investigates, as Guyer rightly states, the conditions of rational agency. There is no serious problem of inter-relation of the formulas once this is grasped.

The argument of *Groundwork* III

It is the task of the third part of the *Groundwork* to show that the principle of autonomy and hence the categorical imperative is a synthetic *a priori* truth. This requires a move from the 'metaphysics of morals' to a critique of pure practical reason. Before turning to an account of how Kant performs this transition, a transition deemed very controversial by most commentators on the *Groundwork* and argued by the majority of them to be a failure, it will first be useful to reprise the results of the second section. Within it we discovered that the categorical imperative must be the form of law that was involved in moral principles and that this imperative could be connected analytically to the concept of a rational will. We thus disclosed that the supreme principle of morality must be the principle of autonomy if rational agency exists at all. What we have not uncovered is that such agency does in fact exist and in lieu of such a demonstration we have not secured any real validity for the moral principle since all we have thus done is specify to what kind of being it would apply if there are such beings but not that we are such beings ourselves or that there are any such beings in existence. What is described in this work as a 'metaphysics of morals' is thus akin to what Kant in the First Critique terms a 'metaphysical deduction'. The pure concepts of morality have been demonstrated but that we are justified in applying them to ourselves in our experience has not. Hence if a critique of pure practical reason is to be undertaken now, it must be the task of such a critique to demonstrate the limits of claims that could be made by a pure practical reason but also to demonstrate that we have such a reason ourselves. So the argument of the third section must be akin to what Kant terms in the First Critique a 'transcendental deduction' which demonstrates the right by which we apply such concepts to ourselves as we have uncovered to be necessary in moral thinking.

The opening of the third section is still contained within the boundaries of a 'metaphysics of morals' that is, an analytical inquiry into rational agency. It follows the pattern of explicating what must be involved for the principle of autonomy to be stated as a property of rational nature. For rational nature to be autonomous it must be free. Freedom can be understood purely negatively as absence of compulsion or positively as a special kind of causality immanent to the will. Since we have identified the principle of autonomy with the categorical imperative, an identification Kant now repeats (Ak. 4:447), there is a strict correlation between a will governed by moral laws and a free will. Hence if there is freedom then there is morality. But to state that there is free will is to state that someone possesses the property of acting under moral laws and this is a synthetic proposition. That this synthetic proposition *must* be stated would be to say that it is not only synthetic but also *a priori*.

If the notion of freedom can be justified then it must be a property of all rational beings that have a will since it is the relationship between the notion of the will (discussed in *Groundwork* I) and the categorical imperative (discussed in *Groundwork* II) that has to be demonstrated. 'I say now: every being that cannot act otherwise than *under the idea of freedom* is just because of that really free in a practical respect, that is, all laws that are inseparably bound up with freedom hold for him just as if his will had been validly pronounced free also in itself and in practical philosophy' (Ak. 4:448). Thus, if there are beings who cannot act except under the idea of freedom, we will assess them to be free practically even if we cannot prove them to be free theoretically. Since we saw in the examination of the Third Antinomy that there is no way of proving freedom theoretically this precaution is necessary and we also saw in the discussion of the Canon of Pure Reason that practically freedom can be assumed even if transcendentally it cannot be proved as all that we require to assume freedom practically is that it not be impossible transcendentally not that it can be proved transcendentally.

To this point Kant now adds that if we have the concept of a rational being with a will then we must attach to this concept the notion of freedom as a notion under which such a being acts and the basis of this is clear if we remember that action requires having an end in view and to have an end in view is to form representations of purposes. Since to act in accordance with a purpose is to select an end then, if there is a will there is practical reason and hence freedom. This demonstrates in effect that the notion of morality requires the concept of freedom as its condition. However, this is all still merely analytic and we have in presenting the idea of freedom presupposed that the moral law has reality. Until we can demonstrate that we are free the demonstration that the moral law is binding upon us will not have been done.

> It must be freely admitted that a kind of circle comes to light here from which, as it seems, there is no way to escape. We take ourselves as free in the order of efficient causes in order to think ourselves under moral laws in the order of ends; and we afterwards think ourselves as subject to these laws because we have ascribed to ourselves freedom of will: for, freedom and the will's own lawgiving are both autonomy and hence reciprocal concepts, and for this very reason one cannot be used to explain the other or to furnish a ground for it but can at most be used only for the logical purpose of reducing apparently different representations of the same object to one single

concept (as different fractions of equal value are reduced to their low-
est expression). (Ak. 4:450)

What is the objection Kant here makes to his own argument as given
thus far in the third section? We will see in due course that there are
sharply differing answers to this question and it will be important to
indicate our reply in a preliminary fashion now in order to test it subsequently against other accounts. Briefly, the situation appears to be of
the following kind. Kant undertakes at the beginning of the third section to set out an account of what enables us to state that a rational
being is, *qua* rational agent, autonomous. The reply is that to be
autonomous such an agent must be free. Autonomy can be thus
grounded on freedom and we can assert freedom as applicable if we connect to the notion of rationality the capacity to act, that is, the possession of a will. Whilst the possession of a will does lead us to the notion
of freedom this is not a clear proof that the rational agent is free however as the notion of freedom is simply deduced here analytically from
the concept of willing. But since the notion of freedom in fact implicitly
assumes the notion of autonomy it can hardly ground it. The circle
thus objected to is one that arises from assuming freedom to ground
morality when in fact for morality to be possible the notion of freedom
must already be given and hence it can hardly be the basis of morality.
*Thus what we require to be given to escape the circle is a reason for thinking
of ourselves as free.*

This requires the step into a critique of pure practical reason as is sig-
nalled by Kant's statement that we must inquire 'whether we do not
take a different standpoint' when we think of ourselves as free than
from taking ourselves as determined (Ak. 4:451). Although Kant does
not here use the term 'critique of pure practical reason' this must be the
point at which we make the transition. The analytic argument thus far
presented which ran into a circle was still within the province of a
'metaphysics of morals' or analytical inquiry into rational agency. The
basis for claiming this is that it traded on definitions that concerned the
understanding of rational agency. But this inquiry into rational agency
is clearly a pure inquiry and one into practical reason. Now we can
begin to see Kant's departure from tradition as he now presents the critique into the claims of such a pure practical reason to ground itself on
definitions and the application of the principle of contradiction alone.
This cannot get past the objection of logical circularity.

The adoption of a 'different standpoint' requires looking anew at the
conditions of freedom. What is the difference between the standpoint

adopted when we view ourselves as free from that adopted when we view ourselves as mere effects of remote causes?

> No subtle reflection is needed to make the following remark, and one may assume that the commonest understanding can make it, though in its own way, by an obscure discrimination of judgment which it calls feeling: that all representations which come to us involuntarily (as do those of the senses) enable us to cognize objects only as they affect us and we remain ignorant of what they may be in themselves so that, as regards representations of this kind, even with the most strenuous attentiveness and distinctness that the understanding can ever bring to them we can achieve only cognition *of appearances*, never of *things in themselves*. (Ak. 4:450–1)

The reference to this crucial critical distinction is here made by reference to the heteronomy of these representations. They come from beyond us and, since they have in them something quite alien to us, we cannot know them in their immanent nature but merely through the veil of our own possibilities of awareness. Thus the distinction between appearances and things in themselves is here motivated by the observation of a difference in kind between that which is aware of something external to it and that external something in its pure externality. Given this ontological division there is a difference in principle between that which *is* aware and that *of which* it is aware. This gives a crude distinction between passivity and activity and through this distinction an awareness that the world of sense is not strictly equivalent to that which understands it. This distinction must even apply to self-awareness inasmuch as the self is grasped as possessed of the same external properties as objects and hence there is a difference between the self-in-itself and the self as it appears, the difference described in the First Critique as the distinction between empirical character and intelligible character.

These critical distinctions are used to provide us with the grounds for conceiving of ourselves as possessed of a rational nature. Kant moves on from the points raised thus far to state the properties of our capacity of awareness:

> a human being really finds in himself a capacity by which he distinguishes himself from all other things, even from himself insofar as he is affected by objects, and that is *reason*. This, as pure self-activity, is raised even above the *understanding* by this: that though the latter is also self-activity and does not, like sense, contain merely representa-

tions that arise when we are *affected* by things (and are thus passive), yet it can produce from its activity no other concepts than those which serve merely *to bring sensible representations under rules* and thereby to unite them in one consciousness, without which use of sensibility it would think nothing at all; but reason, on the contrary, shows in what we call 'ideas' a spontaneity so pure that it thereby goes far beyond anything that sensibility can ever afford it, and proves its highest occupation in distinguishing the world of sense and the world of understanding from each other and thereby marking out limits for the understanding itself. (Ak. 4:452)

We can distinguish three different types of awareness. There is the passivity of sensory impressions, which refer us always to something beyond knowledge. Distinguished from this and capable of grasping the distinction between an event and its law of operation is the understanding, which grasps the laws of nature and sets the laws for nature. Lastly, distinct entirely from sensibility is reason, which is the power to mark the limits of understanding and provide us with thoughts, which we can term 'ideas', that reach beyond sensory representation of any kind and are not even grasped in the laws of sensibility.

It is the capacity to have ideas – that is, the power of reason – that entitles us to describe ourselves as intelligences. It is this capacity that allows us to think of ourselves under the idea of freedom. Since we have seen from the analytical argument at the beginning of the third section that the notion of autonomy is bound up with the idea of freedom, then if we are in possession of a capacity that enables us to think of ourselves as free, we are in possession of autonomy and hence the universal principle of morality. This takes us beyond the circle to which we were inevitably led when we moved only within the circle of analytical definition. 'For we now see that when we think of ourselves as free we transfer ourselves into the world of understanding as members of it and cognize autonomy of the will along with its consequence, morality; but if we think of ourselves as put under obligation we regard ourselves as belonging to the world of sense and yet at the same time to the world of understanding' (Ak. 4:453).

Thus far we have demonstrated a reason for thinking of ourselves as free and hence with this have now a reason for thinking of the categorical imperative as something that applies to us. Kant follows this demonstration of the condition of the application of the categorical imperative to us which took place by showing us that we possessed the conditions of being able to think of ourselves as free with a demonstration of the syntheticity of the categorical imperative. This is required to fill out the critique, as this principle whilst now demonstrated to be applicable to us has still not itself been demonstrated synthetically but only analytically. Kant now remedies this situation:

> this *categorical* ought represents a synthetic proposition a priori, since to my will affected by sensible desires there is added the idea of the same will but belonging to the world of the understanding – a will pure and practical of itself, which contains the supreme condition, in accordance with reason, of the former will; this is roughly like the way in which concepts of the understanding, which by themselves signify nothing but lawful form in general, are added to intuitions of the world of sense and thereby make possible synthetic propositions a priori on which all cognition of a nature rests. (Ak. 4:454)

The 'ought' is here treated like a category of the pure understanding, which itself merely contains the thought of a law in general and is connected to the sensible will by the thought of a pure will that, in accord with reason, gives the condition of the empirical will. The synthesis of the category which is carried out with the intuition in theoretical cognition by the imagination acting in concert with the understanding is carried out in practical cognition by the operation of reason performing a schema of the law itself by setting out a condition for empirical willing and cognition of the interconnection of laws. Hence reason performs in practical cognition the function performed in theoretical cognition by the imagination. Reason as a purely spontaneous power of ideas ties the pure thought of law to the empirical will through providing both the empirical will and the thought of law with their grounds of operation.

Finally, since the opening parts of the analytical argument reminded us that if it is necessary in action to think of oneself as acting under the idea of freedom then in practical terms one is free, we can add for the sake of completeness that in moral experience we continuously do have to so act. Whilst this idea of freedom cannot arise from sensory experience and hence is only an idea it is a practically necessary one. That we must therefore think of ourselves as free is a practical requirement, which we can add to the reasons given us by the distinction between appearances and things in themselves. But how it is possible that we are free is not something that we can undertake to explain. All we can account for is the consciousness of willing, consciousness that requires the idea of freedom. Hence that pure reason is practical can be shown, but how it is the case that it is practical cannot be shown. This takes us to the limit of practical philosophy, a limit at which the critique of pure reason stopped also as the result here matches entirely that which we discovered in the resolution of the Third Antinomy.

Objections to the argument of *Groundwork* III

Despite the consonance of the results of the argument of the third section of the *Groundwork* with the resolution of the Third Antinomy there is considerable dissatisfaction with the argument of *Groundwork* III. Indeed, the response to this argument in the critical literature on the *Groundwork* is almost universally dismissive. This generally negative response to the argument of *Groundwork* III is partly based on a general assumption that Kant himself came to reject this argument when he wrote the Second Critique. I will leave aside consideration of this question until the next chapter. The more serious question, which underlies the dismissal of the argument of *Groundwork* III, is the suggestion that Kant's argument fails in its own terms. In response to this suggestion, widely adopted in the commentaries on the *Groundwork*, and even stated by one of its translators as a footnote to Kant's text,[10] it will be important to state what the argument is that is stated to fail and to assess whether the argument stated to fail is really Kant's argument.

Paton is, once again, the *locus classicus* of this objection to Kant. Paton's basic operative assumption comes from his account of the opening paragraphs of the third section where Kant is moving within the circle of definitions that he is taking here to constitute a 'metaphysics of morals'. Just after the introduction of the idea of freedom in a practical respect as giving us a reason for thinking of a being as actually free has been introduced Kant states the following:

> Now I assert that to every rational being having a will we must necessarily lend the idea of freedom also, under which alone he acts. For in such a being we think of a reason that is practical, that is, has causality with respect to its objects. Now, one cannot possibly think of a reason that would consciously receive direction from any other quarter with respect to its judgments, since the subject would then attribute the determination of his judgment not to his reason but to an impulse. Reason must regard itself as the author of its principles independently of alien influences; consequently, as practical reason or as the will of a rational being it must be regarded of itself as free, that is, the will of such a being cannot be a will of its own except under the idea of freedom, and such a will must in a practical respect thus be attributed to every rational being. (Ak. 4:448)

This passage is clearly an explication of why the idea of freedom in a practical respect should be attributed to a rational being which has a will. For such a being, having a will, has practical reason. Its practical reason must have autonomous judgment as if it did not have such judgment it would of necessity attribute its practical deliberations to impulses rather than reasons. It is something of a surprise to be told by Paton therefore that at this point of the metaphysical argument: 'Kant bases his case, not merely on the nature of practical reason, but on the nature of theoretical reason' (Paton, *op. cit.*, p. 218). The reason for this statement of Paton's is made a little clearer by the fact that when he cites the above passage from the third section of the *Groundwork* he italicises the term 'judgments'. Evidently, Paton takes the reference to 'judgments' to involve theoretical reason as he states that the argument 'applies most obviously to a judgment which is the conclusion of an argument' (Paton, *op. cit.*, p. 218). Kant is not however referring here to the conclusion of arguments but to judgment understood as the process of decision and hence is drawing on the notion of 'motive' which he earlier contrasted with the sensible determination of the *Triebfeder*.

Since there is therefore no reference here to theoretical reason, despite Paton's suggestion to the contrary, there is not here the type of 'surprising turn' in Kant's argument that Paton suggests. Hence Kant does not make the 'mistake' Paton suggests is operative here of supposing that 'morality could be justified by a non-moral concept of freedom established without regard to moral considerations' (Paton, *op. cit.*, p. 221). It would be very surprising indeed if Kant could possibly have made such a 'mistake' in the concluding outline of the 'metaphysics of morals'. Paton's account of this argument has misstated part of it. Paton now describes the discussion of the 'interests' of morality that Kant moves on to and which lead him to the objection from circularity as 'side issues at the best' (Paton, *op. cit.*, p. 223). What is the reason for this attitude of Paton's aside from his false view of the role of theoretical reason in Kant's argument?

The rejection of the discussion of the role of 'interest' in moral consideration comes because Paton rightly takes it to be the case that there is no way of responding to the question why I should do my duty except to state that my duty is necessarily obligatory on me. However, this does not accurately convey what Kant is asking about when he raises the question of 'interest' in morality, as Kant is here in fact asking both am I aware of what my duty consists in, and what power within me operates to make duty a motive force to me? To the first question the categorical imperative is to give the answer but only if it can justifiably be applied to me which justification Kant proceeds to give whilst to the second question there is no answer as it points to the limits of practical philosophy as such, which cannot explain how freedom is an operative power.

Neither of these questions is a side issue therefore as one of them points us to the limit of practical philosophy itself and thus defines the limits of pure practical reason whilst the other leads on to the problem of the justification of the categorical imperative. The objection from circularity is, however, completely misrepresented by Paton. Paton gives the objection and suggests Kant did not take it too seriously despite the fact that it is because of this objection that Kant justifies the move beyond the confines of a 'metaphysics of morals' and to that of a critique of pure practical reason. The reason why Paton thinks that Kant did not take this objection seriously is that he reports Kant's objection as based on a misconstrual of the argument hitherto given when in fact it is merely that Kant does not report himself to have stated his argument in the form Paton took it to have:

> He never argued from the categorical imperative to freedom, but at least professed, however mistakenly, to establish the presupposition of freedom by an insight into the nature of self-conscious reason quite independently of moral considerations. Perhaps when he came to the objection he was beginning to see dimly that the presupposition of freedom of the will really did rest on moral considerations; but it is surely unusual for a man to answer the sound argument which he has failed to put and to overlook the fact that his answer is irrelevant to the unsound argument which alone has been explicitly stated. (Paton, *op. cit.*, p. 225)

Since we have already seen that Kant did not originally state the 'unsound argument' that Paton took him to have given we can neglect this aspect of Paton's charge now. What we can see the objection of circularity to arise from is simply that the citation above given and which is the basis of Paton's original error implicitly introduced the notion of autonomy in the guise of explaining why we should accept it. This is the circle which Kant uncovers as necessarily being a consequence of a purely analytical method as adopted by rationalists of the Wolffian school. Since this objection is compelling it does lead clearly beyond the confines of an analytical method and towards a synthetic one, which has to be justified by the critique of pure practical reason to which Kant then turns. If Paton had been more struck by the paradox of Kant's attempting to object to an argument he hadn't made then he would perhaps have discovered what argument Kant had in fact earlier made and why his objection to it is hence made.

Since Paton thinks that Kant had earlier made reference to theoretical reason he is necessarily at something of a loss to explain why Kant now refers to the distinction between appearances and things in themselves in dissolving the circle that the analytical method has led him to. To this confusion he adds a further one when discussing the conclusion of the argument about appearances and things in themselves where Kant refers to how we transfer ourselves into the world of understanding when we think of ourselves as free. Paton cannot see how this suggestion can be anything other than the suggestion made in the analytical argument that if we are compelled to think of ourselves as free practically then we really are free. There was, however, nothing wrong with this suggestion in itself when it was made in the analytical argument. The difficulty with it in the context of the analytical argument is that we had there no means to demonstrate our freedom except through sleights of hand brought about by definitions. When we have the transcendental distinction in place however we do have a reason to think of ourselves as free and hence the practical necessity of using this idea is suddenly given a new basis which allows us to see how the two standpoints referred to in the opening of the argument actually help us to grasp the nature of freedom.

Similarly, at the conclusion of the argument showing that the categorical imperative is a synthetic a priori, Kant corroborates the results of the argument by referring to the necessity from a practical point of view of considering ourselves as free. But this is not an independent argument for the syntheticity of the categorical imperative but a supporting consideration for thinking of it as applying to us. Paton, however, fundamentally misunderstands the structure of these arguments when he writes: 'If Kant really supposes that he can start from theoretical reason and infer from this to membership of the intelligible world, and from this to freedom, and from this to a justification of the binding character of the moral law, then – however much he may be avoiding a vicious circle – he is falling into a fundamental error. It is manifestly impossible to deduce moral obligation from purely metaphysical or epistemological considerations which have nothing to do with morality' (Paton, *op. cit.*, p. 226).

The final sentence of this quote indicates the reasons for Paton's misgivings about the argument of *Groundwork* III. If Kant were trying to deduce moral obligation from metaphysical considerations then we would have strong reasons to reject his procedure, as it would clearly involve a fallacious assumption of attempting a conclusive indication of a reason for acting in a moral way based on an argument about the nature of where we stood metaphysically. Does Kant attempt this in the argument of *Groundwork* III? No, he does not. The structure of the argument is quite different from Paton's representation of it. The theoretical step in Kant's argument is introduced to show that we have a reason for thinking of ourselves as free as the distinction between appearances and things in themselves applies as much to ourselves as to objects. Since I have a self-in-itself in addition to an apparent self the basis of my possession of a reason is demonstrable. This reason is one which can be shown to necessarily fall into perplexity over the problem of freedom, and it is impossible to demonstrate theoretically that I am free. But since there is also no way of demonstrating that I am not free except by disregarding the transcendental distinction between appearances and things in themselves and since the notion of freedom is one we have demonstrated to be essential to morality then we have no theoretical reason to deny freedom and a practical ground to support it. *This practical necessity of freedom is hence supported and confirmed by the theoretical impossibility of denying freedom.*

Furthermore, the notion which we have defended in theoretical terms of a distinction between appearances and things in themselves indicates the distinction in standpoint between thinking of myself as free and thinking of myself as determined, a distinction which in turn can be used to demonstrate the syntheticity of the categorical imperative. Hence what Kant does is move from the transcendental distinction to the allowance this gives to think in terms of freedom and from there to a ground for thinking of the categorical imperative as synthetic. Kant does not, however, attempt to ground the categorical imperative itself on the transcendental distinction but merely its status as a synthetic a priori proposition. Therefore, the role of theoretical reason in the argument is not to attempt to provide a ground for the categorical imperative as the principle of morality. This argument is entirely conducted within the second section of the *Groundwork* and belongs within the province of a practical metaphysics. Kant merely attempts to show that the categorical imperative applies to us by showing that the characteristics of rational beings discussed in the second section of the *Groundwork* are characteristics we can be shown to have.

Therefore, Kant does what Paton suggests he should have done, namely to use 'metaphysical considerations' (namely, the transcendental distinction) to '*defend* a moral principle taken to be independently established' but not to attempt to use such considerations to establish this principle

(Paton, *op. cit.*, p. 226). These considerations defend the moral principle by showing that it is one that applies to us by demonstrating that we are rational agents. But the moral principle has already been established as such by the analytical arguments given in the second section of the work. Thus Kant's argument is not the 'failure' Paton takes it to be because his argument does not state what Paton takes it to state.

Unfortunately, despite the many confusions evident in Paton's interpretation of the argument of *Groundwork* III his account has proved influential and has been the basis of other declarations of its failure. Thus, Dieter Henrich's article on the argument of *Groundwork* III begins from the same reference to the notion of 'judgments' that Paton makes and similarly suggests that Kant has here confused the notion of practical freedom with an inference from theoretical reason that Henrich terms 'logical freedom'.[11] Apart from Henrich's novel terminology, however, this point is the same as Paton's, based on the same misreading of the same passage and liable to the same objections. Kant does not suggest as Henrich states that 'there can be no rational beings without freedom of the will' (Henrich, *op. cit.*, p. 313), but that there can be no rational *agents* without freedom of the will as such agents must possess a will to be agents and if they are rational must conceive of their action as self-originating in reason as otherwise they will be determined by impulse alone and hence have no awareness and no reason. Whilst Henrich is forced to concede this in the course of his interpretation he still suggests that Kant thinks that 'every rational discourse presupposes freedom of judgment' (Henrich, *op. cit.*, p. 314) as, like Paton, he can only conceive of the notion of judgment as the conclusion to an argument and not as a basis of practical decision.

Henrich assumes that within the text of *Groundwork* III Kant is engaging in some kind of derivation of transcendental freedom despite the fact that the resolution of the Third Antinomy showed this to be impossible. In discussing Kant's turn to the transcendental distinction as a result of the circularity produced by the analytical argument Henrich complains that the laws of the world of intellibility are only introduced 'after a *will* has once again been imputed to the rational being' (Henrich, *op. cit.*, p. 318) as if Kant's argument was an attempt to demonstrate that the rational being *qua* rational rather than *qua* rational agent had to be free. Naturally, it is only through the introduction of the idea of the will that Kant can show a rational agent to be free, but it is only the notion of a rational agent that he is discussing not a rational being *simpliciter*.

Of course, the doctrine of two worlds cannot 'forcibly introduce the idea of the moral law' (Henrich, *op. cit.*, p. 319), but nor is it intended to do so. Kant is not attempting to demonstrate moral freedom logically but rather to show that there are reasons to think of ourselves as free if we can be shown to be rational agents. Kant does not attempt to *demonstrate* that we are agents as the argument of the Third Antinomy has shown that this cannot be demonstrated, but since it can also not be demonstrated that we are not agents then this can be assumed as a logically permissible thought even if its reality can in no way be shown. Henrich's account circles around the argument of the third section but consistently runs into the stumbling block of thinking that Kant in some unsatisfactory sense was trying to establish the moral law independently of moral considerations or trying to show that there are purely theoretical ways of demonstrating moral freedom. Since neither of these tasks are attempted by the argument of the *Groundwork* it is Henrich's interpretation that is clouded with confusions not Kant's argument.

Karl Ameriks is another commentator who assumes the failure of Kant's argument when he presents an argument that does fail but is not Kant's.[12] The first part of the argument of *Groundwork* III is taken to be a demonstration of the reality of transcendental freedom when such a demonstration would violate the resolution of the Third Antinomy. Like Paton and Henrich he makes the same confusion about the notion of 'judgments' assuming some kind of reference to theoretical reason must be made in thinking of practical decisions. The objection from circularity is rather oddly presented by Ameriks as he takes Kant to be suggesting that the problem arises by discussing what is supposed to follow from the notion of freedom that Kant has not established in the analytical argument but which Kant for some reason still wishes to assume as if he had established it (Ameriks, *op. cit.*, p. 204). Since this would be a very odd thing for Kant to do, and since we have a sufficiently cogent alternative account of what Kant's argument has done in the conclusion of his 'metaphysics of morals', we can clearly reject this suggestion of Ameriks.

Ameriks shares in effect Paton's view of the objection of circularity and merely adds confusions of his own. Ameriks real argument, however, seems to be that Kant should have discussed possible compatibilist responses to the problem of freedom and determinism and thus have revised the verdict of the Third Antinomy which indicates that his reservations with the argument are really reservations about the argument of the Third Antinomy and certainly anyone not convinced by the argument of the Third Antinomy would not be convinced of the argument of the third section of the *Groundwork*. Ameriks' reference to the statement of Kant that theoretical philosophy must show that both freedom and necessity are united in the same subject (Ak. 4:456) refers back to the discussion about empirical and intelligible character made within the pages of the Third Antinomy and does not, as Ameriks suggests, add something to the argument of this antinomy. Ameriks' conviction that Kant wished to demonstrate the reality of transcendental freedom despite the conclusion of the Third Antinomy are the source of his conviction that the argument of *Groundwork* III is a failure but this view is not textually based.

Henry Allison, in conclusion, is also of the view that the argument of the third section of the *Groundwork* fails but on very similar grounds to those already discussed.[13] Like Paton, Henrich and Ameriks he is of the view that Kant's reference to 'judgments' involves some reference to theoretical reason and is as such important to the analytical argument. To this he adds the assumption that Kant makes a 'colossal *petitio*' of moving from the practical necessity of freedom to an assumption of the reality of freedom which is not supported in the argument Kant in fact gives (Allison, *op. cit.*, p. 217). Allison adds to this a complaint derived from Henrich that Kant does not demonstrate that 'rational beings such as ourselves possess a will' (Allison, *op. cit.*, p. 218) when it is no part of Kant's task to demonstrate the possession of a will but merely to show that since rational agents possess a will this will must be one that is free.

That Allison takes it to be Kant's argumentative purpose to show that we have a will, underlies his objection to the appeal to the intelligible world Kant can make on the basis of the appeal to the transcendental distinction between appearances and things in themselves. Allison presents no clear objection to this argument except to state that the notion of the intelligible world to which we are led by the notion of reason does not prove that we have a will and thus that the connection between being rational and being agents is not made. But it could not be Kant's intent to *prove* that we are agents as this would simply violate the resolution of the Third Antinomy and the discussion of willing is in fact part of Kant's demonstration of the syntheticity of the categorical imperative. A separate objection which Allison is alone in bringing is made to this argument when he objects to Kant's view that the two standpoints explain the synthetic character of the categorical imperative: 'in order to explain the possibility of a categorical imperative for finite rational beings such as ourselves, it is necessary to show how the moral law addresses beings whose wills are sensibly affected but not necessitated. But such an argument cannot proceed, as Kant here seems to suggest, directly from general considerations about the phenomenal-noumenal relationship' (Allison, *op. cit.*, p. 226).

Allison's concern here seems to be that Kant account for how the categorical imperative affects sensibly conditioned beings. This is not what this argument is intended to show however, as here what Kant has demonstrated is the duality of relationship we have to the categorical imperative as law-givers and as agents legislated to. This dual relationship corresponds to the two standpoints under which we view ourselves as the one who is obligated is placed under a rule of necessity and this rule is analogous to that which we are placed under by natural law so we thinking it (as expressed in the formula of the law of nature) as if it were a natural law. This duality of relation is what enables the categorical imperative to be seen as a synthetic a priori judgment and it is this which Kant is here defending not the question of *how* we are able to view ourselves as placed under the moral law. The question of how we are so placed can rather be viewed either as asking what permits us to view ourselves as the kinds of being to whom the categorical imperative applies which is what the transcendental distinction has given us or what the grounds are for the action of intelligible causation which we know Kant thinks cannot be given.

To these objections Allison adds another concerning the use Kant makes of the transcendental distinction. Allison makes a distinction between *Verstandeswelt* and *intelligibelen Welt* where the former is understood to mean noumenon in the negative sense and the latter noumenon in the positive sense of intelligible character and intelligible freedom. Allison remarks: 'The goal is to show that rational beings, including imperfectly rational beings such as ourselves, are members of such an *intelligibelen Welt* because this would entail that they really stand under the moral law. The problem is that the possession of reason, which is supposed to provide the *entrée* into this world, only gets us to the *Verstandeswelt*' (Allison, *op. cit.*, p. 227). This objection is similar to one voiced by Henrich and is said by Allison to underlie and undermine the entire deduction.

The possession of understanding indicates to us that we are separable from the sensible world that the understanding gives laws to and hence it is the understanding that provides us with membership of the *Verstandeswelt*. Reason, by contrast, as the home of ideas, is precisely what shows us to belong in the *intelligibelen Welt* and this is why it is the home of the most spontaneous aspect of selfhood. Allison and Henrich should not really have missed this point as it is expressly emphasised by Kant in the argument of *Groundwork* III and this argument is supported by reference to numerous passages of the First Critique (Ak. 4:452 and see the account of reason as the home of ideas at A310/B366–A338/B396).

The discussion of the extreme limit of practical philosophy, which closes the argument of *Groundwork* III, is a serious problem for all these commentators as here Kant makes clear that a demonstration of the reality of transcendental freedom cannot be presented in line with the resolution of the Third Antinomy. Since this cannot be presented, Allison assumes that this final section is a kind of self-confession of failure on Kant's part rather than being a closing of the critique of pure practical reason undertaken. As we have seen, all the attempts to show that this argument is a failure rest on misstatements of Kant's argument and whilst the arguments given certainly fail in ways in which these commentators point out they are not Kant's argument. Since the argument of *Groundwork* III does not fail it is unlikely that Kant rejected it when he came to write the Second Critique and it is to an examination of some of the key claims of this work that I will now turn, in the course of which I will demonstrate its essential agreement with the *Groundwork*.[14]

4
The 'Fact' of Reason and the *Summum Bonum*

The *Critique of Practical Reason* presents together a great number of important topics. We are treated here to an account that purports to show how we are justified in making claims practically that we cannot make theoretically, to two distinct and equally important treatments of freedom, to an antinomy that allows Kant to discuss the *summum bonum* in a manner quite distinct from that in the *Lectures on Ethics* and, finally, to treatments of the existence of God and the immortality of the soul. Given that the Second Critique is quite a short book this is a wealth of topics. In the course of this chapter I hope to illuminate some of these matters by describing the basic reason for the work being written and attempting to indicate the nature of the 'critique' here performed. A discussion of the Dialectic of this work will also be given that attempts to respond to some criticisms of its argument.

The 'fact' of reason

A persistent theme in commentary on the Second Critique is the claim that within the Analytic of this work there is an argument that runs decisively counter to the argument of *Groundwork* III. Lewis White Beck presents this view when he describes the argument of the *Critique of Practical Reason* as one in which Kant 'apparently stands the argument of the *Foundations* on its head'.[1] Acceptance of this interpretation of the Analytic of the Second Critique has been widespread and the fullest argument for it is given by Henry Allison who suggests that there is a 'radical difference' between the Second Critique and the *Groundwork* that he also describes as a 'great reversal' of standpoint. Allison presents the difference he takes there to be between the works in the following manner:

whereas in the *Groundwork* Kant takes seriously the possibility that morality might be nothing but a phantom of the brain, even after completing his analysis of its principle (the autonomy of the will), in the second *Critique* he appears (rightly or wrongly) to be burdened by no such concerns.[2]

In addition to the claim that Kant, in the Second Critique, is no longer concerned to demonstrate that the supreme principle of morality applies to us there is conjoined a belief that in the *Groundwork* Kant undertook to provide a deduction of this principle and that he no longer believes such a deduction to be possible when he writes the *Critique of Practical Reason* as is evidenced by the fact that he writes in the latter work that 'the moral law cannot be proved by any deduction, by any efforts of theoretical reason, speculative or empirically supported' (Ak. 5:48).

There are nests of interpretative problems here to address. The reason why Allison thinks that Kant has dropped the concerns he had in the *Groundwork* is due to the use made in the Second Critique of the idea of a 'fact of reason'. What this 'fact' is, how it is described by Kant and its role in his argument are hence key matters that need to be assessed in undertaking to judge the validity of what is clearly now the standard interpretation of the Second Critique. In undertaking to set this out I aim to connect this question with an examination of the rationale for writing this work and to describe the nature of the 'deduction' that is provided within its pages, a deduction undertaken precisely at the point from which a deduction of the moral law is declared unattainable.

The reason for writing the *Critique of Practical Reason*

To address the role of the argument about the 'fact of reason' in the Second Critique requires viewing the general argument of the Analytic of the work. But prior to undertaking this it is first requisite to raise the question as to what the work is intended to accomplish that the *Groundwork* did not. After all, the earlier work already disclosed the supreme principle of morality and provided us with a reason for thinking that this supreme principle applied to us. Unless there is something inadequate in the treatment given in this work what possible justification is there for writing another work that will provide a 'critique' of moral claims rather than proceeding directly now to the setting out of a work that will describe and justify the 'metaphysics of morals'?[3] To provide a preliminary response to this question I will look at the 'preface' and the 'introduction' to the Second Critique.

Kant begins the preface by discussing the fact that this work is not entitled a *Critique of Pure Practical Reason* but merely a *Critique of Practical Reason* and remarks that the task of the work is 'merely to show *that there is pure practical reason*, and for this purpose it criticizes reason's entire *practical faculty*' (Ak. 5:3). This indicates that whilst the *Groundwork*'s task had been to establish what the supreme principle of morality was, the task of the Second Critique is to investigate on what morality itself rests upon, that is, to provide an account of the basis of moral motivation. That we think practically need mean no more than that we have the capacity to think instrumentally, something of which there is little cause to doubt. But that we have a means for postulating a practical reason that is pure implies that there is a manner of relating to action that does not depend upon empirical data. This is precisely denied by empiricist accounts of motivation and is the ground for the scepticism within them as to the efficacy of appeals to reason. Hence, whilst the First Critique was written under the impulse given Kant by Hume to defend metaphysics, the Second is written in response to the claim that morals can be reduced to descriptions of empirically produced feelings.

If pure reason can be shown to be practical (and not merely theoretical), then the notion of freedom that we found in the Third Antinomy to be not disallowed by theoretical considerations would be found to have a reality in action and it is the justification of this notion that Kant reveals here to be at the heart of all his critical endeavour:

> the concept of freedom, insofar as its reality is proved by an apodictic law of practical reason, constitutes the *keystone* of the whole structure of a system of pure reason, even of speculative reason; and all other concepts (those of God and immortality), which as mere ideas remain without support for the latter, now attach themselves to this concept and with it and by means of it get stability and objective reality, that is, their *possibility* is *proved* by this: that freedom is real, for this idea reveals itself through the moral law. (Ak. 5:3–4)

The argument of *Groundwork* III relied upon a repetition of the Third Antinomy to show the syntheticity of the categorical imperative. By contrast, in the Second Critique, Kant wishes to demonstrate the basic case for thinking of pure reason as of itself practical and in the process show that, since there is a moral law, there must be freedom (and with freedom, a basis for thinking the possibility of the transcendental Ideas being given). The relationship between freedom and the moral law is an intricate one as Kant immediately concedes when stating that 'whereas freedom is indeed the *ratio essendi* of the moral law, the moral law is the *ratio cognoscendi* of freedom' (Ak. 5:5). It is because there is freedom that it is possible for there to be a moral law, but if it were not for our awareness that there is a moral law we could never justify the notion of freedom. This mutual relationship between freedom and the moral law touches on the fundamental questions that caused (and still cause) objection to the *Critique of Pure Reason*: the assertion of a means of thinking the noumenal that does not depend upon contravening the critical boundaries presented within the work to the thoughts of metaphysics. 'Only a detailed *Critique of Practical Reason* can remove all this misinterpretation and put in a clear light the consistent way of thinking that constitutes its greatest merit' (Ak. 5:7).

The response to the empiricist destruction of metaphysics is not complete unless the concept of freedom can be given a justification that involves *more* than the argument of the Third Antinomy. As we have seen, the account of freedom in the third section of the *Groundwork* offers nothing more than was given in the Third Antinomy and is hence insufficient to meet the demand for a clear demonstration of the reality of freedom, being intended only to remind one of the earlier argument of the First Critique in order, by means of it, to justify the assertion of the categorical imperative's syntheticity. So, this work is intended to show that pure reason is practical of itself and that the concept of a causality of freedom 'does in fact belong to the human will' (Ak. 5:15). Having established the reason for writing this work it is now time to turn to the argument given in the Analytic for these conclusions.

The practical nature of pure reason

The order of the Analytic's treatment is quite distinct from that of the First Critique. The reason for the difference in order is that whereas the First Critique was dealing with the relationship of reason to objects, the Second Critique is instead relating to the will and thinking the conditions for its causality. The opening of the Analytic with the principles of reason concerns the setting out of the application of concepts as we were informed in the First Critique that an analytic of principles concerns a canon of judgment about application of concepts (A132/B171). This arises immediately when we are considering practical reason, as the question of the application of its concepts is the first that has to be considered.

The Analytic hence opens with a definition and the consequences of it are then set out in three Theorems. The definition concerns the province of practical principles, which are defined as consisting in two kinds: subjective and objective. Subjective principles are *maxims* or rules taken only to apply to a particular actor whilst objective principles are *laws* or taken to hold 'for the will of every rational being' (Ak. 5:19). Since all practical rules involve the thought of a relation of means to ends they are all products of reason. Another name for the objective type of practical principle is an imperative but only if they are seen to have necessity and do not apply merely contingently. The Theorems then follow from these definitions and can be spelled out quickly. Theorem I states that if a practical principle presupposes in its formulation an object independent of its own statement then it is grounded on experience and will involve the notion of a *pleasure* in the object. Theorem II adds that practical principles of an empirical kind all follow a principle of self-love, which can be encapsulated in the desire for happiness. Theorem III restates Theorem II in positive form by declaring that a practical law can only be said to consist in statements that, in their very formulation, without reference to any independent data of experience, provide a universal ground of action. The result of these three Theorems is the statement of two problems. The first problem is what is the character of a will that would be determinable by the mere form of a law? This is answered:

> if no determining ground of the will other than that universal lawgiving form can serve as a law for it, such a will must be thought as altogether independent of the natural law of appearances in their relations to one another, namely the law of causality. But such independence is called *freedom* in the strictest, that is, in the transcendental, sense. Therefore, a will for which the mere lawgiving form of a maxim can alone serve as a law is a free will. (Ak. 5:29)

A will that could be determined by a practical law would be a free will. This gives us a second problem. This is, given that a will is free, what kind of law could have a necessary relationship to its operation? This is answered by stating that the only type of law that could be necessarily connected with a free will would be one that was independent of anything empirical which would require it to be based purely on its own lawlike character. Put together the notions of freedom and a law that is given only in form give us what Kant terms the 'unconditionally practical'. The notion of it is the basic notion of a pure practical reason.

Kant now states this law of pure practical reason: 'So act that the maxim of your will could always hold at the same time as a principle in a giving of universal law' (Ak. 5:30). The law of pure practical reason is hence no other than the categorical imperative. After stating the law Kant goes on to make a fundamental claim for it:

> Consciousness of this fundamental law may be called a fact of reason because one cannot reason it out from antecedent data of reason, for example, from consciousness of freedom (since this is not antecedently given to us) and because it forces itself upon us of itself as a synthetic a priori proposition that is not based on any intuition, either pure or empirical, although it would be analytic if the freedom of the will were presupposed; but for this, as a positive concept, an intellectual intuition would be required, which certainly cannot be assumed here. However, in order to avoid misinterpretation in regarding this law as *given*, it must be noted carefully that it is not an empirical fact but the sole fact of pure reason which, by it, announces itself as originally lawgiving ... (Ak. 5:31)

Hence the consciousness of the moral law is the fact of reason. It is 'of reason' as we arrive at its notion without reference to any data exterior to reason. Its universality is grounded on the conditions of rational agency as such, which conditions can be specified as possession of an autonomous will. The notion that autonomy of the will is the sole principle of morality is then restated as Theorem IV. 'Thus the moral law expresses nothing other than the *autonomy* of pure practical reason, that is, freedom, and this is itself the formal condition of all maxims, under which alone they can accord with the supreme practical law' (Ak. 5:33).

The 'deduction' of the principles of pure practical reason

The argument thus far is equivalent to an *exposition* of the analytical consequences of certain principles. There are a certain number of points made subsequently which are still within this type of demonstration, a demonstration equivalent to what the *Groundwork* termed 'metaphysics of morals'. Subsequently to the completion of this part of the Analytic we have what corresponds to the 'critique' as given in the *Groundwork* or what the First Critique terms a 'transcendental deduction'. Setting out the relationship between these parts of the Analytic should clarify the nature of the 'fact' of pure reason and the reasons we have for thinking that the moral law applies to us.

The remaining parts of the analytical demonstration belong within the opening stages of the section entitled a 'deduction'. Kant here describes the 'fact' of reason as 'autonomy in the principle of morality', a description which accords with the demonstration of Theorems I–III combined and was stated as such in Theorem IV. This 'fact' is identical with 'consciousness of freedom of the will' as it follows from understanding that the condition for a will to be determined by a law without reference to empirical conditions is to state no other than that the will so determined is free. As a law it provides us with the form of a type of nature, namely a supersensible nature that is nothing other than '*a nature under the autonomy of pure practical reason*' (Ak. 5:43). The problem, which is the real problem of this particular 'critique', is how pure reason 'can be an immediate determining ground of the will' (Ak. 5:45). With the statement of this problem the analytical argument is complete and we can begin the key part of the Analytic, setting out the synthetic argument, otherwise described by Kant here as the 'deduction'.

What is the deduction here a deduction of? It is not the moral law as such that is being deduced, we have this already given from the analytical argument so far. Rather it is the 'objective and universal validity' and 'possibility' of this law. This transcendental deduction of the universal validity and possibility of the moral law cannot take the form of the transcendental deduction of the categories of the pure understanding as this latter proceeded by demonstrating that the thought of objects required the categories. Here however we have no objects to deal with. Nor could an empirical proof suffice, as the law is declared independent of all experience. It is because of the impossibility of providing a deduction of the possibility and validity of the moral law by reference to the categories or by reference to the method of empiricism that Kant declares that the objective reality of the moral law cannot be shown 'by any deduction, by any efforts of theoretical reason, speculative or empirically supported' (Ak. 5:47), a declaration generally interpreted to mean that Kant here rejects the approach attempted in the third section of the *Groundwork*.

It should be clear, however, that this statement does not affect the argument of the *Groundwork*. That argument did not depend on theoretical reason, did not refer to the categories of the understanding and did not support some kind of empiricist justification of the moral law. The argument of the *Groundwork* provided instead a basis for presenting the categorical imperative as a synthetic *a priori* proposition. In fact, as Michael McCarthy states, 'the deduction denied in the second Critique is also denied in the *Groundwork*'.[4] Within the *Groundwork* Kant also denied the possibility of showing the moral law by appeal to data of theoretical reason and the argument of the third section did not attempt to provide the account Kant denies is possible in the Second Critique.

Instead of attempting to use the procedures of theoretical reason to show the validity, possibility and hence reality of the moral law, something else is possible, namely to use the moral law itself to provide its own condition. This appeal has a remarkably similar structure to that of the argument of *Groundwork* III:

> But something different and quite paradoxical takes the place of this vainly sought deduction of the moral principle, namely that the moral principle, conversely itself serves as the principle of the deduction of an inscrutable faculty which no experience could prove but which speculative reason had to assume as at least possible ... namely the faculty of freedom, of which the moral law, which itself has no need of justifying grounds, proves not only the possibility but the reality in beings who cognize this law as binding upon them. The moral law is, in fact, a law of causality through freedom and hence a law of the possibility of a supersensible nature ... (Ak. 5:47)

Within the *Groundwork* Kant set out that what enabled us to think the categorical imperative as a synthetic a priori truth was the thought of freedom and here what is done is to show that what enables the thought of freedom to be understood as real is the fact that the moral law is equivalent to a principle of reason's autonomous power. The two arguments are hence not contradictory but mutually reinforcing.

The moral law is the principle that enables us to deduce freedom as a causality of pure reason. The 'objective validity' of the moral law is hence shown through this notion of a causality of freedom and its 'possibility' indicated to reside in the possibility of the thought of freedom, which possibility was guaranteed by the Third Antinomy. But the *reality* of the notion of freedom is then shown by the possibility of thinking the moral law, which possibility is no other than pure reason's own operation. The concept of a will already contains the notion of causality, so the notion of a pure will involves a causality through freedom, a causality admitted in the resolution of the Third Antinomy on the grounds of the transcendental distinction. Since the concept of causality is a pure concept (as demonstrated in the Metaphysical Deduction of the First Critique) it can be understood beyond the conditions of sensible employment but only if such non-sensible employment is not taken to describe theoretical objects. The only other possible thing being described would be the action of a pure subject operating under the conditions of a pure will and this is equivalent to the immanent operation of reason.

The notion of a fact of reason thus expresses the moral law itself which is self-grounded as it cannot be explained theoretically but how it is given to us as necessary can be set out through a deduction. This result is the same in both the arguments of the third section of the *Groundwork* and in the deduction of the Second Critique. There is therefore no 'great reversal' between the two works. The concept of a practical causality involves first, the use of the pure concept of causality. That causality is a pure concept is sufficiently shown by the demonstrations of the *Critique of Pure Reason*. Second, we need to find the ground that allows us to use causality without reference to the conditions of its legitimate use as provided within the *Critique of Pure Reason*. This possibility of an extension of the use of the concept of causality is given by practical reason as practical reason has to use the concept of a will and the notion of a will already contains the notion of causality. Since a free will is a pure will and the notion of a pure will can be presented as given earlier in the Analytic then with this pure will comes the basis of a causality that operates in a manner that is not circumscribable by the understanding.

The 'aesthetic' of pure practical reason

Having provided the transcendental deduction of the possibility and validity of the moral law by showing that it provides a deduction of freedom a notion it makes thinkable (and hence that it is self-authenticating) Kant turns to providing a 'metaphysical deduction' of the categories of freedom, categories that can only arise here once the notion of a world to which they belong has been justified. Effectively, therefore, what the 'deduction' provided was the demonstration that the moral law provides of itself the conditions for a description of the world to which it applies, an intelligible world in which the causality of freedom is operative. Once this world has been demonstrated to be a valid possibility the reality of the categories of freedom has been guaranteed and these categories are then provided on the basis of the moral law.

The categories of freedom are the concepts of the 'object' of pure practical reason, commonly referred to as goodness and evil. These categories are then set out in a table akin to that provided for the categories of pure understanding but the application of these concepts in a moral world is naturally described in a different manner to the categories of pure understanding. Whilst theoretical categories apply to the sensible world through a schematism, the place of this is taken in practical reason by what Kant terms a 'typic'. This 'typic' is a 'schema of the law itself' and is stated in terms of what readers of the *Groundwork* know as the formula of the law of nature formula. This formula is the 'rule of judgment', which is just how it is described in the Second Critique. By means of it the law of nature is made 'merely the type of a *law of freedom*' (Ak. 5:70). The methodological basis of the moral law is then defined as rationalism of judgment as 'it takes from sensible nature nothing more than what pure reason can also think for itself, that is, conformity with law, and transfers into the supersensible nothing but what can, conversely, be really exhibited by actions in the sensible world in accordance with the formula of a law of nature in general' (Ak. 5:71).

If, in the realm of theoretical reason, the real problem is presented by rationalist temptations to overstep the boundaries of the legitimate application of concepts, in the realm of practical reason by contrast, the real problem is presented by empiricism. Empiricism was identified as the principle that supported the antithesis in the Third Antinomy and its basic operation is to reduce reason to the understanding, in the process repudiating any notion of immanent justification of reason that is rather left subordinated to pathologically determined passions.

Since the principles of empiricism depend upon presenting practical motivation as grounded on feeling and in arguing for feeling to be understood exclusively pathologically it is of the utmost importance that Kant concludes the general argument of the Analytic with a presentation of an 'aesthetic' of practical reason. In doing this Kant addresses the question of how the law can be said to motivate us. Whilst the moral law is set in opposition to the circuit of self-love it also radically interrupts the circle that hedonic principles set up. The moral law strikes down self-conceit but this is a merely negative effect upon inclination. The key matter of the effect of the moral law on motivation arises when we transcend this negative effect:

> since this law is still something in itself positive – namely the form of an intellectual causality, that is, of freedom – it is at the same time an object of *respect* inasmuch as, in opposition to its subjective antagonist, namely the inclinations in us, it *weakens* self-conceit; and insasmuch as it even *strikes down* self-conceit, that is, humiliates it, it is an object of the greatest *respect* and so too the ground of a positive feeling that is not of empirical origin and is cognized a priori. Consequently, respect for

the moral law is a feeling that is produced by an intellectual ground; and this feeling is the only one that we can cognize completely a priori and the necessity of which we have insight into. (Ak. 5:73)

The feeling of respect is a feeling that is *non-pathological* in the sense of being the product of an intellectual cause. This feeling, described by Kant as *'moral feeling'*, arises from the consciousness of the moral law, particularly as exemplified in another person. This feeling gets its representation in the person of someone acting in accordance with their rational nature, in the sense of the 'personality' of a rational subject. The presentation of this in the 'aesthetic' of practical reason is the occasion for Kant re-presenting the formula of humanity as an end-in-itself.

The concept of freedom

The Analytic closes with a discussion of freedom that Kant asks that we not 'pass lightly over' (Ak. 5:8). Here Kant reviews the question as to why of all rational Ideas it is the notion of freedom that is so fruitful. In thinking of freedom we have to connect it with a category and here the category is given in the notion of causality. No intuition can be given to a rational concept but we can see that causality, as a dynamical concept, involves a relationship between condition and conditioned. In place of an intuition we search for the unconditioned which finally provides the condition for all that is conditioned. It is this that generates the Third Antinomy. We resolve this antinomy by leaving open the possibility of an unconditioned as the ultimate condition for all that is conditioned. But within the realm of theoretical reason this possibility could be given no scope. Within the realm of practical reason however we need to be able to think this possibility in order to provide us with a basis for showing the validity of the moral law. The moral law thus provides the concept of freedom with its basis of cognition as an effective concept. 'The concept of freedom alone allows us to find the unconditioned and intelligible for the conditioned and sensible without going outside ourselves' (Ak. 5:106). Freedom provides us with this unconditioned thought because it is the basis for thinking the moral law as a valid and possible notion, but it does this by demonstrating the immanent justification of morality.

Through the moral law we can cognize freedom positively, a cognition impossible for theoretical reason. This positive cognition of freedom is the advance made over the position of the Third Antinomy. Whilst the argument of the third section of the *Groundwork* concerned the notion of autonomy, the argument within that section did not revert to the demonstration of the principle of autonomy as the self-given 'fact of reason' that had already been prepared in the second section. Due to the basis of division of material in the *Groundwork* there is no setting out of how the moral law provides us with the positive notion of freedom. Rather, this positive notion is simply taken over in the third section of the *Groundwork* from the second section. The reworking of the organization of the 'critique' undertaken in the *Critique of Practical Reason* depends on an argument that shows that practical reason has a pure component and it is this demonstration that leads to thinking the moral law as a 'fact of reason'. This difference in methodological approach constitutes the difference between the *Groundwork* and the Second Critique.

Is freedom a fact?

Whilst the argument of the Analytic has now been reconstructed and the suggestion of an incompatibility between it and the account of the third section of the *Groundwork* has been demonstrated to be false there is a curious seeming anomaly about the status of freedom in the Second Critique with a claim made towards the close of the Third Critique. In the Analytic of the Second Critique the sole fact of reason is stated to be the consciouness of the moral law although this is also identified as the principle of autonomy of the will. Freedom is given its reality as this notion of autonomy as we discovered from the deduction. But freedom itself is not explicitly declared by Kant to be a 'fact' in this argument. By contrast, in section 91 of the Third Critique, Kant writes:

> It is very remarkable, however, that even a rational idea is to be found among the matters of fact (even though it is intrinsically impossible to exhibit rational ideas in intuition, and hence also intrinsically impossible to prove theoretically that they are possible): the idea of *freedom*; the reality of this idea, as [the idea of] a special kind of causality (the concept of which would be transcendent if we considered it theoretically), can be established through practical laws of pure reason and, [if we act] in conformity with these, in actual acts, and hence in experience. Among all the ideas of pure reason this is the only one whose object is a matter of fact . . . (Ak. 5:469)

Is this statement a departure from the view of the Analytic of the Second Critique? Some philosophers have thought so.[5] However, shortly after this statement, in the context of reiterating the notion that freedom is a 'fact' Kant goes on to state a reason for thinking of it as so when he states that this concept 'establishes its [own] reality in [our] acts' (Ak. 5:474). Since this statement entails that it is through the application to our acts of the notions of morality that freedom establishes its credentials as a thought, the passage in question seems to assert no more than is given in the context of the 'deduction' of the Second Critique. This is why Kant refers afterwards to 'laws of pure reason' and action in conformity with them as the basis of establishing the 'fact' of freedom. Kant also declares here that freedom is the only Idea whose 'object' is a fact but the 'object' of freedom is no other than the possibility of its operation which requires no other than the causality of reason immanently understood, this latter being no other than the moral law itself. Hence, this citation from the Third Critique no more gives us a contradiction with the argument of the Analytic of the Second Critique than does the argument of the third section of the *Groundwork*.[6] The description of freedom as a 'fact' is no more than a description of the principle of autonomy, the principle that is identical with the moral law.

The dialectic of pure practical reason

If there have been recurrent attempts to suggest some difficulties with the argument of the Analytic the presentation of such views has been mild by comparison to the reception accorded to Kant's account of the Dialectic. Problems begin with the very name of this section. After all, in the opening of the preface of the Second Critique Kant stated that once it had been shown that there is a pure practical reason there was 'no need to criticize the *pure faculty itself*' (Ak. 5:3). The principal opponent on the ground of practical reason was the empiricist view that practical reason could not be pure and this is disposed of by the argument of the Analytic. Why then do we need a Dialectic in addition and how can this Dialectic be 'of' pure practical reason?

Lewis White Beck offers one possible response when he claims that the concern of the Dialectic is with 'theoretical *illusions about morality*, not *moral illusions*' (Beck, *op. cit.*, p. 241). This would suggest a reason why the Dialectic is of 'pure reason', but the notion that there could be theoretical illusions about morality would undercut the notion that this Dialectic concerns practical reason at all. This would be surprising given that the Antinomy presented in the course of the Dialectic is stated to be of 'practical reason'. Beck's suggestion is unlikely to be correct, therefore.

Kant introduces the Dialectic by reminding us that pure reason, whether theoretical or practical, always has a dialectic as 'it requires the absolute totality of conditions for a given conditioned, and this can be found only in things in themselves' (Ak. 5:107). The demand of reason itself was described in the antinomies of the First Critique as presenting this concern for a totality of conditions to be given in order for the unity of laws to be manifested at least in their ideality. The nature of this demand in relation to practical reason is then indicated to follow this general pattern:

> reason in its practical use is no better off. As pure practical reason it likewise seeks the unconditioned for the practically conditioned (which rests on inclinations and natural needs), not indeed as the determining ground of the will, but even when this is given (in the moral law), it seeks the unconditioned totality of the object of pure practical reason, under the name of the *highest good*. (Ak. 5:108)

Thinking the Third Antinomy gave us the unconditioned for all that is conditioned in relation to causality and it is the demonstration of the necessity of thinking this that was self-given to reason in the thought of the autonomous immanent principle it disclosed to itself. But once this principle has been given a new dialectic arises as with this principle we discern a practical 'object' in the thought of the good. This 'object', like the objects of theoretical reason can be thought under the condition of totality and so thinking it gives us the notion of the highest good.

The 'object' of pure practical reason can only be presented under the supreme condition of the moral law but, once it is so presented, 'the concept of it and the representation of its existence as possible by our practical reason are at the same time the *determining ground* of the pure will because in that case the moral law, already included and thought in this concept, and no other object, in fact determines the will in accordance with the principle of autonomy' (Ak. 5:109–10). So, although the only motivation for acting morally can be given by the moral law, this law enters into the notion of the highest good and in so doing it also presents the highest good to us as something that we would wish to will the realization of. To repeat: the supreme condition of the *summum bonum* is given in the supreme principle of morality, that is, autonomy. But when we are discussing practical reason we are engaging in an account of the nature of desire as all volition involves a orientation towards the achievement of a close relation to that wished for, namely an attainment of an end in some form. We have another name for the attainment of our ends; we describe it as a state of 'happiness'. The combination of happiness in accordance with our worthiness to enjoy it is what Kant terms the 'complete good'.

Unlike the ancients, however, Kant does not believe that the relationship of goodness to happiness can be presented as analytical. Unlike the Epicurean reduction of morality to prudence or the Stoic reduction of happiness to moral contentment Kant argues for heterogeneity between goodness and happiness, a heterogeneity that entails that the concept of the *summum bonum* is a synthetic concept, just like the moral law itself.

> But because this combination is cognized as a priori – thus as practically necessary and not as derived from experience – and because the possibility of the highest good therefore does not rest on any empirical principles, it follows that the *deduction* of this concept must be *transcendental*. It is a priori (morally) necessary *to produce the highest good through the freedom of the will*: the condition of its possibility must therefore rest solely on a priori grounds of cognition. (Ak. 5:113)

We arrive at the notion of the *summum bonum* by a transcendental means through the thoughts produced by the moral law's relationship to its object, the 'good'. This metaphysical deduction of the notion of the *summum bonum* to be complete requires a demonstration of the validity and possibility of the thought thus given, that is, a transcendental deduction. Such a deduction demonstrates the possibility and validity of the concept in question but since this concept is, in fact, produced by the combination of Ideas the deduction of it can only take place through an antinomy.

The antinomy of practical reason

How does the deduction of the *summum bonum* take the form of an antinomy? Since we are clear that the concept of the *summum bonum* is a synthetic one and since we are dealing with a combination of terms that concerns a practical good then the combination has to be thought in a causal manner. 'Consequently, either the desire for happiness must be the motive to maxims of virtue or the maxim of virtue must be the efficient cause of happiness' (Ak. 5:113). The first possibility is ruled out strictly by the demonstration of the Analytic and is '*absolutely* impossible'. The second possibility cannot be given within the conditions of the sensible world as within this world the rule of causality operates mechanically. The problem is that the notion of the *summum bonum* is 'inseparably bound up with the moral law' and if it is not possible to realize then there is a problem with the law that seems to require this realization.

The 'resolution' of the antinomy

Kant, in setting out a preliminary 'resolution' of the antinomy, a 'resolution' we will soon discover to be insufficient, refers once again to the Third Antinomy. The Third Antinomy was resolved by reminding us of the transcendental distinction between appearances and things-in-themselves, a distinction used again in the argument of the third section of the *Groundwork*. The reference to this distinction occurs again in pointing out a difference in principle between the two forms of causal connection between virtue and happiness.

> The first of the two propositions, that the endeavour after happiness produces a ground for virtuous disposition, is *absolutely false*; but the second, that a virtuous disposition necessarily produces happiness, is false *not absolutely* but only insofar as this disposition is regarded as the form of causality in the sensible world, and consequently false only if I assume existence in the sensible world to be the only kind of existence of a rational being; it is thus only *conditionally false*. (Ak. 5:114)

The problem arises, therefore, from thinking of the connection between virtue and happiness as something that can be observed under sensible conditions in accordance in some sense with natural causes. This error underlay both the Epicurean and the Stoic approaches to the problem of the *summum bonum*. Whilst the feeling of respect has been revealed to be a feeling produced by an intellectual cause, and whilst this feeling is therefore, as Kant states, a 'moral feeling', this feeling is not, therefore, to be taken as pointing us to a possibility of practical pleasure as occurring in a lasting manner in this world. Respect itself is far from being a feeling of pleasure and as such it suggests to us a disproportion between feelings and morality, a disproportion we think should be overcome if there is such a thing as moral feeling at all.

To an extent this disproportion is overcome in the feeling that Kant dubs a practical pleasure, namely the 'consciousness of mastery over one's inclinations' that takes place when, despite feelings to the contrary, one does in fact act in accordance with the moral law. This consciousness is described by Kant as 'intellectual contentment' (Ak. 5:118) and the possibility of this feeling, a feeling of a practical pleasure indicates the basis for a 'resolution' (Ak. 5:119) of the antinomy. It involves a further extension of the 'aesthetic' of practical reason or what we might term a transcendental anthropology. Pointing to this feeling on the same basis as the feeling of respect draws us once again to the transcendental distinction that Kant always makes the basis of the resolution of the antinomies. However, this feeling itself is hardly, despite the revelation of its possibility, a lasting response to the problem presented in the antinomy. This practical pleasure is in competition with sensible inclination and the latter has a constant power over us. The pointing to this feeling is at best a partial account of a resolution, if that. Fundamentally, it simply restates, in the register of an 'aesthetic', the dependence of the *summum bonum* on the supreme good as stated in the supreme principle of morality. Pointing us to this extension of the practical aesthetic has not closed the gap between the conditioned state of the moral actor and the unconditioned demand for the *summum bonum*.

The true resolution of the antinomy is not immediately presented by Kant, who instead reminds us of a basic principle of procedure in transcendental investigations. This concerns the relationship between pure practical reason and theoretical (or 'speculative') reason. Can pure practical reason suffer an extension of principles that theoretical reason could not afford? The answer to this question is evidently in the affirmative as this extension has already been given in the 'fact' of reason itself. Since this extension is possible for pure practical reason despite not being possible for theoretical reason the question arises as to whether in the resolution of the antinomy of practical reason it is not permissible to utilize notions of a theoretical type, giving them an extension not possible for theoretical reason. Should this utilization of theoretically illegitimate notions be noticed to be necessary practically then there is a practical reason for undertaking it. Further, since the interest of practical reason can be demonstrated to be an interest of pure reason itself, as has been shown in the Analytic, then there is a ground within the resources of pure reason for an extension in practical terms not permissible in theoretical terms. This is so given one proviso that this extension is 'based a priori on reason itself and therefore *necessary*' (Ak. 5:121). This gives us a principle of the primacy of practical reason over theoretical reason in the case of pure reason having a practical part whose demands therefore express something necessarily.

The postulates of pure practical reason

The true resolution of the antinomy hence emerges from combining the thought of the practical aesthetic with that of the primacy of practical reason. This combination leads us to postulating a *theoretical* proposition 'though not one demonstrable as such, insofar as it is attached inseparably to an a priori unconditionally valid practical law' (Ak. 5:122). The theoretical propositions in question had been discussed in the *Critique of Pure Reason* where the impossibility of stating that they could be known was part of the limitation of metaphysical claims. Considering them again from the standpoint of practical reason they remain strictly undemonstrable but their practical necessity emerges as the only thoughts that can resolve the antinomy of practical reason, an antinomy that it is necessary that we resolve if the notion of a moral world that we had clearly justified in the Analytic is to be defended from the immanent tendency of reason to undermine itself by totalization. The manner in which the postulates given resolve the antinomy should now be stated, Kant's discussion of the notion of such postulates visited and the objections to his procedure here reviewed.

> The production of the highest good in the world is the necessary object of a will determinable by the moral law. But in such a will the *complete conformity* of dispositions with the moral law is the supreme condition of the highest good. This conformity must therefore be just as possible as its object is, since it is contained in the same command to promote the object. Complete conformity of the will with the moral law is, however, *holiness*, a perfection of which no rational being of the sensible world is capable at any moment of his existence. Since it is nevertheless required as practically necessary, it can only be found in an *endless progress* toward that complete conformity, and in accordance with principles of pure practical reason it is necessary to assume such a practical progress as the real object of our will. (Ak. 5:122)

The *summum bonum* really involves more than the passing contentment that practical pleasure gives. It requires a lasting settlement between the moral feeling and the harmony of the soul. This lasting settlement is what Kant terms here 'holiness' and which we can also see as practical perfection. Since such practical perfection is not possible for us under any conceivable sensible conditions we have to think of a progress towards it as a proximate possibility. Such progress would have to be in principle endless in scope given the limitations of our reason as revealed to us in the *Critique of Pure Reason* and this endlessness of scope can be summarized as a request that our soul be given in principle forever to approximate to this standard, in other words that it be freed from the condition of mortality in order to envisage the conditions necessary for the realization of this thought. In other words, for the task of realizing the highest good to be attained requires a series that extends beyond that given in the sensible world, just as the resolution of the Third Antinomy did. This series can only be given in an intelligible world, that is, a world in which the constraint placed upon desire by the finitude of our constitution can be superseded. Under such conditions the moral actor would be immortal.

The conditions for the attainment of the realization of the *summum bonum* thus require the postulation of a theoretical object that cannot be theoretically justified, but is practically required for the coherence of pure practical reason and this theoretical object is an immortal soul. The notion of the immortal soul provides us only with the conditions for the first part of the *summum bonum*, namely a perfect harmony of the will with the moral law. For this to be joined to happiness a further postulate is required. For happiness to be proportionate to the perfection of the will we require 'the supposition of the existence of a cause adequate to this effect', a postulation that there exists a God, a notion that is revealed to be 'morally necessary' (Ak. 5:125). This moral necessity of a belief in the existence of God is clearly not a duty of belief as there can be no duty to presuppose the existence of an object but there is a duty to promote the *summum bonum* as this latter contains within itself, as its condition, the totalization of the supreme good. For this *summum bonum* to be realized in relation to its completeness however there must be presupposed the theoretical grounds of this completeness and these can only be given with the existence of God and the immortality of the soul, two theoretical postulates which are adopted for the sake of practical coherence.

After the postulate of the existence of God has been presented Kant states he has completed his deduction of the *summum bonum* (Ak. 5:126). This concept can now be identified with the Christian notion of the 'kingdom of God' and this latter be seen to be the total conception of the moral world. The basis for the claim that this moral world is essentially identical with the Christian conception requires however thinking the latter as a rational system of belief, a contention which we will need to examine in much greater detail in Kant's works on rational religion to which I will turn in the next chapter. It is however clear that the resolution of the antinomy in the deduction of a 'kingdom of God' moves us to what Kant terms the 'final end of pure practical reason' which is religion or the *'recognition of all duties as divine commands'* (Ak. 5:129).

In summarizing the notion of postulates of pure practical reason Kant indicates that there are three such postulates, immortality, freedom considered positively and the existence of God. Whilst immortality and the existence of God have been dealt with in the resolution of the antinomy, freedom is not there presented as it has been justified already on the basis of the deduction in the Analytic. These three postulates were set out initially in the *Critique of Pure Reason* where, when treated purely theoretically, they were all seen to lead to great difficulties. The notion of the immortality of the soul, if treated only theoretically, can do no more than produce a paralogism, whilst the idea of freedom inevitably leads speculative reason into an antinomy and the existence of God was presented there only as a transcendental ideal whilst now it is adopted as a notion with practical significance 'as the supreme principle of the highest good in an intelligible world' (Ak. 5:133).

All these notions, which theoretically could be given only the most liminal significance, gain great illumination when viewed from the vantage of pure practical reason. The notion of freedom viewed positively was deduced directly from the thought of the moral law and is a postulate in the sense of requiring a thought of causality but a 'fact' as involved in the necessary self-apprehension of reason. The other two ideas by contrast emerge only as the deduced conditions of thinking the *summum bonum*, the practical totality.

Objections to the argument of the Dialectic

The argument presented in connection with the *summum bonum* and the antinomy of practical reason has drawn a wealth of commentary, the majority of it extremely unfavourable.[7] The objections raised have covered a range of questions, from the consideration of whether the antinomy generated within the Dialectic is genuine to the suggestion that the postulates are strictly unintelligible. The most important difficulties raised, however, concern the question of whether Kant's procedure can be said to be legitimately critical and whether it is consistent with the arguments of the Analytic. It is on these objections that I will focus.

Lewis White Beck's objections to the Dialectic form a considerable element of his commentary on this part of the Second Critique. Beck launches so many objections in fact that it would be the work of a considerable article to review and reply to them all. Here I will discuss only those that touch on the consistency and coherence of Kant's account. The first such claim is that Kant's suggestion in the statement of the antinomy of practical reason that if the *summum bonum* is shown to be impossible then the moral law is null and void is directly contradicted by him elsewhere, a claim Beck makes at the very beginning of his consideration of the Dialectic (Beck, *op. cit.*, p. 244). Beck suggests, in citing passages, this claim is denied within the very pages of the *Critique of Practical Reason*. This would be quite extraordinary if true. The basis for this suggestion is the following point made in the Dialectic after the discussion of the antinomy has been completed and when Kant is describing the notion of a 'need of pure reason':

> a need *of pure practical* reason is based on a *duty*, that of making something (the highest good) the object of my will so as to promote it with all my powers ... This duty is based on something that is independent of these suppositions and of itself apodictically certain, namely the moral law; and so far it needs no further support by theoretical opinions as to the inner character of things, the secret aim of the order of the world, or a ruler presiding over it, in order to bind us most perfectly to actions unconditionally conformed to the law. But the subjective effect of this law, namely the disposition conformed with it and also made necessary by it to promote the practically possible highest good, nevertheless at least presupposes that the latter is *possible*; in the contrary case it would be practically impossible to strive for the object of a concept that would be, at bottom, empty and without an object ... This is, accordingly, a *need from an absolutely necessary point of view* ... (Ak. 5:142–3)

Here what Kant states is that the moral law, as a self-given 'fact of reason', is certain as a law without recourse to the *summum bonum*. But he goes on to add that the law is grasped as promoting in us an orientation towards a perfect state and that this perfection requires it to be possible that the supreme good of attaining to the state of moral perfection be at least possible. As such, it requires these conditions to be given as possible, which is what is done through recourse to the postulates of practical reason. The insistence on the independent standing of the moral law does not undercut the point that this law leads us to be motivated to attain a condition which we cannot reach under sensible conditions. Hence this quotation does not contradict the opening statement of the Analytic but rather confirms it.

Beck also repeats the objection of Wizenmann, an objection already addressed within the *Critique of Practical Reason,* when he writes that seeking the *summum bonum* is only based on the 'natural character of man' (Beck, *op. cit.,* p. 253) and hence not different in kind from an inclination. To this claim Kant already replied when he stated in response to Wizenmann's claim that one might wish for something impossible that this could not apply to 'an *objective* determining ground of the will' as provided by the moral law, a law 'which necessarily binds every rational being and therefore justifies him a priori in presupposing in nature the conditions befitting it and makes this latter inseparable from the complete practical use of reason' (Ak. 5:143n). The 'need' set out as that of pure reason arises from its maximal setting forth of the command that is given in the moral law, a maximal setting forth that it is reason's basic condition to give in the form of an unconditioned for every condition. The notion of this unconditioned is practical perfection, a perfection that would reveal the maximal state of morality. Such a condition is basically given within the law itself as our orientation in action and unless it is possible that it be achieved, then morality is as such not pure as it is not capable of maximization but if it is not pure then there is no real moral incentive at all but merely heteronomous motivation.

Having stated the basis of Kant's reply to Wizenmann it now becomes possible to address a point that Beck is not alone in setting out which is the view that Kant has committed a central 'confusion' of the supreme condition of the *summum bonum* which is the moral law 'with the supreme perfection of virtue' (Beck, *op. cit.,* p. 268). That practical perfection is Kant's thought is not however due to a confusion such as the one that Beck insinuates. The antinomy concerns maximalization and it does this in two ways. First, the supreme condition of goodness as set out in the moral law is determined as the condition of the *summum bonum.* Second, this supreme condition is determined in accordance with its own highest condition as unless it was so how could we think of a 'highest' good? If the moral law was not presented in the antinomy in terms of a practical perfection, we would merely be asked to think a proportion between morality and happiness without having determined that proportion to the 'highest' extent and thus we would only be thinking of the notion of happiness in accordance with moral motivation. This would be sufficiently addressed by the aesthetic of practical reason except for the fact that any such proportion would only be momentary. The condition for thinking this condition as other than momentary and hence as applicable in general is the removal of the condition of mortality that is presented in the first postulate. But removal of this is also undertaken in order that the ideal that is promised within the maximal condition of the moral law can be presented as attainable. There is therefore no 'confusion' between the supreme condition of the *summum bonum* and practical perfection, rather it is only the supreme condition thought as practical perfection that really provides us with the total conception of morality at all.

Beck's next objection concerns the postulate of the immortality of the soul and the assumption of Kant's that it addresses the difficulty of attaining the state of practical perfection. Beck writes that this will not do as: 'If, I say, the soul is no longer under the temporal condition, it is not possible to understand what is meant by "continuous and unending progress"' (Beck, *op. cit.*, p. 270). The removal of sensible conditions would seem to remove temporal constraints but in that case how can we think of an 'unending progress'? The answer to this objection is to say that it requires us to think that when Kant speaks of such 'progress' he is conceiving of the sensible conditions continuing to apply when in fact what he is doing is applying the conditions of sensibility as a 'type' of the thought of free causality. Free causality is not a temporal series as, if it was, then it would not be a *free* causality, but since such causality necessarily transcends our capacity of comprehension we can only speak of its operation analogically. This analogical thought of causality is permitted from a practical point of view, but should not be regarded as actually approximating to the conditions of sensibility as this would be to commit a gross subreption. Beck's point here is based on simply forgetting the condition of thinking the supersensible. It is true that having pointed this out does not enable one to conceive clearly the type of 'progress' Kant describes but necessarily this is not possible as the noumenal notion of free causality is not comprehensible, only presentable analogically.

Beck's arguments against the coherence and consistency of the postulates do not succeed therefore. The place of happiness within the *summum bonum* seems to be the prime matter motivating Beck's objections however due to a worry that in some sense heteronomous motivation has been reintroduced with it. What has been introduced is the thought of a proportion between happiness and morality and this proportion attends to our thought of the completest good. Naturally, the supreme good is attained in following the moral law, maximally to the point of practical perfection. But, if it is perfectly legitimate to think that the notion of desert is a moral requirement for the coherence of the system of morality, then it should be pointed out that the inclusion of happiness within the complete good involves no more than specifying this.

The major source for a critical treatment of the postulates is Hegel.[8] In the section of the *Phenomenology* entitled 'Spirit that is certain of itself, morality' Hegel provides an account of the postulates that suggests that they undermine the notion of morality itself as argued for by Kant. Since the antinomy of practical reason can be seen to turn on the thought of the maximal conception of virtue and its proportionate relationship to happiness Hegel presents it as requiring us to think of the moral sphere itself as only given if there is a perfect accord with the moral law. Since this is never given under sensible conditions, Hegel suggests that the 'moral consciousness' is driven to the view that moral existence has no reality. But Hegel notes that acting in accordance with the moral law, whilst never conceivable as actual under sensible conditions, is nevertheless constantly the command made at each point of action and he discerns therewith a contradiction between the postulation of this perfection in a beyond and the actuality of operating now in accordance with a command that cannot be granted now.

> What consciousness really holds to be the truth of the matter is only this intermediate state of imperfection, a state nevertheless which at least is supposed to a *progress towards* perfection. But it cannot even be that; for to advance in morality would really be to move towards its disappearance. That is to say, the goal would be the nothingness or the abolition ... of morality and consciousness itself; but to approach ever nearer to nothingness means to diminish. Besides, 'advancing' as such, like 'diminishing, would assume *quantitative* differences in morality; but there can be no question of these in it. In morality, as in consciousness, for which the moral purpose is *pure* duty, there cannot be any thought of difference, least of all the superficial one of quantity; there is only one virtue, only one pure duty, only one morality. (Hegel, *op. cit.*, para. 623)

This statement can be seen to be the ultimate source of Beck's argument that the notion of the immortality of the soul involves a reference to a 'progress' that makes no sense. Whilst Hegel is right to present moral situations as constantly involving negotiation with the imperfect condition of approximation to behaviour entirely in accordance with the moral law this does not itself amount to an admission that there is no moral action simply because practical perfection is an ideal. Rather, the notion of practical perfection provides the maximal conditions of coherence for moral action. Hegel suggests that such a maximal condition is equivalent to the destruction of morality itself but this suggestion undercuts his argument that the negotiation with imperfection involves a resignation of morality as it commits him to the view that only practical perfection would be moral whilst involving him in the denial that such perfection amounts to anything. The argument about quantity is entirely of a piece with Beck's argument about sensible conditions involving as it does a denial of the analogical status of the manner of thinking the supersensible and insisting on viewing this thought as based on a real transplantation of categories.

If these criticisms are therefore weak, Hegel's subsequent claim that the notion of desert cannot apply if morality is not real cannot work as it is based on these earlier poor arguments intended to show the lack of reality of morality. Hegel's implicit commitment to the notion that only the perfection described in the antinomy would be moral follows from his tracing of the thought of pure duty to its ultimate condition, but does not respect the problem of the relationship between the moral command and the world in which this command is placed. Failure to do this commits Hegel to simply denying that moral action ever takes place simply because it does not take place constantly. This follows only part of the logic of Kant's perfectionism and does not respect the relationship between the postulates that give us the grounds for such perfection and the condition of moral action that Kant describes in his transcendental anthropology and which I will discuss at more length in the next chapter.

5
Radical Evil and Moral Redemption

The treatment of Kant's works on religion is not well integrated in the current secondary literature into the account of his practical philosophy. Whilst pioneering works on Kant's writings on religion have been written these writings are still largely framed as contributions to 'philosophy of religion' and not thought of as performing a significant role in the development of Kant's practical philosophy. It will be my contention in this chapter that these writings do in fact perform an important role in Kant's practical philosophy. The Second Critique closes with the account of the postulates and the Third Critique culminates with an account of moral faith. I wish to demonstrate in this chapter that *Religion within the Limits of Reason Alone* and the *Conflict of the Faculties* should be seen as an extension of topics broached in the Second and Third Critiques, an extension which enables Kant to significantly expand his conception of rational religion and enables him to outline a form of rational eschatology. This notion of rational eschatology will be demonstrated to provide Kant with a treatment of history that is significant for comprehending the relationship for him between ethics and politics.

Moral teleology: the context for Kant's writings on religion

The Dialectic of the Second Critique introduced the notion of postulates of practical reason, a notion that enabled reason in its practical use an extension not permitted it in its theoretical use. These postulates all related to the thought of the *summum bonum* and the culminating postulate is the existence of God considered as a practical thought. Within the pages of the Second Critique however the *summum bonum* is motivated by considering an unconditioned goodness and this latter is thought in terms of the elements of what would be requisite to think of a complete good. The existence of God hence often appears to readers of this work as a thought insufficiently justified.

In the *Critique of Teleological Judgment* Kant returns to the notion of a practical justification for the existence of God but arrives at it only after having set out in considerable detail a critique of teleology. Within this critique Kant delimits the claims that can be made for teleology within the investigation of nature and presents reasons for thinking that teleology is not a part of science. Kant revisits here the 'proof' for the existence of God based on physicoteleology and adds a new element to his rejection of this proof when considering the relationship between the idea of God and the existence of rational beings under moral laws. In doing so Kant makes the following striking remark:

> *moral teleology* compensates for the deficiency of *physical* teleology and for the first time supplies the basis for a *theology*. For physical teleology on its own, if it proceeded consistently instead of borrowing, unnoticed, from moral teleology, could not provide a basis for anything but a *demonology*, which is incapable of [providing] a determinate concept [of the deity]. (Ak. 5:444)

The basis of theology arises from moral teleology as physical teleology could only provide a *demonology*. Why does Kant suggest this? Because, even if, *per impossibile*, a successful proof of the existence of God could arise from physical teleology, all this would prove would be an intelligent being capable of constructing a purposive order. But such a being would not be shown thereby to have any moral relationship to the order thus created and hence could be conceived as a mere demiurge or, as Descartes suggests, an 'evil demon'. To be persuaded that the relationship of a creator to a purposive order is moral implies a demonstration of the morality of this creator and this cannot be given from physical teleology. Therefore, there is a need for a moral teleology in addition to the physical teleology that the majority of the *Critique of Teleological Judgment* has set out.

To supply this moral teleology Kant sets out a moral proof for the existence of God. The argument in the Second Critique for the postulate of the existence of God showed that the idea of God's existence was necessary for the thought of the *summum bonum* to be given coherence and Kant essentially restates this argument in the Third Critique (Ak. 5:448–50). In the later work Kant makes the point that this proof for the existence of God has been present to people from as long as they have reflected on the evidence of right and wrong actions as a 'supreme cause that rules the world according to moral laws' (Ak. 5:458) is the only principle that can reconcile nature with the moral law. Hence we have faith in the existence of God as a condition for the possibility of achieving the *summum bonum* even though we have no insight into whether this can be achieved. The basis for thinking the existence of God is through an analogy, an analogy that is grounded on thinking the being in question by comparison with an attribute of our own. Not a natural attribute however but rather the singular fact of reason:

> among the three pure ideas of reason, *God, freedom,* and *immortality,* that of freedom is the only concept of the supersensible which (by means of the causality that we think of in it) proves in nature that it has objective reality, by the effects it can produce in it. It is this that makes it possible to connect the other two ideas with nature, and to connect all three together to form a religion. Therefore, we have in us a principle that can determine the idea of the supersensible within us, and through this also the idea of the supersensible outside us, so as to give rise to cognition [of them], even though one that is possible only from a practical point of view; and that is something of which merely speculative philosophy (which could provide also merely a negative concept of freedom) had to despair. Hence the concept of freedom (the concept underlying all unconditioned practical laws) can expand reason beyond those bounds within which any concept of nature (i.e., theoretical concept) would have to remain hopelessly confined. (Ak. 5:474)

The nature of the type of analogy in question here is significantly returned to in *Religion within the Limits of Reason Alone* and will be discussed below. It is worth making the point here, however, that it was demonstrated in the Second Critique that freedom is the key postulate of pure practical reason. This key postulate is the autonomous capacity to act in accordance with the moral law. It shows that there is nothing impossible in freely choosing to ground action in rationality and since through this notion we have granted ourselves an immeasurable power that the thought of the immortality of the soul accords with there must needs be a thought of that which enables it to be possible and this is the notion of the existence of God. Since the thought of freedom gives us a sense of the supersensible character of ourselves it is by an analogy that we can conceive of the nature of the supersensible beyond us, a supersensible beyond us that as a thought in fact allows us to conceive of an ultimate unity of freedom and nature.[1]

If the Third Critique culminates by restating the argument for the existence of God given in the Second Critique, it adds to this argument the thought that moral teleology is the only basis for a theology (understood as the basis for thinking that there is a moral creator of the world). This is further here justified by showing a connection between ourselves as bearers of the moral law, a purely supersensible principle and the character that would have to be imputed to the 'supersensible' external to us (figuratively presented as God). Freedom comprehended as both an original fact of our reason and as also the ground for action motivated by incentives of a non-sensuous kind provides the basis for thinking of a non-pragmatic anthropology or in other terms for thinking character according to transcendental determinations. This is part of the point of *Religion within the Limits of Reason Alone* as is the outlining of the theology that moral teleology has made it possible to conceive of. It is therefore now time to turn to how the relationship between a transcendental philosophical anthropology and theology is stated in the pages of this work.

In justifying the notion of moral teleology Kant stated in the Third Critique that a righteous atheist would have to confront the problem of desert that is addressed by the *summum bonum* and that this would necessarily lead such a one to despair (Ak. 5: 452–3). Similarly, in the opening pages of *Religion within the Limits of Reason Alone*, Kant presents a thought experiment:

> Assume a human being who honours the moral law, and who allows himself to think (as he can hardly avoid doing) what sort of world he would *create*, were this in his power, under the guidance of practical reason – a world within which, moreover, he would place himself as a member. Now, not only would he choose a world precisely as the moral idea of the highest good requires, if the choice were entrusted to him alone, but he would also will the very existence of [such] a world, since the moral law wills that the highest good possible through us be actualised, even though, in following this idea, he might see himself in danger of forfeiting much in the way of personal happiness, for it is possible that he might not be adequate to what reason makes the condition for it. (Ak. 6:5–6)[2]

This thought experiment basically restates in a vivid fashion the typic of the moral law that is given in the universal law of nature formula. In restating the typic in this fashion however Kant utilizes the argument we have just discovered in the Third Critique to the effect that there is a manner in which we can conceive of the character of the Supreme Being, viz. by thinking it in accordance with our own super-sensible aptitude, the power of freedom. This procedure not only allows us to think of a means of conceiving the character of this being however, it also prompts us to think of ourselves after its pattern (a two-way analogical procedure). The effects of this analogical transfer-ence and the type of character of it in Kant's system of rational religion form one of the key topics in elucidating *Religion within the Limits of Reason Alone*.

The schematism of analogy

The place of schematism in the theoretical philosophy of the First Critique has drawn much attention and critical commentary. The role of schematism in the practical philosophy of Kant has, by contrast, been scantly noticed. Whilst the role of the typic as a type of practical schema is described in the Second Critique and this schema is already utilized prior to being named in the account of the law of nature for-mula in the *Groundwork* it would be worth pausing before treating the major themes of *Religion within the Limits of Reason Alone* to recall another thought of schema that is discussed in the First Critique but not within the pages of the section devoted to schematism. This is the notion introduced towards the close of the work, whilst Kant is describ-ing the nature of architectonic. Kant writes here that a schema is neces-sary for a system to be constructed and he describes the schematization necessary for systematization as involving 'an essential manifoldness and order of the parts determined *a priori* from the principle of the end' and states that this arises from 'a single supreme and inner end, which first makes possible the whole' (A833–4/B861–2). I would describe this schema as a final end schema as whilst it makes possible the whole through determining it by reference to an idea it is also a form of sub-sumption which is altered in the process of execution as the original purposive notion of the system is one that is open. Improvement in the conception of the system is possible and this improvement re-deter-mines the 'origin' of the system at each point or to put it otherwise the idea only becomes clear in a progressive fulfilment (A834–5/B862–3).

Within the pages of *Religion within the Limits of Reason Alone* the notion of a practical schema is also referred to, albeit in passing and the description that is given of it is not sufficient to describe the practice of schematization that Kant in fact sets out within the work. In a footnote describing the way in which God is described after the pattern of an account of emotions Kant states that this is a '*schematism of analogy*' with which we cannot dispense. But the introduction of the notion by name is mainly done to warn against thinking that within such a practical area it is possible to think the schema in question as one of object-determination, which would involve simple anthropomorphism. In rejecting this, Kant adds little by way of description of the correct procedure for such practical schemas. It would be my contention, however, that it is best pictured not after a manner of pathological motivation but through practical feeling, the very practical feeling that it is a major task of the *Religion* to describe. However, the pattern of determining this practical feeling in the divine and ourselves is in accord with a final end schema such as is described in the First Critique and it is this that describes the true schema of analogy. Only, that is, through a developing account of the nature of practical feeling can we form any conception of the appropriate analogy between the supersensible within us and the supersensible beyond us. This developing account alters the analogical procedure adopted ensuring it has greater sophistication as it is developed, but part of this sophistication is a concomitant setting forth of the divine nature, a setting forth that in its turn alters the pattern of the description of practical feeling. This schematism of analogy will further the final end schema by utilizing the procedure described in the Third Critique: 'judgment performs a double function: it applies the concept to the object of a sensible intuition; and then it applies the mere rule by which it reflects on that intuition to an entirely different object, of which the former object is only a symbol' (Ak. 5:352). Hence the concept of 'practical feeling' (as given most particularly in the notion of 'respect' but, as we shall see, also in manifold other terms) is applied to the sensible intuition of persons. Then the rule of reflection on persons is applied without the intuition that guided the application of this rule to a quite different object: the supersensible outside us that is judged in accordance with the rule that applied to the supersensible within us. This 'double function' shows the symbol of God to be given through the traits of personality and it is this symbolization of the supersensible without us that gives us the peculiar supersensible figuration we term 'God'. If to this we add from the notion of schematism of analogy that the traits of this figuration are then by a reference back towards ourselves involved in a recursive analogical connection with us we then have the key to the descriptions of the intimate relation between practical feeling and the divine that are set out in *Religion within the Limits of Reason Alone*.

Radical evil

The first part of *Religion within the Limits of Reason Alone* is without doubt the most famous part of it. It is here that Kant conducts his enquiry into 'the radical evil in human nature'. The question of the characterisation of the human race is in fact not, despite appearances to the contrary, a mere pragmatic anthropology. This becomes clear when Kant informs us how we are to understand his use of the expression 'human nature':

> lest anyone be scandalized by the expression *nature*, which would stand in direct contradiction to the predicates *morally* good or *morally* evil if taken to mean (as it usually does) the opposite of the ground of actions [arising] from *freedom*, let it be noted that by 'the nature of a human being' we only understand here the subjective ground – wherever it may lie – of the exercise of the human being's freedom in general (under objective moral laws) antecedent to every deed that falls within the scope of the senses. But this subjective ground must, in turn, itself always be a deed of freedom (for otherwise the use or abuse of the human being's power of choice with respect to the moral law could not be imputed to him, not could the good or evil in him be called 'moral'). Hence the ground of evil cannot lie in any object *determining* the power of choice through inclination, not in any natural impulses, but only in a rule that the power of choice itself produces for the exercise of its freedom, i.e., in a maxim. (Ak. 6:20–1)

The subjective ground of the 'nature' of human beings is what Kant wishes to uncover. This entails that the type of enquiry that would need to be undertaken to discern the answer to this problem would have to be a *transcendental* philosophical anthropology. Since it would wish to uncover an origin within the realm of freedom it must of necessity come to a bedrock with the description of the adoption of maxims as to attempt to discern the basis of ultimate maxims would simply be to reduce freedom to natural necessity and hence partake of a subreption. Hence appeal to the operation of sensuous feeling within the moral actor cannot be allowed an ultimate purchase as the allowance of this feeling as a basis for action requires the incorporation of it as an incentive into a maxim. It is the adoption of the maxim 'I will be moved by this feeling' that is the ground of action in this case rather than the feeling itself. As described in the aesthetic of practical reason the moral law is itself an incentive if it is taken as a 'drive'. Since the operation of the law (or its converse) within the actions of a moral agent cannot be said to originate in anything other than the adoption of a maxim 'we call it a characteristic of the power of choice that pertains to it by nature' or describe it as indicative of the *moral character* in question.

The account of *moral character* is the outlining of the transcendental philosophical anthropology previously mentioned. The basis of this transcendental anthropology is the discussion of what belongs to the experience of the moral actor and belongs to it by necessity such that, although this experience is governed by laws of freedom, there are invariant patterns which appear *as if* they were elements of nature (another type of schematism of analogy although with less complexity than the one described above). These invariant patterns are described by Kant as 'original' parts of human nature and are divided into two kinds: predispositions to good and propensities to evil. Although the predispositions to good are treated first and given as existing in three different types (with reference to animality, humanity and personality), only the third of these is truly moral and it is revealed in turn not to be the basic orientation of our moral nature. The predisposition to animality is described by Kant as 'merely *mechanical* self-love' (Ak. 6:26) and involves self-preservation, the desire for propagation and a social drive.[3] Whilst this predisposition falls generally within the 'natural' or purely empirical characteristics of humanity for Kant the vices that can arise from this predisposition are actions of freedom and include '*gluttony, lust and wild lawlessness*' (Ak. 6:27), clearly extreme attachments to appetite in the first two instances and involving the tendencies to utilize the social drive in ways that militate against the social bond in the last.

The predisposition to humanity is basically the comparative form of self-love that we call generally 'seeking a good reputation'. This is grouped under the notion of 'humanity' rather than 'animality' as whilst it clearly is part of the social drive it does not involve the indiscriminate yearning for company and togetherness that characterizes that drive, but instead grows out of the reasonable desire to make distinctions between persons and to be included in the group of the 'best' of them. If this desire for reputation and distinction is related to moral ends then this predisposition is clearly towards the good but since it is also the basis for rivalry and jealously, 'vices of secret or open hostility' can arise from it. Whilst Kant describes the vices that arise from the predisposition to animality as 'bestial' because they are grounded in overweening appetite the vices that arise from the predisposition to humanity are termed 'vices of *culture*' as they emerge from the furtherance of a reasonable relationship to others become unreasonable. However, in concluding the description of the vices of culture, Kant makes an intriguing comment that relates to the central problem of radical evil that we have yet to uncover when he states that in their extreme degree they are 'simply the idea of a maximum of evil that surpasses humanity' or are termed *'diabolical vices'* (Ak. 6:27). (Kant includes here the notion of joy in others misfortunes.)

Whilst the predisposition to humanity does describe both a moral motivation and the distortion of it in terms that make clear that with this we have truly begun to set out the promised transcendental philosophical anthropology it is really only with the predisposition to personality that we discern this notion becoming clearly concrete. The predisposition to personality is nothing other than the taking of the moral law as a drive described in the *Triebfeder* of the Second Critique and now described simply as 'moral feeling' (Ak. 6:27). This is a practical reason considered unconditionally and on the basis of this no vices can grow. It is hence the truly original predisposition to good and the two former predispositions are strictly good only in relation to its guidance as the first operates as an impulse and the maxim of guidance of this impulse is requisite for it to be conceived as good, whilst the second is truly moral only if the distinction sought for by it is comprehended in moral terms.

Kant separates these 'predispositions' from the 'propensity' to evil as he wishes to suggest that whilst the former are 'original' to humanity the latter are 'acquired' by beings that could have avoided the acquisition. It is only what Kant terms 'genuine evil, i.e., moral evil' (Ak. 6:29) that belongs under the heading of a propensity. There are three grades of this propensity, however, just as there were three predispositions towards the good. The first type is termed 'frailty' and involves the indecisive incorporation of the moral maxim which maxim is then often experienced as weaker in effect than sensuous incentives. This form of the propensity to evil is the temptation to take sensuous incentives as determinative for action and to deny the prior incorporation of them into a maxim of action. It is followed by the second degree: the adoption of impure maxims or a mixing of moral with non-moral motivations in the same maxim so that 'actions conforming to duty are not purely from duty' (Ak. 6:30), which involves interpreting the moral law as if it were an external law of the state rather than an internal one of reason itself. This produces outward conformity but inward hypocrisy, and given the mixed nature of the motivation thus allowed freely can grant self-exception to that which seems not to fit with the sensuous element allowed place in the maxim.

The third degree of this propensity is the most complete one. Kant terms this 'depravity' or 'perversity' and it involves reversal of the ethical order so that sensuous incentives are given priority over the moral law. With this ordering of the elements of the maxim we have an attitude that is corrupted at root and hence 'the human being is designated as evil' (Ak. 6:30). The notion of a propensity to evil involves a 'choice that *precedes every deed*' or is a 'deed in the first meaning (*peccatum originarium*)' (Ak. 6:31), an intelligible deed. This account of the origin of evil is basic for Kant since although, as we shall see, he can add more to this in a certain expansive figuration, nothing can be added by way of explanation as freedom naturally cannot be explained.[4]

Having described the predispositions to good and the propensity to evil Kant returns to the question of whether the human race should be described as 'by nature' good and evil. In accordance with a long tradition, Kant describes the human race as 'evil' by nature.[5] The reason for this verdict is unusual by Kant's standards as he appeals here to examples, albeit not just to any such. The tradition from Hobbes to Rousseau of establishing an account of the political order by reference to a 'state of nature' is the basis of the examples utilized. First, Kant interprets this expression with a literalness not intended by representatives of this tradition by referring to 'vices of savagery' (equivalent to the bestial vices just described) in 'the scenes of unprovoked cruelty in the ritual murders of Tofoa, New Zealand, and the Navigator Islands, and the never-ending cruelty (which Captain Hearne reports) in the wide wastes of northwestern America from which, indeed, no human being derives the least benefit' (Ak. 6:33).[6] Whilst these examples however might be thought to partake of a merely pragmatic anthropology Kant's subsequent references are more skilfully brought to bear on the issue in question. The reference to the aforementioned vices of culture is brought back as widely observed phenomena and to these is then added the more significant reference to the fact that the state of nature is yet to be overcome in terms of 'external relations' between states of which Kant writes that in these relations states adopt policies that no philosopher has yet been able to bring into accord with morality. Of this situation, which indicates the persistence of a state of nature between peoples, Kant writes:

> So *philosophical chiliasm*, which hopes for a state of perpetual peace based on a federation of nations united in a world-republic, is universally derided as sheer fantasy as much as *theological chiliasm*, which awaits for the completed moral improvement of the human race. (Ak. 6:34)[7]

The uncovering of the persistence of the state of nature is the real evidence for Kant's assertion and this persistence cannot be viewed as a mere empirical fact of historical development but must itself be grounded on a reason. The reason in question will be returned to below in accounting for the movement of history within the pages of *Religion within the Limits of Reason Alone* and the *Conflict of the Faculties*.

A provisional response is, however, unveiled in the question for the persistence of evil that the failure to abolish the state of nature between states suggests. Kant rejects the account of the 'fall' that is traditional in terms of a pure giving in to appetite as this would not be sufficient to account for evil. However, he also veers away from the notion that moral reason is capable of destroying the appeal to the law since this law has been uncovered as an original property of reason (such that we can term it, as was done in the Second Critique, a 'fact'). The suggestion that the appeal of the law could be uprooted from our reason would be equivalent to thinking of ourselves as 'diabolical' beings and this would be too much of an account, as it would deny the basic place of the moral law within our reason. Kant in rejecting the notion of a corruption that would destroy the moral law does not however reject the account that evil is based on corruption. Rather, he interprets corruption in the sense of 'perversity', that is as based on a preference for the appeal to sensuousness over the moral law so that the former is made '*the supreme condition*' of the latter (Ak. 6:36).

Since the origin of evil lies within freedom it is also not a historical question to inquire into this origin. 'Every evil action must be so considered, whenever we seek its rational origin, as if the human being had fallen into it directly from the state of innocence' (Ak. 6:41). At each time that actions based on maxims that are not grounded on the moral law are performed they are such as *could have been avoided* and must have been based each time on a simple acceptance of the propensity towards evil so that evil 'can only have originated from moral evil' (Ak. 6:43). This origination is even the basis for the appeal in the Scriptures to the notion of an 'evil spirit' (Ak. 6:43–4). In discussing the considerable number of objections that are raised in contemporary works to Kant's treatment of evil it will be worth looking also at this figurative notion of an 'evil spirit'.

Kant's 'evil spirit' and diabolical evil

In two separate places of the text of *Religion within the Limits of Reason Alone* Kant makes reference to a figurative notion that can be set alongside the notion of God. The first occurs towards the close of the First Part of the work shortly after making the point that evil can only have originated from moral evil. Kant amplifies this by stating that the incomprehensibility of the origin of evil is expressed in the Scriptures by reference to 'a *spirit* of an originally more sublime destiny' who is represented as tempting human beings into evil. Kant adds: 'The absolutely *first* beginning of all evil is thereby represented as incomprehensible to us (for whence the evil in that spirit?)' (Ak. 6:44). The reference to this notion of an evil spirit whilst clearly signalling the incomprehensibility of the origin of evil *qua* evil does nonetheless indicate its super-human character suggesting that the basis of evil itself may well lie as far beyond rationality in its principle as is the divine.

The second use of this figurative notion of an evil spirit is even more instructive. This occurs in the context of stating at the beginning of the Second Part of the work a disagreement with the Stoic view that evil lies merely in omission of good acts and is not itself a special positive principle.[8] By contrast with this view Kant again appeals to the Scriptures:

> We should not therefore be disconcerted if an apostle represents this *invisible* enemy – this corrupter of basic principles recognizable only through his effects upon us – as being outside us, indeed as an evil *spirit*: 'We have to wrestle not against flesh and blood (the natural inclinations) but against principalities and powers, against evil spirits' [Ephesians 6:12]. This expression does not appear to be intended to extend our cognition beyond the world of the senses but only to make intuitive, *for practical use*, the concept of something to us unfathomable. It is all the same to us, so far as this practical use is concerned, whether we locate the tempter simply in ourselves, or also outside us; for guilt touches us not any the less in the latter case than in the former, inasmuch as we would not be tempted by him were we not in secret agreement with him. (Ak. 6:59–60)

This second reference to the figurative notion of an 'evil spirit' is of a piece with the first reference. Kant here explicitly refers to this notion as an intuitive presentation of a concept that is unfathomable for the purposes of practical thinking. The 'unfathomable' nature of this evil spirit is just as clearly stated as in the earlier quote only this time two further uses of this figure are made. The notion of an 'evil spirit' helps to set forth the fact that the ground of evil is not sensuous and it also brings out an intriguing element involved in the story of the 'temptation' of humanity. To be tempted implies a 'propensity' in common with that which tempts and hence, in this sense, it is the case that we must be taken to tempt ourselves even if another is the occasion for the temptation in question. This element of the thought of temptation should also make clear why the 'evil spirit' is capable of being placed within ourselves just as easily as without us. Since evil is a product of freedom the 'evil spirit' has in fact to be given our qualities as it is our own supersensible characteristic that is super-human (in the sense of pointing beyond pragmatic anthropology to transcendental anthropology).

The two uses of the figure of the 'evil spirit' demonstrate that it performs a function of a piece with the intuitive presentation of the supersensible without us in the intuitive form of God. Just as God can be presented only by analogy with our own supersensible characteristic and it is this that enables the personification involved in the notion so also with the thought of an 'evil spirit'. The procedure of a schematism of analogy is at work in both cases.[9] The first reference to the notion of an 'evil spirit' is less telling than the second, however, as in the second we learn clearly *about ourselves* on the basis of the figure whose character has been constructed in fact *by analogy* with ourselves and thus this presentation marks an extensive and sophisticated use of analogy of the type we would expect from Kant's discussion of the term in the Third Critique.

It is when we touch on the nature of Kant's use of this figure of an 'evil spirit', however, that we can begin to appreciate the nature of contemporary objections to Kant's treatment of radical evil. These objections have sources both in reference to historical developments since Kant and in an extension of the notion of an 'evil spirit' beyond that allowed by Kant. The historical developments have a particular locus in the attempted destruction of the European Jews during the Second World War.[10] Since the events in question certainly appear to touch the very limits of rational discussion (as would be expected from a situation where evil reigns) they have often be taken to rule out any type of account that does more than simply appeal to a need for 'witness'.[11] Whilst this response is motivated by a notion of respect for the victims that clearly has Kantian correlates it tends also to obscure the nature of thinking evil in responding to unique events at the expense of thinking evil *per se*.

Alongside this reference to twentieth-century history, however, has arisen a wider discussion which, whilst partially grounded on thinking the nature of modernity, is also based on relating to post-Kantian notions of evil.[12] One of the reasons for the appeal to post-Kantian accounts is due to a sense of dissatisfaction with Kant's view. A predominant source of this dissatisfaction is the sense that in some way Kant has not taken evil seriously enough. The suggestion is that the reference to an 'evil spirit' should be taken further than Kant wants to take it and we should think evil not as *radical* but as *diabolical*. This hypothesis of a *devilish or malign reason* is one that Kant is keen to reject if it is interpreted as a possibility for humanity and it is only introduced in passing in his text as a heuristic device that enables the deployment of a schematism of analogy.

The refusal of Kant's account in favour of a notion of 'diabolical evil' is widespread, but I will here mention just one of the representatives of this view. Alenka Zupančič bases her amendment of Kant on a reading of him that is intended to respect the purity of the account of morality in Kant. In describing a different account of evil from Kant Zupančič presents a case of someone who, whilst satisfying a sensuous desire, does so in the full knowledge that this will lead to the ending of any sensuous desires stating: 'if – as Kant claims – nothing but the moral law can induce us to put aside all our pathological interests and accept our own death, then the case of someone who spends a night with a woman, even though he knows that he will pay for it with his life, *is the case of the moral law*'.[13] Here the crux of Zupančič's argument appears to be that if acting in accordance with a sensuous desire to the point of death can be taken on knowingly, then this indicates that such a desire has in accepting itself as engaged to the point of death become an action according to principle of a type with the action according to the law. Hence there is contained within such an act the principle of a diabolical reason.

Whilst I will be suggesting a problem with this argument I do not think that the argument is one that can be lightly brushed aside. Joan Copjec, in reply to theories of the type advanced by Zupančič, presents a reply that seems to be insufficient to this challenge. Copjec writes:

> In order to elevate resistance to the law into a maxim, it would be necessary to phenomenalize the law, but, as we have seen, the moral law resists phenomenalization. In fact, it is this very resistance that is responsible for the radicality (or ineradicableness) of evil in the first place .... The attempt to think diabolical evil turns out to be another attempt to deny will's self-alienation, to make of will a pure, positivized force; this reading, then, offers a voluntarist alternative to Kant. But since the fault in human will cannot be repaired, it is apparent that this alternative wrongly credits man with a power for pure destruction, that is, with a power in the first instance to destroy himself, to annihilate his own freedom.[14]

Whilst Copjec's argument is a general one and is in fact being responded to by Zupančič rather than being a response to Zupančič, it is, I think, correct to present the arguments in the order that I have. Copjec's response to the arguments in favour of 'diabolical evil' would apply, given the nature of her argument, to Zupančič. On Copjec's construal attempts to think 'diabolical evil' have about them a Romantic aura and really simply repeat the phenomenalization of practical feeling that Kant intended to resist. In such an argument the distinction between the *peccatum originarium* and the particular decision has been annihilated with the result that the intelligible ground for practical reason and practical feeling has been removed. This hence culminates in a simple failure to note the inescapability of freedom.

To this argument – an argument that does repeat some aspects of Kant's account in a telling manner – Zupančič appears to me to have a clear reply. Since both lying (the destruction within the moral actor of the basis of their personality) and suicide (the wilful self-removal of a moral actor from the stage of action) take place, then it is absurd to state that there is no possibility of 'diabolical evil' and Kant himself, whilst declaring 'devilish vices' outside the realm of human action, in fact illustrates their prevalence in his notion of the vices of culture.

To these arguments in favour of Zupančič can be added the further consideration that it is not a phenomenalization of the law to imagine a situation of pure desire in which the desire in question is wished for even to the point of assenting to death. Rather, it is a purification of the notion of desire to think this, a purification of a piece with Kant's own notion of practical feeling but incorporating within this notion desires that Kant would have to view as evil given their direction towards an action that does not conform with the moral law. These replies that are open to Zupančič whilst not without problems do enable her to reply comprehensively to the objections of Copjec. Hence to find a Kantian reply to Zupančič's argument will require further investigation of the nature of moral teleology in order to bring out the nature of the deep response there can be on Kant's behalf to a desire that asserts itself even in the face of death.

Kant's 'evil spirit' revisited, or further thoughts on the relation between moral teleology and demonology

In order to set out the nature of the response open to Kant to the thought of 'diabolical evil' as presented by Zupančič I wish to take a route that will appear paradoxical to many contemporary Kantians. Rather than setting out a reply that will concentrate mainly on the thought of the vices of culture and engage in an extended discussion of the nature of Kant's thoughts on suicide and lying and minimizing the reference to an 'evil spirit' in Kant I wish rather to proceed in an inverse order. I will first set out an extension of the thought of the 'evil spirit' in relation to some remarks made by Walter Benjamin and on the basis of this extension of the thought of the 'evil spirit' will connect Kant's moral teleology to a thought of demonology. This connection will enable revis-iting the type of maxim at work in those who commit suicide and adopt a stance of perennial lying. However, I will not treat these latter topics at as much length as they deserve in this chapter, as that would require discussing the account Kant gives in the Doctrine of Virtue.

To set out a connection here between Kant's notion of an 'evil spirit' and the work of Walter Benjamin will appear unusual both to Kantians and to those who study Benjamin.[15] In his account of German Baroque drama, however, Benjamin discusses the figure of Satan and he writes:

> What tempts is the illusion of freedom – in the exploration of what is forbidden; the illusion of independence – in the secession from the community of the pious; the illusion of infinity – in the empty abyss of evil. For it is characteristic of all virtue to have an end before it: namely its model, in God; just as all infamy opens up an infinite progression into the depths. The theology of evil can therefore be derived much more readily from the fall of Satan, in which the above-mentioned motifs are confirmed, than from the warnings in which ecclesiastical doctrine tends to represent the snarer of souls. The absolute spirituality, which is what Satan means, destroys itself in its emancipation from what is sacred. Materiality – but here soul-less materiality – becomes its home. The purely material and this absolute spiritual are the poles of the satanic realm; and the con-sciousness is their illusory synthesis, in which the genuine synthesis, that of life, is imitated.[16]

This presentation of the figure of Satan in is terms of his appearance as an allegorical figure. It can therefore be legitimately seen as an exten-sion of Kant's use of the figurative device of an 'evil spirit'. I will inter-pret this passage in this sense and draw out from it how the thought of 'demonology' in the Third Critique can be shown to relate to it.

In the above passage Benjamin presents Satanic consciousness in terms of a set of transcendental illusions. The illusions cited include two practical elements and one theoretical. The practical elements refer us to the notions of freedom and independence and the theoretical one to a thought of infinity and Benjamin seeks to suggest that the unity between these three illusions presents a synthesis that mirrors that given in 'life'. It is the unification of the three in this synthesis that is the most interesting element of Benjamin's account but I want first to focus on the separate elements. The illusion of freedom is not an illusion in the sense that there is not freedom to explore 'what is forbidden'. Rather, it is an illusion to assume that this exploration constitutes a free exercise of free choice. This goes to the heart of Zupančič's objection. According to Zupančič the choice of what is forbidden by the moral law cannot be regarded as a failure to freely exercise free choice (in the sense that asserting a sensuous inclination is determinative for a choice of maxim is) if this choice of the forbidden is *assented to to the point of death*. Given that Benjamin sees the unification of Satanic consciousness as having something to do with death it would be appropriate to hold off the full reply to Zupančič here until reaching the point of being able to describe this unification.

The second illusion, also a practical illusion, concerns the notion of 'independence'. This illusion is based on the notion that there can be a true realization of personality separately from communal moral life. Since the refutation of this illusion depends on a further exploration of Kant's account of the *summum bonum* within the text of *Religion within the Limits of Reason Alone* I will also not fully set out this response yet. The third illusion however is theoretical and involves the notion that it is possible to have an 'infinite progression into the depths' which progression lacks an object (as this object is lost in the straying from virtue, a path that always requires relation to an object or, as Kant would put it, a matter). This illusion will suffice at present to determine the nature of the Satanic consciousness and the type of synthesis it involves.

In this illusion of an infinite progress that lacks an object we have the thought of progress that is purely given in a means–end relation without the end being anything other than an empty search that lacks any determinate object. The abandonment of virtue involves the abandonment of its matter and paradoxically this ensures that the search for vice is the 'formless abstraction' that Kant's ethics is often taken to involve. Kant in fact insists within the pages of *Religion within the Limits of Reason Alone* and elsewhere that there can be no ethical maxim that does not have a matter (Ak. 6:4). By contrast the abandonment of virtue in favour of vice will involve a type of thought of progress that will be precisely involved with a type of subreption. Joan Copjec recognizes this when she writes: 'the historical subreption that attempted to redefine our ethical vocation as the pursuit of happiness and the cherishing of well-being, or physical life, has brought us the most unimaginable horrors and an undeniable 'contempt for life'

(Copjec, *op. cit.*, p. xxii). Kant also sets out the opposition to action in accordance with virtue in terms of a pure commitment to 'happiness' that separates this from and sets it against the moral law (whilst the thought of the *summum bonum* is an attempt to unite happiness with the moral law).

The rejection of the moral law as the basis of the maxim of action does not, despite appearances to the contrary, open the maxim in question to the possibility of complete indetermination. Without the moral law as a form for maxims of action the moral actor must substitute something else. This something else is found in the matter of inclinations. The inclinations, when lifted to a higher power, operate on the moral actor in one of two variable and oscillatory ways: via hedonism and world-denying pessimism.[17] The oscillation is caused by the inherently variable nature of happiness in combination with the endless quality of physical inclination. For the hedonist there are innumerable ways of 'improving' pleasure particularly when this 'improvement' is comprehended technically. There are elaborate techniques of relating to sexual combinations and pleasures from the descriptions of the *Kama Sutra* to the most modern advices on concentration on 'technique'. There are also innumerable ways of 'improving' the functioning of the body through prosthetic replacements of organs. The failure of the attachment to these 'improvements' due to the incessant quality of the 'progress' involved in the thought of them leads, through its unsatisfactory character, to a pessimism that involves theoretical or practical commitments to suicide.[18]

The synthesis that is Satanic consciousness of these elements hence involves a combination of a spirituality that would be absolute, which is another way of saying a freedom that wishes to be 'more' free than the law will permit, with an absolutization of 'matter' (which is as much to say taking the inclinations as a second power or as themselves *principled*). This synthesis clearly matches Zupančič's suggestion of a commitment to inclination to the point of death.

To round out the problem with this synthesis and to elucidate a Kantian reply to it will require returning to the thought of 'demonology'. This notion is mentioned by Kant in the Third Critique to characterize a being who is grounded purely on the argument of physico-teleology. We can now see the nature of Kant's suggestion. It is plausible to construe the argument from physico-teleology to refer us to a being who has or could create or sustain the perfect state of physicality. However, this perfect state must push physicality to its completion given that the progress that could be had by physicality whilst limitless can only reach satisfaction in death.[19] Death is such a satisfaction as at this point there is no separation between the body and all other bodies and this lack of separation is correlated with the realization of the aim of stilling the desires in question by giving them a final satisfaction. Hence this 'synthesis' mirrors that involved in 'life' but does so in the satisfaction of death.

In the discussion of organisms in the *Critique of Teleological Judgment* Kant describes organisms as involving a recursive connection between parts such that the whole body is a product of mutual interaction and imbrication of its components. Within the Satanic consciousness by contrast there is a fixation on parts at the expense of the whole and in favour of the destruction of the whole. This consciousness hence involves the commitment to seeing an organism as a mechanism, an error that is involved in many theoretical construals of organisms within contemporary thinking and which enables the understanding of the connection between such and the practical refusal of the authority of the moral law.[20]

If the *assent to desire to the point of death* is in fact constitutive of the Satanic consciousness, just as Zupančič in a way suggests, then what is to prevent this from being confused with the moral law in the sense that it could be taken to purify desire in a manner correlative with Kant's notion of 'practical feeling'? It should now be clear that what prevents this is precisely the emptiness of the form of the desire involved. Certainly the *matter* of such a desire has a precise correlate with the *matter* of action in accordance with the moral law in the sense that in both cases inclination is raised to the level of practical feeling and this helps us to understand how Kant's notion of 'vices of culture' can be seen to involve these latter in the transcendental philosophical anthropology that he is setting out. But the 'form' of the 'principled' commitment to inclination is precisely lacking. Such a maxim *lacks form* in the sense that there is no rule regulating it. This maxim has to be comprehended through the notion that it includes a commitment to dividing the body of the desirer such that the body has to be falsely pictured as a mechanism. This false picturing of the body leads to the necessity of seeing the body as matter to be sacrificed in favour of an endless approximation to a model that cannot be described. The endless sacrifice must involve the replacement of the body with the partial drives and hence must complete itself in denial of the pleasure that it ostensibly wishes to state itself in favour of. This denial of the pleasure asserted in the assertion thereof is the contradictory synthesis that we can term *desire for death*. By contrast with this the moral law requires commitment to the unification of the body in terms of a logic of life and this logic is consummated in the moral safeguarding of life, which is why it includes explicit prohibition of suicide (and since suicide can only be rendered permissible morally through the lying assimilation of the organism to a mechanism this connects suicide quite intimately to lying).

There is therefore a principal difference between action in accordance with the law and action in accordance with a 'principled' commitment to inclination even though the law can lead us to commit actions that will certainly lead to our death as it is not the case that the law implies *desire for death* but rather commitment to life, even if this life in certain situations has to take on the figurative status of the life of the moral community. This commitment to life in the moral law ensures a continuity between physical teleology and moral teleology whilst physical teleology adopted purely for its own sake must involve denial of the *teleology* of physical teleology, a denial all too prevalent in contemporary circumstances.

If it is therefore not the case that the level of purity of malign maxims can be taken to render them equivalent to moral maxims does not this reply to Zupančič at least demonstrate that the notion of 'malign reason' has to be taken more seriously than Kant took it? In the sense of demonstrating that it is possible for people to commit themselves to action on behalf of such a maxim there is a ground for saying this. If Kant resisted making this concession it is possible to state why in terms of an example from his own work that is sometimes cited as evidence of his failure to follow his own thought to its logical conclusion.[21]

This is the example of the executions of Louis XVI and Charles I to which Kant refers in a celebrated footnote to the Doctrine of Right. Kant refers here to a 'horror' felt in contemplating the formal execution of a monarch and he writes of this 'horror':

> But how are to explain this feeling, which is not aesthetic feeling (sympathy, an effect of imagination by which we put ourselves in the place of the sufferer) but moral feeling resulting from the complete overturning of all concepts of right? It is regarded as a crime that remains forever and can never be expiated (*crimen immortale, inexpiabile*), and it seems to be like what theologians call the sin that cannot be forgiven either in this world or the next (Ak. 6:321)

In placing this feeling of 'horror' within practical feeling Kant makes clear that this is a moral feeling. But in indicating the nature of the feeling Kant reaches for theological language which he interprets in the sense of rational religion. This indicates the fact that the 'horror' in question has something clearly to do with evil. The type of evil here indicated is connected to the notion traditional theology terms the 'sin against the Holy Ghost' (and the rational explication of the notion of the Holy Ghost will be given below but we can immediately understand that this problem must be connected with the sacrifice of hope).

If we turn now to the basis of this 'horror' and note the manner in which Kant deals with it we will get to the central point of why Kant is reluctant to grant that 'diabolical evil' is a possibility for human beings (even if a 'diabolical reason' can be envisaged as we have noted). Kant writes:

> The reason for horror at the thought of the formal execution of a monarch *by his people* is therefore this: that while his *murder* is regarded only as an *exception* to the rule that the people makes its maxim, his *execution* must be regarded as a complete *overturning* of the principles of the relation between a sovereign and his people (in which the people, which owes its existence only to the sovereign's legislation, makes itself his master), so that violence is elevated above the most sacred rights brazenly and in accordance with principle. Like a chasm that irretrievably swallows everything, the execution of a monarch seems to be a crime from which the people cannot be absolved, for it is as if the state commits suicide. There is, accordingly, reason for assuming that the agreement to execute the monarch actually origi-nates not from what is supposed to be a rightful principle but from fear of the state's vengeance upon the people if it revives at some future time, and that these formalities are undertaken only to give that deed the appearance of punishment, and so of a *rightful procedure* (such as murder would not be). But this disguising of the deed miscarries; such a presumption on the people's part is still worse than murder, since it involves a principle that would have to make it impossible to generate again a state that has been overthrown. (Ak. 6:322)

The nature of this passage requires some considered thought. In describing the formal execution of a monarch Kant describes the dif-ference between such an act and an assassination as being like the difference between begging exception to the law in terms of self-interest and directly rejecting it in a principled manner. But whilst Kant is keen to point out a problem with the latter it is worth noting what this prob-lem is. For the people formally to execute the monarch is to commit an act akin to suicide. The reason for this comparison is that, just as with suicide, it involves the self-immolation of a personality (given Kant's claim that the state is a moral personality, a claim central to *Perpetual Peace*). This act of self-immolation, like the *desire for death*, described by Zupančič is a free choice for the cessation of the conditions of freedom. Without a principle of executive power there is not a state but, if the sovereign power is itself capable of being judged, then it is not a sovereign power or a rival sovereign has overcome it. The latter occurs in warfare but the basis of civil war is a challenge to the power that determines the range and scope of rights. Hence, a civil war is not a rightful state of affairs (nor, of course, is a war between nations which is why there is a state of nature between them). This absence of a rightful state is equivalent to the return to a state of nature but if brought about via the assassination of a ruler it can at least be located as not based on the principle of opposition to a state of right as such.

The presentation of the formal execution of a monarch hence *should be seen* states Kant on the model of the wrongdoer who makes an exception to the law on their own behalf. This is why Kant presents it as an act brought about by fear of retribution and disguised in legal form. The reason why it *should be seen* this way, however, is because an act of suicide cannot be redeemed. There is no way to reinstate the rightful state if the principle of a rightful state has been destroyed. Hence the execution if interpreted in terms of a 'diabolical evil' would extinguish any ground for hope in history as it would render plausible the extirpation of the grounds of state development in terms of removing the basis for such development (by removing the concept of right as such from the grounds of formation of common enterprises in any one case then one renders them unstable in every case as someone can always claim grievance). This is the reason for Kant's unwillingness to admit that there is diabolical evil amongst humans. Once admitted and there is no clear return to a thinking of 'progress' other than on the terms of malign reason and hence with the collapse of the moral law so goes the commitment to life (which is why it is a 'suicide').

These connections hence justify Kant's contention that diabolical evil is not a possibility in terms of a historical perspective on the nature of right. To further comprehend the basis for this rejection it will be necessary to view Kant's positive view of historical progress and to connect this intimately with his understanding of right. It should be clear from this initial view however that the example in question is one that raises important questions about the moral grounding of political arrangements. By contrast with this example, the example used by Zupančič to demonstrate the conceptual conceivability of malign reason is of small purport. The example used by Zupančič does demonstrate the conceptual conceivability of such a reason, but does so through a necessary indication that the reason in question is one that is deathly in principle. Similarly, at the level of political history, an action of diabolical evil would involve a principled commitment to the destruction of the grounds of action. Since such destruction cannot take place without destroying the moral life in which it occurs it is not a possibility for humanity in the sense of indicating an enduring relation that could be established. Within human affairs generally it is hence a practical requirement to presume that such a principle is not the basis of any action as it prevents there being any question of redemption arising for the no longer moral actor in question. But with regard to moral actors there is always such a possibility for redemption hence the blocking of it attempted in the case of the malign reason is not a basis for comprehension of a maxim even if it is conceptually conceivable. Within the realm of political history it is not conceivably the basis of action either as it would prevent the prospect there also of the moral regeneration of peoples which regeneration we have grounds to hope for. I will turn to the nature of these grounds for hope in relation both to moral actors and the movements of history.

Redemption and the hope of historical progress

The contemporary concentration on the problem of radical evil has not been matched by an equivalent attention to the problem of 'redemption'. By the problem of 'redemption' I mean the problem of the ascent from basing action on evil maxims to basing it on good ones or converting oneself to acting in accordance with the moral law. The reason for this lack of equivalence in attention has partly been because of the belief in an evil that is more deeply rooted than in Kant's conception of it, but also partly because of despair over the possibility of overcoming the conditions of nihilism. To offset this latter concern it will be necessary to reprise Kant's positive conception of progress and to rehearse the reasons why it escapes the charges brought against the notion of progress. But it would be well to discuss first the difficulties of comprehending the redemption of the moral actor in relation to the action of any particular actor, as we will discover Kant's treatment of this is intricate.

Kant initially turns to addressing this question towards the close of the first part of the *Religion*. In doing so Kant immediately indicates a difficulty in understanding the nature of a conversion to morality when he states that it requires a 'revolution' in modes of thought although in terms of sense it can only be understood as involving a 'gradual reformation':

If by a single and unalterable decision a human being reverses the supreme ground of his maxims by which he was an evil human being ... he is to this extent, by principle and attitude of mind, a subject receptive to the good; but he is a good human being only in incessant labouring and becoming i.e. he can hope – in view of the purity of the principle which he has adopted as the supreme maxim of choice, and in view of the stability of this principle – to find himself upon the good (though narrow) path of contrast *progress* from bad to better. (Ak. 6:48)

This combination of 'revolution' and 'gradual reformation' has a very paradoxical character to it. It both requires a commitment to a decisive change and involves seeing this change as part of a process, a process of 'moral education'. In this initial introduction to the problem of this redemption it is a brief sketch of this 'moral education' that Kant is more concerned with, the nature of the elucidation of the paradox in question involves tying this education to a 'revolution' in disposition. In the second part of the *Religion*, however, Kant turns to giving a fuller explication of this paradox through a decisive reinterpretation of the figure of the Son of God in the terms of rational religion.

Before the figure of the Son of God is introduced however Kant makes quite clear once more the perfectionism of his outlook, a point that is once more worth drawing attention to. Kant describes here the 'end of creation', a topic that was also visited in *The Critique of Teleological Judgment* and, as in that work, he describes this 'end' as humanity (conceived as rational being *qua* moral) *'in its full moral perfection'* and he adds: 'it is our universal human duty to *elevate* ourselves to this ideal of moral perfection, i.e., to the prototype of moral disposition in its entire purity' (Ak. 6:61). The thought of this ideal itself can give us impetus to attaining it once we present it with 'force'. This 'force', however, requires another resort to the schematism of analogy by which means we can present this ideal in the figurative form of the Son of God.

We can only represent this ideal of a humanity in full moral perfection in the idea of a human being, as through this representation we can set the ideal before us in a form that enables it to be one that we can figure to ourselves as capable of our imitation. It is this need to comprehend the figure in question after the pattern of the form of a human being that leads Kant to refer indeed to the very notion of the schematism of analogy (Ak. 6:65). Having made this point, however, Kant sets himself the task of describing three difficulties that attach to the problem of realizing this good principle. The first difficulty connects back to the description of radical evil given in the first book of the *Religion*: 'The distance between the goodness which we ought to effect in ourselves and the evil from which we start is, however, infinite, and, so far as the deed is concerned – i.e. the conformity of the conduct of one's life to the holiness of the law – it is not exhaustible in any time' (Ak. 6:66). This first difficulty in realizing the good principle is what I would term a difficulty of series. It arises from the defective nature of our disposition and the immense gulf that exists between this and the good principle. Whilst Kant can and does refer to the fact that a good predisposition must lie at the heart of the possibility of realizing the good principle this first difficulty is then expressed anew by him in the following sharp formulation: 'How can this disposition count for the deed itself, when this deed is *every time* (not generally, but at each instant) defective?' (Ak. 6:67).

To this first difficulty Kant's solution is to use the same device that enabled him to resolve the antinomy of teleological judgment: the distinction between our own form of conception which, relying on a difference between intuition and conception, creates this form of infinite representation (on which the 'technical' notion of progress relies) whilst for an intuitive intellect it would be possible to look beyond the defective nature of the 'each time' towards the 'perfected whole' from which the good disposition would in principle arise, even though this dispositions whole would never appear in the series as other than defective. The super-session of serial representation by the intuitive intellect also refers us to the harmony between the resolution of the antinomy of teleological judgment with the resolution of the Third Antinomy presented in Chapter 2 above.

Kant's second difficulty with the realization of the good principle concerns the synthesis of elements required by the thought of the *summum bonum*, a synthesis now described in lapidary form in the expression '*moral happiness*' (Ak. 6:67). The problem here is, on what basis can we be assured that such a state could be achieved by us? It can by no means be understood as a certainty that we will achieve such a blessed state as this would be sufficient to cancel out the effort and persistence required for its achievement and promote a self-consciousness that might see itself in the light of a purely imaginary and 'enthusiastic' purity.[22] By contrast to have no assurance at all might render the coherence of moral life nugatory and throw into despair any who had thought to try attainment of its goal.

Kant's resolution of this second difficulty, which I would term 'the difficulty of happiness', is to point beyond the dogmatic constitutive elements of this antithesis towards a regulative construal that permits its correct statement. This permits a further use of the schematism of analogy figuratively to represent the good and pure disposition as the Holy Spirit. The comfort we can derive from our persistence in effort towards attainment of the good principle is one that is as if sent by the divine to give us aid in facing the difficulty of the resolution of this principle. It is a comfort grounded securely in the effort that is involved in the struggle itself and the figurative representation employed here points us from this struggle to the principle of its resolution and operates as a recursive figuration of the situation.

The third difficulty is the most serious and allows us to get to the setting of the problem on a wider stage than henceforth. This third difficulty concerns what I would term the problem of infinite guilt:

> Whatever his state in the acquisition of a good disposition, and, indeed, however steadfastly a human being may have persevered in such a disposition in a life conduct conformable to it, *he nevertheless started from evil*, and this is a debt which is impossible for him to wipe out. He cannot regard the fact that, after his change of heart, he has not incurred new debts as equivalent to having paid off the old ones. Nor can he produce, in the future conduct of a good life, a surplus over and above what he under obligation to perform each time; for his duty at each instant is to do all the good in his power. (Ak. 6:72)

The radicality of evil points us to the debt that has been incurred in all actions prior to the moral revolution of adopting the good principle as one's aim and since the operation according to this principle is at infinite remove from the orientation prior to its adoption it cannot be wiped out by continuous future action in accord with the good principle as this will still be the obligation at each future moment, not merely one adopted to render past action reparable. Nor can the debt I have to repay the actions in accord with the evil principle under which I previously acted by taken on by another, as it is not transmissible due to its personal character for each one of us (Ak. 6:72). This third difficulty arises, like the first, from a serial representation of our situation. The appeal to the intuitive intellect that resolved the first problem does not here immediately help however, but rather multiplies difficulties. Since the intuitive intellect must judge the person as now based on the good disposition it is appropriate to think of the person as now new-born in the sight of this representation and hence as being a different person from the one who committed the acts that are judged as based on the evil maxim. Since this would be a clear basis for the intuitive intellect to have a relation to the moral actor in question that would not be determined by our temporal ordering there would be a problem as to how it could render justice as to apply just reckoning to the person who acted wrongly can hardly be done in punishment of the new-born person. Since it cannot be correct to punish *after* the moral conversion, it can also not be presented as fully carried out on the person who existed *before* this conversion it becomes unclear at what point the punishment requisite for the judgment of the offender could be said to be carried out. Kant hence does not resolve the third problem as he did the first, as in this case the problem persists even in the application of the schematism of analogy. Hence Kant's solution here has to open a new vista:

> As an intellectual determination ... this conversion is not two moral acts separated by a temporal interval but is rather a single act, since the abandonment of evil is possible only through the good disposition that effects the entrance into goodness, and *vice-versa*. The good principle is present, therefore, just as much in the abandonment of the evil as in the adoption of the good disposition, and the pain that by rights accompanies the first derives entirely from the second. The emergence from the corrupted disposition into the good is in itself already sacrifice (as the 'death of the old man', 'the crucifying of the flesh') and entrance into a long train of life's ills which the new human being undertakes in the disposition of the Son of God, that is, simply for the sake of the good, yet are still fitting *punishment* for someone else, namely the old human being (who, morally, is another human being). (Ak. 6:74)

The earlier denial of transmissible liability, which applied to the notion that another could take on one's own debt is somewhat revised in the comprehension of the adoption of the good maxim as a conversion which makes a new person. The new person arises from the sacrifice of the old and this sacrifice of the old person is the punishment of that person for what they did and the maxims on which they acted. This sacrifice of the old person in the birth of the new marks a continuity between them but the revision of the denial of transmissible liability is contained in the figurative notion of the Son of God. The Son of God (a forceful presentation of the disposition now adopted) bears as '*vicarious substitute*' (Ak. 6:74) the debt of sin that has accumulated. The new person born from the conversion bears the punishment in the following sense: 'he willingly takes upon himself, as so many opportunities to test and exercise his disposition for the good, all the ills and sufferings that befall him; these 'the old man' would have to impute to himself as punishment, and he too actually imputes them to himself as such inasmuch as he still is in the process of dying to "the old man"' (Ak. 6:75). The sufferings that are befallen in the action according to the good principle are actively taken on by the new person that arises from the conversion, sufferings that the old person would certainly regard as punishments and which the new person could still perceive as such insofar as they are not entirely reborn.

Kant declares this resolution of the third difficulty the 'deduction of the idea of a *justification*' (Ak. 6:76). This new form of practical deduction concerns a speculative problem that is nonetheless of practical interest in its resolution. What its resolution points to is the necessity of representing the possibility of a good disposition only on the grounds of a revolution of disposition (even though for our serial presentation we can only discern a gradual reformation). This double relation to the moral self draws out the notion of intelligible character as something is always viewed in a double aspect. Whilst this character has to be understood as operating according to radically opposed possible maxims and the 'conversion' from the evil maxim to the good one as driving a complete wedge within its development the very notion of development itself (also involved in any thought of moral education) is given to us as a necessary thought only through our entanglement with conditions of intuition, conditions necessary for us to represent such matters at all (and another ground for the use of the schematism of analogy).

Before setting out how this third difficulty and its resolution help to lead Kant to restate his answer to the problem of redemption in wider terms than apply to any given person it is first necessary to consider a recent objection to the treatment of these three self-posed difficulties. John E. Hare presents this objection when he writes:

> The work he [Kant] can assign to God in three persons, as translated within the pure religion of reason, still leaves unresolved the question whether the revolution which produces a disposition pleasing to God can take place. Again we have the dilemma about extra-human assistance. Either it is just humanity that atones, in which case we are not helped to see that we can get into a position in which we are entitled to make vicarious atonement; or something beyond the

human atones for us, in which case we cannot object to transmissible liability. The same is true of the doctrine of election. It can be understood without extra-human assistance as an expression of our ignorance of the causes why one person chooses for good and another for evil, and our need, therefore, to leave judgement to Providence. But this interpretation does not help us with our initial difficulty. To be sure, we are ignorant of the reasons why some people choose for good, and others for evil. The problem, though, is to see how *any* people can choose for good, given the fact of innate (though imputable) depravity.[23]

The problem as posed by Hare is not the same as the problem posed by Kant. For Kant the problem is not how any one can choose for the good. As Hare notes this question of choice between the fundamental maxims is not one that Kant thinks can be explained at all. But the problem arises for Kant then in terms of understanding how what he has to conceive of as a complete transformation can be represented given problems of infinite guilt. This problem is what is then addressed by the deduction of the idea of a justification. This deduction involves, as already pointed out, a revision of Kant's initial rejection of the notion of transmissible liability but a revision that does not admit that the liability is transmitted to anything that would phenomenally appear as a different person but rather through the notion of intelligible character itself being open to alteration even though the notion that alteration is involved arises from our intuitive presentation. Hence there is no problem in revising the notion of transmissible liability without invoking in terms of object-determination a form of extra-human assistance. Since no such object-determination of the divine is open to Hare any more than to Kant he should, like Kant, construe this question in terms of a schematism of analogy on pain of being able to say anything intelligible here at all.

Hare, in stating his objection, referred also to the notion of Providence. In closing this discussion on redemption I would like to consider Kant's treatment of this topic in *The Conflict of the Faculties*. This will enable a return to the description of the notion of an ethical commonwealth in the *Religion* in relation to the correct notion of progress on Kantian grounds, 'moral progress'. In the second part of *The Conflict of the Faculties* Kant poses a question about the nature of human progress. This is put in terms of a moral history.[24] Here Kant raises the problem of how we could have a ground for saying whether or not human history as a whole could be said to be comprehended as progressing. Since we are thinking of progress now in relation to morality this evidently has to be understood to be a question about the possibility of the race as a whole becoming more moral. For this notion of 'becoming moral' to be set out at all coherently we have to connect the hope for moral progress to a ground. Kant describes the ground for such a hope in relation to events contemporary to him but prior to doing so indicates the type of occurrence that would give such ground for hope:

> This occurrence consists neither in momentous deeds nor crimes committed by human beings whereby what was great among human beings is made small or what was small is made great, nor in ancient splendid political structures which vanish as if by magic while others come forth in their place as if from the depths of the earth. No, nothing of the sort. It is simply the mode of thinking of he spectators which reveals itself *publicly* in this game of great revolutions, and manifests such a universal yet disinterested sympathy for the players on one side against those on the other, even at the risk that this partiality could become very disadvantageous for them if discovered. (Ak. 7:85)

It is hence not the deeds that involve physical upheavals that themselves give us a basis for moral hope. It is rather that which is inferable as operative amongst the spectators of such events that does so. The way of thinking that Kant describes is one that involves universality but also disinterestedness. The predisposition involved is one, which in fact not merely involves hope for the better but 'is already itself progress insofar as its capacity is sufficient for the present' (Ak. 7:86). The reason why Kant can make this move from the hope for progress to the indication that the predisposition involved already indicates progress is that this predisposition is itself one with the triumph of the good principle as it motivates one to move in the direction of the good principle.

This discussion, conducted in somewhat enigmatic fashion, clearly involves reference to the French Revolution. Kant refers only to the 'revolution of a gifted people', but goes on to refer to the right of a nation to provide itself with a civil constitution and the end that 'that same national constitution alone be *just* and morally good in itself' (Ak. 7:85). This reference to constitutions whose just basis would be republican can refer only to the events in France. This first reference to a constitution of republican character is a negative basis for the predisposition towards the revolution of the spectators however as the republican constitution is desirable only in its peaceful characterisation.[25] Added to this is the 'passionate participation in the good' revealed by the enthusiasm indicated by spectators of the revolution, a 'genuine' enthusiasm that 'moves only towards what is ideal, and indeed to what is purely moral, such as the concept of right' (Ak. 7:86). As this enthusiasm of the spectators is related to the purely moral element of the revolution it is the truly moral phenomena that gives ground for hope as the revolution itself 'may be filled with misery and atrocities to the point that a right-thinking human being, where he boldly to hope to execute it successfully the second time, would never resolve to make the experiment at such cost' (Ak. 7:85). Beyond the physical revolution the wishful participation of the spectators constitutes a *moral revolution*. In relation to this we have the ground for hope that we sought:

> For such a phenomenon in human history *will not be forgotten*, because it has revealed a tendency and faculty in human nature for improvement such that no politician, affecting wisdom, might have conjured out of the course of things hitherto existing, and which nature and freedom alone, united in the human race in conformity with inner principles of right, could have promised. (Ak. 7:88)

It is the universal tendency towards this participation in the revolution that is noteworthy, the enthusiasm based on purely moral grounds with which it was met. The moral enthusiasm in question enables us to hope as the events within the nation in question itself could miscarry without this enthusiasm having been other than a moral phenomena and one of the widest and most extraordinary kind. This is what Kant terms 'a historical sign' (Ak. 7:84) that recalls the Idea, demonstrates it and yet also anticipates it. This historical sign is in fact yet another schema of analogy although not this time applied to the supersensible in figurative mode, but rather used to discern the pure basis for a phenomenon that appears in empirical circumstances in response to a dramatic set of events. It is hence the events that appear as proximate cause for the hypothesis that what is revealed in the response to them is the true expression of a moral upheaval and hence for thinking this response on an intelligible ground. Since the structure of this thinking gives us grounds for believing in moral progress we witness a type of final end schema being applied by Kant but we have to comprehend now that the condition for application of this is by the method of a schema of analogy.

The *summum bonum* revisited: ethical commonwealths and Kantian ecclesiology

The fact that the account of the response to the French Revolution led Kant to describe in anticipative fashion the notion of the concept of right indicates that we are now on the edge of the breakthrough from the critique of morality to the doctrinal treatment of practical problems. One last point of the critical treatment should be mentioned before turning to these doctrinal works. This concerns the discussion in Part Three of the *Religion* of the ethical commonwealth, a discussion that pushes us towards the doctrinal treatment of virtue. Connected to this treatment and worth also a brief account is Kant's original description of ecclesiology. In the third part of the *Religion* Kant turns to the 'founding of a kingdom of God on earth', a condition which provides the fullest account of redemption as here Kant treats of the main problem any given moral actor has to face in their surroundings: the society of others.

The establishment of the possibility of a situation in which human beings as a group could regenerate and move towards the establishment of the good principle are here set out as 'the setting up and the diffusion of a society in accordance with, and for the sake of, the laws of virtues' (Ak. 6:94). This would be an ethical community, a community that requires a pre-existent political community in order to be able to come into existence and yet which has a special unifying principle of its own, viz., virtue.

Whilst the community of virtue could not occur without a community of a political kind (a priority of strict conception) it cannot be brought about by politicians (Ak. 6:96). It is of wider provenance than a political community as it touches the very ground of maxims in terms of actions towards oneself as well as others, and it is wider in extent since it would have to cover the whole human race. All human beings wish for the *summum bonum* inasmuch as they are motivated by rational morality and this *summum bonum* is now related by Kant to the notion of the kingdom of ends he deployed in the *Groundwork* in order to think of a highest common good. This re-description of the *summum bonum* through the revision of the kingdom of ends is however 'the idea of working toward a whole of which we cannot know whether as a whole it is also in our power' (Ak. 6:98). Here, if anywhere, is where the objection raised by Hare ought to come. For in responding to the question of how we could know whether this whole would be within our power Kant reaches once again for the schematism of analogy.

The legislation that would underpin such a *summum bonum* could not come from any public lawgiver, as it has to affect internal actions such as thoughts and dispositions. Hence the only one who could emerge, as the founder of the legislation of the community, would be the one who could penetrate into all hearts. This hence reveals that the legislator of the moral community would be God 'as a moral ruler of the world' (Ak. 6:99). Therefore, for a moral community to come into existence is for all peoples to submit to the legislation of God, but since the term God is the product of a schematism of analogy, and what we rationally mean by it is the universal aim of perfect moral accord, it would seem to be a statement that the legislation of such a community would be the autonomy of reason itself. However, once we have deciphered the use of the schematism of analogy we may wonder if we have had an answer to our question of how we could know whether we could achieve such a goal.

In further response to the persistence of this question Kant posits a further determination of the thought of the ethical community. Since such a community would be 'a moral people of God', it would be the case that another name for it would be a church, considered however in universal extent and thus after a pattern of rational ecclesiology. Kant deduces the characteristics of this church from the table of judgments (Ak. 6:102). Its constitution is really sharply different from a political one as it is akin to a household rather than any of the forms of political organization (Ak. 6:102). The ground for such a church would be a pure religious faith. Such a faith adopts the final end of morality as its principle in reading holy books of any sort, a description that makes clear the use Kant makes of Biblical hermeneutics (Ak. 6:110). The historical existent faiths need to be reformed in the light of this notion of pure religious faith and made thereby moral. The possibility of this reformation is the hope of the foundation of a moral community.

The possibility of this reformation can be grasped once again however only in the figure of a revolution, a revolution in dispositions and not in physical arrangements. The possibility of it is thinkable but not demonstrable. The grounds for hope in relation to it can however be discerned as Kant points out in his account of the response of spectators to the French Revolution. The eschatological horizon of Kant's critical position is thereby reached. Does it, as Hare would suggest, involve a necessary appeal to extra-human assistance? Yes and no. It involves an inevitable thought of the type that a schematism of analogy represents and which determines the character of the supersensible without on the mould of the supersensible within. This reference is indispensable to the coherence of morality and is what enables a progressive comprehension of human history. But it does not allow for a schema of object-determination that would constitutively try to represent that which we comprehend figuratively as an object of some type of knowledge grounded in a law-governed experience of the type presented in nature. This double response is the reason why it is necessary to have constant recourse to a schematism of analogy that becomes the basis for representation of the final end schema whilst refusing the schema of object determination in the realm of practical thought.

6
Possession, Property and Contract

The treatment of the nature of evil brought us to the very edge of the critical treatment of practical philosophy that has been sketched thus far. Now I want to turn to the work that Kant wished for the longest time to produce and which was the crowning of his practical philosophy: *The Metaphysics of Morals*. There are four distinct problems that have to be addressed in interpreting this work. First, how does the Doctrine of Right relate to the critical treatment of morality? Second, how does the Doctrine of Virtue provide us with the means for connecting the moral law to ethical situations? Third, what is the unity of the whole work of which these two doctrinal treatments are both part? Fourth and finally, what is the connection between Kant's doctrinal works in practical philosophy with his critical work in the most general terms? These questions are all of considerable difficulty. I propose to address the overarching problem about the relationship between critical and doctrinal treatments in the last chapter where I will also give an account of how *The Metaphysics of Morals* is a unified work. The discussion of the Doctrine of Virtue will be undertaken in Chapter 7. In this chapter I propose therefore to undertake an overview of the Doctrine of Right with the problem of its relationship to the critical treatment of morality underpinning this interpretation.

The Doctrine of Right has a very specific place in Kant's practical philosophy. It is the place where Kant sets out a lengthy and complicated account of possession as the basis for a defence of property rights and in which a discussion of the nature of civil society is set forth that draws on the traditions of both contractarian and natural law treatments. Whilst the former is included under the heading 'private right', the latter is contained in the account of 'public right'. However, it is not sufficient to provide an overarching interpretation of the Doctrine of Right in terms of how the notions of the two types of right can be said to relate as there is also a wider question that has been consistently raised in secondary literature on this work, the question of whether the treatment of right is to be taken as belonging within the province of moral philosophy at all. I will begin therefore by setting out this problem as an introduction to the framework within which, in my view, the interpretative dilemmas that arise in reading the Doctrine of Right must be set.

Is the Doctrine of Right independent of Kant's practical system?

In some respects this is a very peculiar question to raise not least because of the fact that the Doctrine of Right is presented by Kant as the first part of his doctrinal treatment of morals. In the preface to the *Critique of Judgment* Kant stated that with its publication he had completed his critical enterprise and intended now to proceed to the doctrinal one (Ak. 5:170). This statement is in some respects peculiar, not least in relation to theoretical philosophy as Kant published *The Metaphysical Foundations of Natural Science* prior to the writing of the *Critique of Judgment*. It is far from clear, however, that this work could be regarded as part of the doctrinal part of theoretical philosophy as this was intended to consist in a metaphysics of nature not in a metaphysics of natural science.[1] Matters are further complicated by the status of the *Opus Postumum*. In the area of practical philosophy, furthermore, as we have noted in the reading of *Religion within the Limits of Reason Alone*, the critical treatment was not completed until this work extended considerably the account of areas first covered in the postulates of pure practical reason. Despite these caveats it is clear that Kant saw a continuity between his critical treatments of moral questions and his doctrinal ones and since the Doctrine of Right is the first part of his work on doctrinal moral philosophy it would seem prima facie obvious that it belongs within the framework of his systematic account of morality.

The reason why there are questions that can be raised here however is that Kant also does wish to separate his treatment of right in some important respects from the treatment of ethics strictly speaking.[2] For example, during the introduction to the Doctrine of Right Kant states that the work will treat 'strict right' by which he means 'that which is not mingled with anything ethical' (Ak. 6:232). This separation of the treatment of right from the ethical is intended as allowing that the basis of right not be grounded on the necessity of incorporating right notions into one's maxims of action for as Kant writes: 'That I make it a maxim to act rightly is a demand that ethics makes of me' (Ak. 6:231). It is not therefore a demand made on me by right itself strictly considered. Since this is so it must be possible to set out the case for strict right as a notion with no reference to the necessities of maxim formation that are so important in the treatment of ethics and this in its turn would suggest that the treatment of right is in some sense constitutively independent of Kant's moral system despite being produced to answer one of the demands of this system. This odd situation can be responded to in two distinct ways. Thomas Pogge provides one of them:

> I believe, that Kant wants his argument for *Recht*, and for a republican instantiation thereof, to be independent from his morality. This morality may well give its adherents moral reasons for supporting *Recht* and a republican constitution in particular. But it does not therefore have a special status with respect to *Recht*, because it is ... just as true that selfishness gives its immoral adherents selfish reasons for supporting *Recht* and a republican constitution in particular.[3]

Whilst Pogge's argument is supported by many considerations drawn from the Doctrine of Right itself, there is also prime evidence for it given in the remark made in the course of *Perpetual Peace: A Philosophical Sketch* where Kant states that the problem of setting up a state could be solved even by a 'race of devils' (Ak. 8:366), a statement that certainly seems to clearly suggest that political arrangements are constitutively separable from considerations of a moral order.

By contrast Katrin Flikschuh has argued the opposing view to this at considerable length. Whilst Flikschuh does not suggest that the account of right is based directly upon the categorical imperative she does argue that adding to this imperative a consideration of economic desiring gives us the basic content of the Doctrine of Right. This argument thus concedes that there is a distinction between ethics strictly speaking and the treatment of right, a distinction that must in some sense be present given Kant's remarks about strict right but it does lead to the view that the appeal to the categorical imperative will be of some importance in the argument of the Doctrine of Right and if that is so then there is a clear problem with Pogge's view that the treatment of right is entirely constitutively independent of Kant's system of practical philosophy.[4]

I assume that the treatments of possession and property in the discussion of private right and the treatment of contract in the discussion of public right will be key tests for the solution of the problem of how we are to tackle this question of the relationship between the account of right and the previously adduced supreme principle of morals. Prior to setting out these questions I will offer a preliminary account of the formulas of right given in the prefatory material of the Doctrine of Right relating it to what is said there of the categorical imperative.

The formulas of right and the categorical imperative

In the introduction to the whole of the *Metaphysics of Morals* Kant sets out a description of what 'metaphysics of morals' itself is. Since metaphysics is itself on Kant's terms 'a system of a priori cognition from concepts alone' (Ak. 6:216) and a practical philosophy is said to be concerned with freedom then we have the basic notion of the type of metaphysics in question if we determine it as a system of the a priori concepts of freedom. Within the treatment of this subject however we need not merely principles of morality but also 'principles of application' so that whilst metaphysics of morals is not based upon anthropology 'it can still be applied to it' (Ak. 6:217). The relationship between these two types of principles is something I will discuss again below. However, in relation to the notion of freedom, Kant goes on in this general introduction to the whole work to make another point of some interest when he states: '*Freedom* of choice is this independence from being *determined* by sensible impulses; this is the negative concept of freedom. The positive concept of freedom is that of the ability of pure reason to be of itself practical' (Ak. 6:213–14). The positive concept of freedom is equivalent to subjecting maxims to the condition of the categorical imperative. Hence the positive concept requires the treatment that strict right will not involve, that of giving a test for the adoption of maxims, the test so laboriously discussed in the *Groundwork*. By contrast the treatment of strict right requires only that we have a basis for assessing whether actions are regulated in accordance with the dictates of sensibility or by reference to something else in public conduct. Hence whilst this treatment does not enquire into the basis of the maxim someone has for the actions they perform it does set the grounds for which that action can in fact take place or in other words sets it into a negatively moral context.

Both positive and negative conceptions of freedom refer to a consideration of an agent in reference to being able to act in such a way that the action done is not determined by sensibility and thus they require for Kant the belief that there is a ground to think that we can so act, a ground first set out in the Third Antinomy and reasserted in the third part of the *Groundwork* (and in the description of the 'fact of reason' in the Second Critique). This is why, in the introduction to the whole work, Kant can state as a clarification of concepts used in both parts of the *Metaphysics of Morals* that obligation is 'the necessity of a free action under a categorical imperative of reason' (Ak. 6:222). The action can be *under* the categorical imperative even if it has not been required that the person so acting has been requested to explicitly and self-consciously adopt as the maxim of this action that it be *in accord* with the categorical imperative. Later, within the same introduction to the whole work, Kant states that the categorical imperative, which he restates there, only affirms what obligation is (Ak. 6:225 and see also Ak. 6:226 where Kant offers the supreme principle of the doctrine of morals as equivalent to the categorical imperative).[5]

Kant also makes clear the difference between the considerations of action that are involved in ethics by contrast with those operative in strict right when he distinguishes between the law and the incentive that is related to it.

> That lawgiving which makes an action a duty and also makes that duty an incentive is *ethical*. But that lawgiving which does not include the incentive of duty in the law and so admits an incentive other than the idea of duty itself is *juridical*. (Ak. 6:219)

The juridical law is hence based upon an operation upon incentives that is not directly based upon the law although the law will produce outward action that, whilst regulated by an effect on inclination (in terms of fears and benefits), will produce action that can be viewed *as if* it came from the subject's own reason as it will be in conformity with the nature of the moral law rather than inclination.

If we turn from this material in the introduction to the whole work to the specific introduction to the Doctrine of Right itself then we will find there much that helps to buttress the view that is gradually being developed of the reasons why we can treat strict right as belonging within the province of morality even though it is distinct from ethics strictly so called. In answering the question he poses himself, 'what is right?', Kant sets out the moral notion of this in terms of three elements that belong to the notion. These three elements are: first the external relations of one person to another; second, the relation to another's choice; and third, to the *form* of this choice (that it is free). This gives him his notion of what right as a combination of these three elements is when he states: 'Right is therefore the sum of the conditions under which the choice of one can be united with the choice of another in accordance with a universal law of freedom' (Ak. 6:230).

This inclusive description of the notion of right indicates that it is intended as an account of the conditions that allow free action to be expressed. This is why Kant gives the universal principle of right in the formula immediately subsequent to this setting out the notion of right in the following manner: 'Any action is *right* if it can coexist with everyone's freedom in accordance with a universal law, or if on its maxim the freedom of choice of each can coexist with the everyone's freedom in accordance with a universal law' (Ak. 6:230). Note the negative nature of this formulation, a negative characteristic that shows it to conform to the negative concept of freedom, as the action is one that 'can' coexist with the freedom of others, not one that is necessarily intended to so coexist. That is why it is no part of this law that it be adopted explicitly as a basis for maxims, it is rather a law that enables the judgment of the actions adopted but gives no license to investigate the basis on which they are adopted. Hence Kant specifies that this principle is analytic (Ak. 6:396) by which he means that it states only: 'freedom *is* limited to those conditions in conformity with the idea of it' (Ak. 6:231).

Thus far all that we have is an explication of the notion of freedom when considered in relation to outer actions. This explication proceeds a step further when Kant adds that since what hinders freedom, even if it should be the action of a free being, is wrong that 'coercion that is opposed to this (as a *hindrance of a hindrance to freedom*) is consistent with freedom in accordance with universal laws, that is, it is right' (Ak. 6:231). Since strict right requires 'only external grounds for determining choice' (Ak. 6:232) the element of coercion is not extrinsic to it, but rather integral to its statement as it is this that separates it from ethical lawgiving. This is the reason why Kant can state boldly and clearly that: 'Right and authorization to use coercion therefore mean one and the same thing' (Ak. 65:232).

Reciprocal coercion is thus the basis of a rightful state of affairs. This is stated again when Kant explains that there is only one 'innate right'. Since Kant takes an innate right to be that which belongs by nature to all it is not surprising that this innate right is freedom. We are now clearly aware however of the intimate connection of external freedom with coercion so that the specification of this freedom in accord with conditions of equality and independence is a further extension of how this internal unity of freedom and coercion is expressed.[6]

One point remains to state as not clearly expressed in this prefatory material and as very helpful for the basic enquiries of private and public right. Mary Gregor makes the point that there is throughout the Doctrine of Right an appeal, sometimes implicit, sometimes explicit, to the notion of humanity as an end-in-itself as given in the *Groundwork*.[7] This is less surprising than it might seem as in the *Groundwork* Kant writes that 'there is still only a negative and not a positive agreement with *humanity as an end in itself* unless everyone tries, as far as he can, to further the ends of others' (Ak. 4:431) and he also describes the principle of humanity as 'the supreme limiting condition of the freedom of action of every human being' (Ak. 4:431). If we take these statements together we can see that the principle of humanity as an end in itself conforms to a merely negative notion of freedom (by contrast with the principle of autonomy's positive conception of freedom which requires a commitment to self-legislation). Further, we can also see that this principle as the 'supreme limiting condition' of freedom is equivalent to strict right.

Hence we should expect the invocation of this principle at key stages of the argument of the Doctrine of Right as the manner in which the categorical imperative is given its application. This form of application will be worthy also of comparison subsequently with that of the Doctrine of Virtue. Since the Doctrine of Virtue, as we will see in due course, explicates a moral teleology that is of a piece with the central aspects of Kant's general moral philosophy and adopts the positive conception of freedom it would appear that it is only at the level of strict right that Kant sets out a key element of his practical philosophy that is not clearly connected to a perfectionist teleology.

Private right and public right

The last point to be addressed prior to looking at the central notions of the Doctrine of Right is the conceptual division of the work between a treatment of private right and one of public right. The nature and justification of this division is worthy of a short explanation. What Kant terms private right is what is often referred to as 'natural right'. Under this classification fall the rights that can be said to be based on the natural conditions of humanity irrespective of the existence of political communities. Hence another name for this area could be 'pre-political right'. Since Kant understands the 'natural' condition of humanity to be one of rational agency it would be expected that under the heading of private right he will treat the conditions for such agency in the broadest external sense. This is why it is here that Kant provides a justification of possession that enables a defense of property rights. By contrast public right treats of the civil condition. Under public right we thus discover the rightful basis of civil society in terms of the form of government and the general basis of social arrangements, a basis given for Kant in the form of contract. Whilst this has the appearance of suggesting that Kant is a contractarian thinker the relationship to the tradition of natural law will also be discerned here in relation to the previously given discussion of private right. The treatment of both in this chapter will of necessity be given in broad terms as the intricate discussions conducted here would not be available for treatment within the space of one chapter but I hope to bring out at least the general basis of Kant's treatment so that the relationship between this characterization and some of the details can be given on another occasion.

The justification of possession

It has been generally agreed in the commentaries and responses to the Doctrine of Right that the treatment of possession and property is the key to the work. This is despite the fact that there are recognized to be considerable problems with interpreting the argument Kant gives about these topics. Some of these difficulties are text-philological.[8] Even without discussing these however there are competing interpretations of the nature of this argument that indicate quite different verdicts of the philosophical import of Kant's discussion. Katrin Flikschuch for example suggests that an antinomy is discussed in the seventh section of the first chapter of the Doctrine of Right and she suggests this is connected to the Third Antinomy and that grasping this connection will give the real import of the argument.[9] By contrast, Kenneth Westphal does not refer to this antinomy and suggests that the argument should be read only as justifying the notion of possession and not as giving a ground for property rights.[10]

Clearly, if we conceive of the relationship of possession to external freedom on the one hand, and to property rights as durable rights on the other and hence as requiring a civil society, then we will have reason to think that the argument concerning property has some considerable significance in taking us beyond the analytic level of the prefatory material and towards being able to grasp how Kant will subsequently treat public right. The opening part of Kant's argument is given in the notion that to claim something as rightfully mine involves me in the claim that another's use of it without my consent would be a wrong. This minimal definition becomes immediately complicated:

> But something *external* would be mine only if I may assume that I could be wronged by another's use of a thing *even though I am not in possession of it.* – So it would be self-contradictory to say that I have something external as my own only if the concept of possession could not have different meanings, namely *sensible* possession and *intelligible* possession, and by the former could be understood *physical* possession but by the latter a *merely rightful* possession of the same object. (Ak. 6:245)

This distinction between sensible possession and intelligible possession is evidently of a piece with the distinction between sensible character and intelligible character as given in the First Critique. Sensible possession is clearly empirical possession but the claim that is made to possess something that is not currently held must of necessity point beyond this and what it points to is intelligible possession.

The philological discussion about the text does converge with philosophical considerations in the sense that the appeal that is subsequently made in what was originally printed as the second paragraph of chapter 1 refers to the postulate of practical reason. If we follow the emended text by contrast we move from this argument about the distinction between empirical possession and intelligible possession to an exposition of the notion of external objects. The argument for emending the text here is clear as this move to an exposition of the notion of external objects would seem analytically the right next step of the argument with considerations about the postulate of practical reason only really having a place after this discussion. This exposition is in fact a type of 'metaphysical exposition' as described in the First Critique (B38) and explicated in the Jäsche logic as 'the connected (successive) representation' of the marks of a concept, as found through analysis (Ak. 9:143). Hence the exposition is still a part of Kant's analytical presentation and it sets the stage for how the treatment of property rights will subsequently be developed as Kant distinguishes here three external objects of my choice: '1) a (corporeal) *thing* external to me; 2) another's *choice* to perform a specific deed (*praestatio*); 3) another's *status* in relation to me' (Ak. 6:247) and these three types of object are located in relation to the table of categories of the First Critique, interestingly picking out from this table the three categories that are re-treated in the Analogies of Experience.

With relation to the *thing* external to me Kant repeats the importance of the distinction between two types of possession. Since this type of possession requires a view of occupancy that does not require present-ing spatial relation the justification of it requires an intelligible exten-sion of the notion of substance in practical terms that was precisely not permitted in theoretical terms. By contrast, the possession of another's choice to perform a specific deed or in simpler terms the holding of their promise requires a view of causality that is not restricted by time and allows simultaneity of transfer in practice even though this is impossible in theory. Finally, the right I have to the possession of another's status (as wife or child) is one that I possess irrespective of the presence of the one held to me and hence this allows a relation of com-munity between myself and this other despite temporal and spatial dis-tinction, an allowance that requires the extension of this category practically that cannot be allowed theoretically.

Having set this set out once more in an analytic argument, albeit one that makes clear the relationship of the matters under consideration to metaphysics, Kant proceeds to present first a nominal and then a real definition of the notion of external objects as material for possession prior to his deduction of the concept of rightful possession. A nominal definition is described in the Jäsche logic as 'those that contain the meaning that one wanted arbitrarily to give to a certain name, and which therefore signify only the logical essence of their object' (Ak. 9:143). This is the type of definition that was at work in the meta-physical deduction of the First Critique (A66/B91–B116).[11] Hence the nominal definition is still part of the analytical argument presented thus far and it is given by Kant in the following manner: 'that outside me is externally mine which it could be a wrong (an infringement upon my freedom which can coexist with the freedom of everyone in accor-dance with a universal law) to prevent me from using as I please' (Ak. 6:249). If it would be a wrong to prevent me from using this exter-nal object then it is externally mine. This is a simply logical definition.

Immediately after this, however, Kant gives a real definition of the notion of an external object that is mine. A real definition is described in the Jäsche logic as one that suffices 'for cognition of the object according to its inner determinations, since they present the possibility of the object from inner marks' (Ak. 9:143). Since Kant describes a real definition, as that which also suffices for the deduction of it, this real definition is one that will, when fully understood, enable us to comprehend by what right we claim an external object as ours and hence it belongs to the level of a transcendental deduction. The real definition that Kant gives of the notion of an external object that is mine is: 'something external is mine if I would be wronged by being disturbed in my use of it *even though I am not in possession of it*' (Ak. 6:249) and this hence demonstrates that the real definition of external possession must correspond to the notion already given of intelligible possession. Whilst this is an illuminating step in Kant's argument the key stage is clearly the one where this definition is demonstrated to be one that we can rightfully claim to have, i.e., its transcendental deduction.

At this point the argument takes a decisive turn as Kant now phrases the problem as follows: 'The question: how is it possible for *something external to be mine or yours?* resolves itself into this question: how is *merely rightful* (intelligible) *possession* possible? and this in turn, into the third question: how is a *synthetic* a priori proposition about right possible?' (Ak. 6:249). Whilst all questions about right are a priori questions as the notion of right is itself a priori the questions that arise with regard to purely empirical possession are entirely contained within nominal definitions, as they are purely analytic demonstrations of that which is contained merely in the logical concept of possession. But if we transcend the boundaries of space and time, we make a claim that puts aside the boundaries of the nominal definition and this is what leads us to the notion of intelligible possession. Whilst Kant has thus only analytically set out what this notion involves and hence has thus far only given an analytic argument this argument has expounded a concept that we can now see to be a *synthetic* one.

We have thus moved effectively within the space of a metaphysical deduction going from the nominal definition, which holds an equivalent place to the logical notion of judgment, to the real definition that holds the place of the category. The category now has to be given its rightful basis. The argument for this takes the form of presenting a postulate. The postulate is presented in negative form as simply stating that if an object of choice would in itself have to belong to no one we would have a state contrary to right. The negative presentation of this postulate is connected to the negative account of freedom at work in the treatment of strict right. Kant's developed argument is here very simple:

> if the use of it could not coexist with the freedom of everyone in accordance with a universal law (would be wrong), then freedom would be depriving itself of the use of its choice with regard to an object of choice, by putting *usable* objects beyond any possibility of

being *used*; in other words, it would annihilate them in a practical respect and make them into *res nullius*, even though in the use of things choice was formally consistent with everyone's outer freedom in accordance with universal laws. (Ak. 6:250)

Since we derived the concept of external freedom analytically from the notion of freedom in general we have a merely negative sense of freedom. But this sense is sufficient for us to be able to test by use of the principle of contradiction maxims that would pretend to regulate right. A maxim that attempted to regulate right by ruling out external possession in intelligible form would fall under the test of the principle of contradiction since we would then be ruling out of use something that is clearly available for use according to the notion of external freedom. Thus we operate here in accord with laws of thought that are always governed by the principle of contradiction (Ak. 6:247 is here thus connected clearly to Bxxvi). We thus extend beyond the mere concept of right as such (this is why it is a *synthetic* claim that is being justified) by testing whether the objection to this extension could be justified according to laws of thinking (but not of cognition). This extension of the concept of right by virtue of the postulate is what Kant terms a 'permissive law' of practical reason and this notion is a principle of application of the concept in question, a principle of application akin to a schema, namely a typic of this concept. This is clearly stated by Kant when he writes:

In an a priori *theoretical* principle, namely, an a priori intuition would have to underlie the given concept (as was established in the *Critique of Pure Reason*); and so something would have to be *added to* the concept of possession of an object. But with this practical principle the opposite procedure is followed and all conditions of intuition which establish empirical possession must be *removed* (disregarded), in order to *extend* the concept of permission beyond empirical possession and to be able to say: it is possible for any external object of my choice to be reckoned as rightfully mine if I have control of it (and only insofar as I have control of it) without being in possession of it. (Ak. 6:251–2)

The extension of the concept of possession beyond empirical conditions hence takes place by testing whether objection to this extension is consistent with application of the principle of contradiction, that is, by testing the concept of a world that would be produced by the objection. The world that would be so produced is presented in accordance with a typic and this typic is revealed to be necessarily inconsistent so that the opposite world is the consistent one and hence the permissible extension of the concept is given.

The argument for the possibility of intelligible possession is thus presented via this negative characterization of the postulate and it is now possible to re-present the postulate in positive form (Ak. 6:252). The possibility of intelligible possession thus cannot of necessity be shown directly; it has to be demonstrated indirectly as we have no cognition of intelligible possession but that it is a necessary extension of the concept of possession we can demonstrate by negating its contrary. The inference for intelligible possession is hence based upon the application of the categorical imperative (Ak. 6:252). Along with the notion of external possession of a thing in accordance with the concept of intelligible possession Kant takes it to be the case that this argument simultaneously justifies the notions of promising and rightful possession of the status of a person (Ak. 6:254). It is only after the argument is given however that he presents the antinomy that Flikschuh presents as so central (Ak. 6:254–5) and this antinomy in fact simply represents the distinction between empirical and intelligible possession given in the first section and really adds nothing to the argument thus far given.

This general argument about possession is however only preliminary to Kant's attempt to establish property rights.[12] This is shown by the fact that immediately after presenting the antinomy Kant proceeds directly to the need for a civil condition. The connection between the argument concerning possession and the justification of property rights takes three stages: first, Kant gives a negative argument for the necessity of a civil condition; second, he connects this argument with a characterization of how natural right relates to civil right; and third, he sets out the general principle of external acquisition.

The necessity of the civil condition

In the first stage of this argument Kant draws out the implications of the postulate of practical right. The point is that the postulate declares an obligation, and obligation was expressed in the prefatory material as requiring universality. Hence if, in accordance with the postulate, I express the point that others have an obligation to recognize my right to intelligible possession, I must in accordance with the law of non-contradiction also accept the right of all others to make the same claim upon me. But for this requirement to be upheld as a claim there needs to be coercive possibility to uphold the claim. A unilateral will cannot be the basis of coercive law alone since that is not consistent with the nature of freedom. So only a collective will could do this. 'But the condition of being under a general external (i.e., public) lawgiving accompanied with power is the civil condition' (Ak. 6:256). Thus the first negative argument is based purely on the fact that if intelligible external possession is a right, then this right requires universal application but such application requires a power in accord with both its range and its right. The only power that fulfils this role is the power of a civil condition.

The second stage of this argument concerns a characterization of how to view the nature of the relationship between natural right and civil right. The laws of a civil constitution have to conform with the requirements of natural right, as this constitution is the way in which it is possible to secure natural rights. Hence rights are pre-political in the sense they are not grounded on the civil constitution itself, but rather provide it with its basis. However, prior to the constitution, intelligible possession is held in accord only with the possibility of this constitution being achieved. Prior to the civil constitution there is a rightful presumption to intelligible possession but since this possession has no secure way of being maintained it is only a provisional right.

The second part of Kant's argument hence states that the civil constitution is only the manner in which the coercion that accompanies right is given. But since the coercion that accompanies right is integral to right any held right prior to the existence of such coercion cannot be more than a presumption. Thus Kant both makes clear that right is essentially pre-political in form and yet also indicates the necessity of political organization for right to be effectively established.

The final part of Kant's argument towards property rights is in his statement of the general principle of external acquisition. In discussing this principle Kant writes of the acquired right that is intelligible possession in terms of its original acquirement. The condition of this original acquisition of intelligible possession is that it is not derived from another. Kant determines the act that establishes the acquired right of intelligible possession in relation to three aspects. The first aspect is apprehension of an object that involves simple physical taking of an object in physical terms. The second aspect is declaring this possession and my intention to exclude all others from it. The third aspect is the key one however as this involves appropriation through the act of a general will. These three aspects correspond very closely to Kant's description of the three syntheses in the Transcendental Deduction of the First Critique. Synthesis of apprehension is described in accord with the act of apprehension that merely involves physical taking. The synthesis of imagination requires a rule that regulates serial reproduction and this is in accord with the declaration or statement that must accompany rightful possession in original terms. The synthesis of conceptual type is a synthesis of recognition through universal marks, and this accords with the universal will that has to operate the universal recognition that is given in appropriation. The addition of this third part of the argument towards property rights is to restate the necessity of a general assent in order for rights to possession to have their rule-governed claim to physical things recognized.

Exposition of the 'right to a thing'

Kant now returns to providing a further exposition of the nature of what is involved in the claim to 'right to a thing'. Whilst the nominal definition of this is that it is 'a right *against every possessor of it*' (Ak. 6:260) it is not the case that what enables me to have this right is that I have a direct claim over the thing in question. That would have the absurd consequence of making the thing appear in some sense under obligation to me so that my right would be 'a *guardian spirit* accompanying the thing' (Ak. 6:260). Since the right I have is not therefore conceivably a direct claim over it, there must rather be an indirect claim over it that is mediated through something. Thus the real rather than nominal definition of a right to a thing is that it is 'a right to the private use of a thing of which I am in (original or instituted) possession in common with all others' (Ak. 6:261). This notion of an original possession in common thus emerges as an intermediary between the thing and myself and is the basis of my rightful claim.

This adds considerably to the argument already provided for intelligible possession. Kant, in writing about this notion in general, did not thereby bring in the reference to original possession in common and now that he does so in the further exposition of the notion of 'right to a thing' he connects this claim to external intelligible possession to the natural law tradition. Hugo Grotius, the main source of this tradition, argued for a notion of original possession in common of all the earth in order to give an account of natural justice as the basis of social order.[13] Kant aims to show that the notion of a right to a thing 'is only that right someone has against a person who is in possession of it in common with all others' (Ak. 6:261).

After introducing this notion of an original possession in common Kant discusses the nature of original acquisition. Original acquisition would have to concern land, as without ownership of land there is nothing to prevent anything that is claimed as one's own from being removed. That a piece of land can be acquired follows from the postulate of practical right as the claim to it is a claim in accordance with the notion of intelligible possession. But the ability not merely to have this claim even in a provisional sense but its true meaning goes beyond what Kant has established prior to this point.

The reason why it does this is because the type of possession involved in the original acquisition of land depends *directly* and not *indirectly* (as with the case of intelligible possession *per se*) on the relationship to others. That is, the notion of ownership of land includes in its very notion the agreement of all others, as all others have a direct interest in the land and its products so that the acquisition of it includes relation to their consent in its very notion whereas in the case of intelligible possession *simpliciter* the possibility of it merely involves its universality but not a direct thought and conception of the united will of all others, merely the possibility of accord therewith.

The place in Kant's text that seems to me to accord with my presentation of it is in his exposition of the concept of original acquisition of land. Kant here writes:

> The law which is to determine for each what land is mine or yours will be in accordance with the axiom of outer freedom only if it proceeds from a will that is united *originally* and a priori. . . . Hence it proceeds only from a will in the civil condition . . . which alone determines what is *right*, what is *rightful*, and what is *laid down as right*. – But in the former condition, that is, before the establishment of the civil condition but with a view to it, that is, *provisionally*, it is a *duty* to proceed in accordance with the principle of external acquisition. (Ak. 6:267)

Prior to the civil condition there is a duty to proceed in accord with the principle of external acquisition that is given in the postulate of practical right but for this duty to bring about the secure relation that is required to say that we have property we need a civil condition and hence the civil condition is what establishes right to *property*, that is, to the secure holding that is needed. Prior to the civil condition the right to property is not given, as there is only provisional acquisition, not conclusive acquisition. Whilst the acquisition is in conformity with right as it proceeds in accordance with the postulate of practical reason and hence is an intelligible possession that points in its very notion to the civil condition it is not truly property as it lacks the secure characteristic that is required to speak of property. Hence property as secure possession is only given in the civil condition.

The notion of property cannot be regarded as based in labour, as this would be to repeat the notion that right is grounded directly in a relation to the thing. But nor is it based on a real historical notion of possession in common as it was for the theorists of natural law. Rather it is based on original right, that is, the right to intelligible possession but it also gives this right its conclusive basis. The passage to this would require going beyond the boundaries of private right as we can see that property is only given in the civil condition whilst the condition of natural right provides only the provisional basis on which the right to presumptive claim to property is given but not really property right itself.[14]

Contract rights

The notion of contract is the last notion treated with any length in Kant's account of private right. Once more the notion really requires the transition to public right and Kant's treatment of it explicitly includes recognition of this. Kant describes what the notion of a contract involves in the following manner: 'An act of the united choice of two persons by which anything at all that belongs to one passes to the other is a *contract*' (Ak. 6:272). Some of the detail of the manner in which contract is characterized involves difficulties too intricate to treat here.[15] The key aspects of it that I wish to discuss involve the manner in which this notion extends the account given thus far of the rights of possession and how the account necessarily moves us towards the considerations of public right. Included under this latter heading are also the peculiar status of a *social contract* in Kant, a notion that surely needs to be related to the account of contract in the treatment of private right.

In describing a contract as involving the passage of something from one person to another Kant is obliged to discuss the conditions under which this passage has to be conceived: 'what belongs to the promiser does not pass to the promisee (as acceptant) by the *separate* will of either but only by the *united will* of both, and consequently only insofar as both wills are declared *simultaneously*' (Ak. 6:272). As with intelligible possession generally so a contract that involves a passage of claim from one person to another must extend beyond the conditions of space and time that are required for theoretical comprehension. This is how Kant interprets the symbols that are used in contractual agreement to indicate the joint consent of the parties to its terms such as the shaking of hands as a way of manifesting the simultaneous nature of the declaration. However, since such symbols in fact are only apprehended under the conditions of experience that accord with theoretical conditions of cognition they never succeed in manifesting the practical nature of the promise here made. Kant indicates that this reveals that there does need to be given a transcendental deduction of the conditions of contract formation.

The deduction involves, however, a simple pointing to the conditions that have to be given to describe the nature of a contract. Such an involvement as a contract specifies can only be described in intelligible terms, as it is only under these terms that it is possible to suspend the involvement of spatio-temporal determinations. Kant states this when speaking of the departure from these determinations in contractual relations: 'The theory that it is possible to abstract from those conditions without giving up possession of the promise is itself the deduction of the concept of acquisition by contract' (Ak. 6:273).

The possibility of promising is itself based upon the categorical imperative (Ak. 6:273) and the notion of this can be applied to relations as we are aware from the Second Critique only in the form of a typic (not a schema of object-determination) or, more expansively, in a schematism of analogy. A contract is in fact only the rightful possession of another's promise (Ak. 6:274). Hence a contract is not a right to a thing directly any more than property rights are to be regarded as such and like property right contract right involves a necessary reference to the 'idea of the *choice of all united* a priori' (Ak. 6:274). I have a right *to* the thing only once it has been delivered, until this point it is a right to the promise that has been acquired. 'My right is only a right against a person, to require of the seller performance (*praestatio*) of his promise to put me in possession of the thing.' (Ak. 6:275).

The question of the exercise of contract right, however, leads us very easily to the boundary between private right and public right. Under the heading of contract right Kant includes marriage right. Marriage right, which involves mutual acquisition of each other's sexual organs (Ak. 6:278), is grounded on the notion of humanity in our own person and hence on universal claims to the condition of external freedom as expressed in rationality.[16] But Kant's statement that a mere contract without physical interaction does not constitute a marriage contract requires him to state that this contract is not merely '*pacto*' or a contract *simplicter* but also '*lege*' or something that requires an actual law to govern it and a law that specifies physical actions in conformity to it.[17] Since this is so it follows that although marriage right as an example of contract right is a natural right and hence pre-political, it is in fact only under the condition of the civil condition that it can really be said to exist, just as property rights depend also on this condition.

Since parental right, which Kant treats next, is only guaranteed as a stable condition of marriage right it must also be the case that it depends upon the civil condition (although Kant does not mention this in his exposition of it). Similarly, the right of a head of the household, a right that includes contractual control of servants requires recourse to lawful force and this can only be guaranteed if there is a lawful state to regulate and inform its operation. The operation of contract right hence really requires a civil condition just as property right can only be said to be existent as secure holding of rightful possession in this condition. The basis of the exchange that is at work in contract requires a law that enables the enforcement of the contract in question and it also requires a medium in which exchange can be given an abstract form. There are two such mediums: one for the representation of how things are moved from one to another (money) and the other for how ideas in general are conveyed (books). Both these mediums of abstraction require and yet also enable the regulation of exchange itself in a lawful form.

The transition from private right to public right

It is already clear that whilst possession in general can be justified outside of the civil condition that its security and hence its conversion into property requires the civil condition. This is even more apparent when we look at the basis of regulation of property claims in the notion of contract. If intelligible possession is itself pre-political then so should be the contractual transfer of such. But just as intelligible possession is completely insecure unless it can be made so by a coercive power that guarantees it so also a contractual exchange requires a medium in which it can be given universal form and this medium itself requires guarantee of its operation. The guarantee is a system of public laws. Hence it is no surprise that Kant writes: 'A rightful condition is that relation of human beings among one another that contains the conditions under which alone everyone is able to *enjoy* his rights, and the formal condition under which this is possible in accordance with the idea of a will giving laws for everyone is called public justice' (Ak. 6:305–6). Public justice involves protection of the status of what is held, regulation of contractual exchange and interconnection of laws into a unitary whole.

Prior to the rightful condition that is public there is only a state of nature. Kant indicates that there could be in such states provisional holding of right perhaps in terms of domestic right only. But even domestic right is in fact, as we have seen, in need of external forces that enable it to be held together (not least in the personal relation that is marriage right). The real problem with the state of nature is now stated by Kant to be that in such a state there is no 'distributive justice' by which he means an interconnection of laws in a unitary whole. The rights that we have deduced in the discussion of private right and which could be discussed prior to an account of political forms are what would have to regulate the political form and make it a rightful form. 'From private right in the state of nature there proceeds the postulate of public right: when you cannot avoid living side by side with all others, you ought to leave the state of nature and proceed with them into a rightful condition, that is, a condition of distributive justice' (Ak. 6:307).

It is not possible – and this is clear from the argument about original possession in common – to live without others. Hence it is not possible to have a rightful state without a civil condition. This is established by thinking of right apart from such a condition and it becoming clear how the securement of right requires this condition. This is sufficient to establish the move to an account of public right. However, in setting out such a discussion two questions must be borne in mind. First, the argument thus far to the condition of public right has turned very much on the notion of possession in common. Whilst this is an idea for Kant not a description of an historical condition does not his use of it involve him in a type of natural law argument not least given his extensive treatment of pre-political conditions of right? Second, what place does the notion of a social contract have in Kant's thinking and how is it related to his description of contract right? These two questions can be simply united in a third: how does Kant succeed in marrying contractarian ideas with ones derived from the tradition of natural law? Before proceeding to attempt to address these questions in terms of accounting for Kant's discussion of public right it is worth finally summarizing the importance of the treatment of private right and how it leads us to the notion of public right. Kant in a powerful paragraph at the beginning of his discussion of public right provides this summary himself:

> If no acquisition were cognized as rightful even in a provisional way prior to entering the civil condition, the civil condition itself would be impossible. For in terms of their form, laws concerning what is mine or yours in the state of nature contain the same thing that they prescribe in the civil condition, insofar as the civil condition is thought of by pure rational concepts alone. The difference is only that the civil condition provides the conditions under which these laws

are put into effect (in keeping with distributive justice). – So if external objects were not even *provisionally* mine or yours in the state of nature, there would also be no duties of right with regard to them and therefore no command to leave the state of nature. (Ak. 6:312–13)

The statement of the importance of the account of private right here is significant. The civil condition is itself only possible because of the rights that can be established as necessary even without it being invoked. The civil condition provides the conditions of securing rights not the basis of rights themselves. It is only because rights are justified separately from the civil condition that there is a real basis to the command to enter this condition in the first place.

The nature of the state

The description of public right turns on the account of the state. The notion of the state involved in Kant's account is clearly the state as an idea based on norms that are the way in which we can regulate the operation of any existent state in accordance with pure right. Whilst the state itself is presented as containing three authorities (sovereign, executive and judicial) the key connection between the state and the notion of private right rests within the sovereign legislative authority. Kant characterizes this as belonging to 'the united will of the people' (Ak. 6:313) just as he presented the original possession in common in relation to a notion of united willed action. The key point now is that we are given the shape of the social contract as resting upon this united will because of the fact that it is only such a will that can provide the basis for public right. As the arrangement of affairs on behalf of another is always capable of wronging that other, a state of right is one in which the consent of all is requisite to ground it so that: 'only the concurring and united will of all, insofar as each decides the same thing for all and all for each, and so only the general united will of the people' can found the sovereign legislative authority (Ak. 6:314).

If the notion of original possession in common indicated a connection between Kant's account and that of natural law theory this claim about the legislative sovereign authority having to represent the united will of all to be rightful echoes the claims of the social contract tradition, particularly as found within the work of Rousseau. Whilst the natural law tradition is departed from by Kant's insistence on thinking of the original possession in common as an ideal notion however his relation to the social contract tradition appears to be one of much greater acceptance of the terms given to him by tradition. Rousseau's account of the social contract is extraordinarily similar to Kant's and, given the early impact of Rousseau on Kant, it is difficult not to think that this is a deliberate echo. Rousseau describes the social contract as reducing to the following formula: 'Each of us puts his person and all his power in common under the supreme control of the general will, and we collectively receive each member as an indivisible part of the whole'.[18]

Whilst the natural law tradition is said to tend towards conservatism, the contractarian tradition, not least as represented by Rousseau, points towards a radical notion of republicanism. Kant's difference from both these traditions does not prevent him from borrowing from both in a unique synthesis of elements. After describing the nature of this social contract as involving the notion of a rightful condition as it must have a form that could be consented to by all Kant describes the members of the state thus formed as *citizens* of it. The rights of the citizens require an integral comprehension of them as free in terms of giving laws to which they could consent, equal in terms of moral capacities and independent in terms of owing their existence within the commonwealth thus constituted to their own efforts and not on dependence on others. This last attribute turns out to be important in terms of how Kant's republican constitution is to be located in representative terms. The independence of the citizen from requirement of good offices of others gives the citizen their civil personality. The civil personality is what gives a right to vote but once this is stated it becomes necessary for Kant to distinguish between active and passive citizens and assign this voting right only to the former.[19]

Whilst this description of the nature of citizenry within the state has its difficulties the precise justification of the social contract itself is one that is in accord with Kant's description of the realization of the condition of external freedom. Kant indicates that the relinquishment of the state of nature is not a surrender of freedom but the finding of freedom as 'dependence upon laws' and this is entirely as we would expect from the discussions of private right. Whilst Kant does have clear reasons for thinking that freedom is really based on regulation by law, as it is only in a civil condition that the prime requirements of external freedom can be met, the description of sovereignty to which he is led by the contractarian strand of his argument is arguably in tension with the natural law basis of argument towards the civil condition. This can be seen for example when Kant rejects the notion that it is possible for the citizen to have any rights over the sovereign and is emphatic in the rejection of the right to rebellion (A6: 320–2). On a pure natural law argument the citizen has a clear right against the sovereign and this authorizes the possibility of rebellion, a fact that militates against the conventional assumption that natural law theory is conservative.[20]

Kant here follows Rousseau very closely and in doing so adopted a view of sovereignty that few now find acceptable.[21] However the argument takes a rather surprising turn when it becomes clear that for Kant a successful revolution is one that cannot further be challenged as he rejects the historicist premise on which such a rejection would be based (Ak. 6:323). Hence whilst Kant's position does not authorize any right of rebellion it also disallows any response to successful revolution and thus de-legitimates traditional authority. This double effect of Kant's position attests to the peculiarity of the treatment of the social contract in Kant's account. If we compare the social contract to a contract right then in the case of the latter we possess only a promise and in the case of the former that promise is one of order. If the authority breaks down the promise that it has contractually committed itself to is no longer delivered and hence there is no longer a sovereign to who I am bound. This is one potential line of argument in any case and one that would suggest that the alteration of Kant's argument here indicates the oddity of the type of contractarianism to which he is committed.

That this question in fact has some far-reaching implications in the overall assessment of Kant's position is in my view incontrovertible. I will therefore wish to return to viewing other aspects of it in due course. Prior to doing so it is worth rounding out the nature of state authority and sovereignty in Kant's account. Since the sovereign is the guarantor of social order and since the basis of this in terms of the original agreement is the unified will to possess land it is not surprising that the sovereign is the supreme proprietor of land without of necessity having any private claim to any land (Ak. 6:324). One of the important effects of Kant's formulation here is to prevent there being any claim to an hereditary basis for any corporation or grouping has a claim to land by virtue of perpetual possession (Ak. 6:324). This anti-feudal thrust of Kant's argument may be part of the rationale for the sweeping role given to the sovereign as such power protects the united legislative will from being usurped by a class that would place itself above the law that is given by such a will. This applies as clearly to the church as to any hereditary noble order (Ak. 6:325).

The direct claim of the sovereign over land is the effect of the argument that any particular claim to possession of a right over a thing is only indirect. Whilst this indicates the principal claim of the state authority in positive terms is grounded in the main negative right that underpins the whole Doctrine of Right Kant also maintains that there is an indirect claim that can be made by the sovereign power. What is this claim and what makes it indirect? The claim in question is the right of the sovereign to 'impose taxes on the people for its own preservation' (Ak. 6:326). The preservation in physical terms of the people is a clear duty of the state as it is supposed to be the guarantor of the welfare of the people. The notion of welfare that it is necessary to invoke here however indicates the 'indirect' nature of the claim involved. Kant is clearly setting out a basis for the state as based on concepts of strict right not on the eudaemonistic notion of 'welfare' that accords in political terms to the notion of happiness rejected by him as a ground for the pure principles of morality.[22]

Kant refers here to 'reasons of state' that authorize the government to constrain the wealthy by means of taxes to provide for the poor and needy. The reason of state in question is clearly the necessity for the order that the state is the guarantor for in terms of its protection of property to be fulfilled. But whilst this commitment to guarding welfare is one that the government is hence only indirectly involved with it is none the less a right of state as Kant makes clear by indicating that there is here coercive right involved and that the protection discussed is one that is not to be regarded as voluntary.[23]

The type of indirect obligation that Kant conceives of is however of a very rudimentary emergency kind and does not reach the level of involvement in for example matters of public health that are now routine in Western societies. The degree to which this indirect obligation is capable of being pushed on Kant's account here is unclear not least because of the fact that it involves principles of application and a consistent rule for the use of such, a rule not stated at this point in his account. There is however no principled statement here that would militate against such extensions as Kant, unlike libertarians today, does not issue any stern strictures against such extension on behalf of his prior lexical prioritization of the notion of liberty.[24]

The other aspects of Kant's treatment of the position of the sovereign that are of some interest are his account of the distribution of offices and dignities and the treatment of punishment. With regard to the distribution of offices however Kant imposes a severe constraint on the sovereign's power, a constraint that emerges from his treatment of the notion of the legislative united will of all. This united will, states Kant, must wish for anyone who fills civil office to be qualified for such and since it is clear that such qualification takes many years preparation and training he states there can be no grounds for the sovereign claiming a right to remove any such offices (Ak. 6:328). Since the appeal here is to the basis of sovereign power itself as given in the social contract, this is an element of limitation of sovereignty that is based on the rightful claim of such sovereignty itself.

On the same grounds of appeal to the fact that all laws must be grounded in universally applicable principles as would be assented to directly by the united will of all Kant presents his rejection of hereditary claim to office deeming such claim a 'groundless prerogative' (Ak. 6:329). This is one part of his treatment of dignity and is in accord with the fundamental claim that freedom, as a supreme principle, has to be understood as also involving formal equality. The same point undergirds Kant's rejection of slavery and even of serfdom (Ak. 6: 330). The key claim to dignity that rests upon the principle of humanity in one's own person and hence on the supreme principle of right is one that seems to be tested most delicately by the state's claim of a right to punishment of offenders.

The notion of a right to punishment is one that is grounded only on the fact that the one punished has committed a crime (Ak. 6:331) not on any claim to interest in the welfare of the criminal or interest in his well-being even in a moral sense. The law of punishment is a 'categorical imperative' that has to be applied in terms of the principle of formal equality (Ak. 6:332). This leads Kant to a striking retributivism:

> Accordingly, whatever undeserved evil you inflict upon another within the people, that you inflict upon yourself. If you insult him, you insult yourself; if you steal from him, you steal from yourself; if you strike him, you strike yourself; if you kill him, you kill yourself. But only the *law of retribution* (*ius talionis*) – it being understood, of course, that this is applied by a court (not by your private judgment) – can specify definitely the quality and quantity of punishment; all other principles are fluctuating and unsuited for a sentence of pure and strict justice because extraneous considerations are mixed into them. (Ak. 6:332)

The argument here is illustrated by two key examples. One concerns theft. Since theft is the crime that undercuts the principle of external acquisition it is a crime that makes right in general insecure. The criminal who commits this offence hence in principle challenges any securing of right and because of this must face a loss of rights to the extent that he is 'reduced to the status of a slave' (Ak. 6:333) at least for a time.[25] The other key example is murder. Since the principle of equality ensures that all are treated as alike in terms of rightful appraisal the extinction of a member of the civil order can only be matched states Kant by the capital penalty (Ak. 6:333–4).[26] The only case where Kant indicates exception to this is in terms of seditious groupings of large extent where there may be recourse by executive decree to banishment or deportation (Ak. 6:334). The exception indicated is an interesting one since it does not touch the case of a common murder committed either on grounds of mercenary type or in terms of alleged appeals to passion. Other exceptions that are admitted however as exceptions include cases of infanticide and duelling.[27]

Whilst Kant's treatment of punishment accords in general terms with retributive notions of punishment it is justified clearly in terms of a concern with right rather than a basic notion of belief in punishment as something that is dependent upon results in terms of ordered relations emerging from its use. This neglect of consequentialist arguments for punishment is again in accord with strict right but the adaptation of the principles of retributive punishment is made in accord with principles of application that extend the consideration of right in terms that do include consequentialist elements. This mixture is part of the difficulty of conceiving the Doctrine of Right as a combination of elements as the application of principles is not itself given the level of justification that the principles themselves are.

The conclusion of Kant's treatment is with relations between states. This treatment raises some of the key problems of the Doctrine of Right. I will leave consideration of these problems however until after a treatment of the Doctrine of Virtue as we will note that the unification of the *Metaphysics of Morals* requires an understanding of these matters. Suffice it to say, however, that whilst a state is a law-governed guarantor for right there is still something provisional about right whilst states are still separated from one another and in a state of nature with regard to each other. This indicates the need to think the conditions for overcoming the divisions between states as a way of transcending finally the state of nature. That such a transcendence will require returning to questions about history, moral progress and eschatology should however be clear and this is the reason why I wish to leave consideration of them until Chapter 8.

The social contract, natural law and the ethical nature of right

In setting out an overview of what we have uncovered as the central concerns of the Doctrine of Right it is necessary to return to the vexed question of the relationship between the contractarian and natural law elements of Kant's views. Leslie Mullholland claims, for example, that the difficulties in Kant's treatment of original possession in common indicate the necessity of attributing to Kant the key principle of consistency (rather than universality) and to treating the justification of the rightful claim to property as being based on need: 'He suggests that the unavoidable conflict of wills concerning land leads to the assumed *need* of everyone to have rights to land if they are to live and exercise freedom'.[28] This argument is, however, strikingly implausible since Kant could not commit himself to justifying principles of strict right by reference to principles based on needs. Rather the need that exists to protect life must rather be grounded on a commitment to the value of the life that is being protected and this therefore refers to the principle of the end-in-itself that we have uncovered thus far as the key notion of the Doctrine of Right.

If we think of this principle of the end-in-itself as the notion that allows the categorical imperative application within the boundaries of strict right, then we can immediately see the account of right as being clearly part of Kant's moral philosophy. Whilst this is so there is a distinction to be drawn between moral philosophy and ethics as the latter concerns the validation of all duties as based only upon self-given law whilst strict right is not such that it must be taken as the ground of maxims. If right is a moral doctrine of external relations based upon the fact that persons are ends-in-themselves then the notion of a social contract is one that appeals to this rationality considered as a unitary force (as in the kingdom of ends but without the internal lawgiving comprehended as applicable across inner as well as outer relations and without being considered as explicit law for any one of the wills concerned). This is the reason why the social contract argument in the Doctrine of Right is peculiar. It is not merely that Kant does not present the social contract as something anyone ever assented to, it is also something no one explicitly ever needs to assent to. It is a mere idea, albeit a constitutively necessary one for the very notion of a civil condition.

It is the same with the notion of original possession in common. The invocation of a notion that comes from natural law is not based as it would be within the traditions of natural law in terms of the ends a being must have and is consequently not part of a teleological argument concerning nature. Rather, it is intended to apply the principle of universality to the argument in favour of intelligible possession. That possession has to be conceived of as intelligible enables escape from the antinomy of possession and provides a first justification for the notion of possession. But until the criterion of universality has been applied to the principle of intelligible possession the claim to it has not taken the form of an obligation. Applying the test of universality to the principle of intelligible possession allows this principle to be adopted as the form of a world. This form of a world is however the civil condition. Therefore, Kant's use of this argument differs from the natural law tradition in not being the prime basis for the justification of possession but its secondary basis and being grounded not in an appeal to natural capacities but to criteria of universality.

However, the other interesting aspect of Kant's relation to these two traditions is found in the equivocation over the role of the sovereign. Whilst the sovereign is conceived in keeping with the social contract tradition as an authority that is ultimate there are still grounds for limiting the extent of his power (as with regard to civil offices) and even a justification if not for a right to rebellion at least for a defusing of legitimist counter-revolutionary claims. Here Kant indicates a certain allegiance to the type of thought involved in natural law thinking. This is in the sense that the extensive treatment of private right has provided the basic guard-rails around the sovereign's exercise of authority and in doing so instituted a bulwark against the slide towards absolutism within contract theory. The paradoxical consequence of Kant's theory however is revealed precisely in his ambivalence towards the notion of absolute sovereign power. Unlike many contemporary authors Kant sees the notion of an absolute sovereign power as potentially benign as it is precisely the basis for a response to special claims to rights as hereditary or feudal claims and indicates a potential alliance between the universality of rights and a stable sovereign power.[29] Thus the type of power seen by many today as destroying rights was seen by Kant in an anti-feudal connection.

Whilst this helps to explain the situation within which Kant's account of sovereignty developed and some of the purpose it served it also suggests the contingency of the argument in favour of absolute sovereignty and a needed counter-balance to it. This can be found, however, in precisely the types of argument that Kant believed help sustain the notion of absolute sovereignty. Just as the basis of rights is universal application of them so also the rejection of a power that attempted to distort the principles on which its own power was grounded can be given as based on the universal united will of all as no sovereign has, on Kant's own account, the right to impose laws that the will of all could not possibly consent to. But abrogation of the condition of right in terms of the destruction of security in possession would be such an attempted legislation and would therefore be a case in which the sovereign power could be rightfully resisted. This would point again however to a need to think the principles of application further. Finally, Kant's resistance to such a right of rebellion is clearly based on the conviction that a state of nature is a worse condition even than despotism as it provides even fewer protections for right and that any rebellion could lapse into such a state of nature. Whilst this argument has much merit it is not as powerful as the observation that lack of security in a despotism is no improvement upon a state of nature, at least for substantial groups and that these groups therefore have the right, if necessary by force, to institute a civil condition.

In response to the questions of Thomas Pogge it is clear that Kant's account of right is part of his moral philosophy and that it is comprehensive. Difficulties of application do abound and need to be given further treatment but that the account harmonises with and requires Kant's previous account of freedom is evident and this indicates the comprehensiveness of Kant's treatment. I will now turn to providing a similar overview of the Doctrine of Virtue preparatory to the concluding consideration of the unity of practical reason in Kant's treatment.

7
The Ends of Virtue

The Doctrine of Virtue, the second part of Kant's *Metaphysics of Morals*, is, without doubt, the work in which the greatest number of statements supporting the interpretation of his practical philosophy as I have presented it can be found. It is also the culminating treatment of strictly ethical questions that Kant had for many years been labouring to produce. It is hence of prime importance in my treatment, as it was for Kant himself. In recent years, after two centuries of almost total neglect, this work has begun to receive critical attention. The nature of this attention has been such however as to concentrate primarily on 'problems' with this work rather than attempting to set out the prime principles underlying its architectonic. A prime reason for this has been a noted failure to reach consensus concerning this architectonic. Hence the prime task of this chapter is to present an account of the principles underlying the division of the material in this work and in the process to discuss some of the key features that come to light once this is done. I wish also to present a 'difficulty' of my own, a 'difficulty' concerning the treatment of one of the perfect duties to oneself and to trace the source of the unease I have with the treatment Kant gives to the area in question to some of the earlier statements of his position in lectures on the same area. The purpose of presenting this difficulty in the context of a chapter that is designed primarily to clear up difficulties is to begin the task of probing the resources of Kant's treatment of ethics once this treatment has been clarified in its principles.

Virtue: a combination of teleology with perfectionism

In the prefatory material to the Doctrine of Virtue Kant sets out an unmistakable case for viewing ethical considerations in terms of teleological standards that involve an orientation towards perfectionism. In contrasting the Doctrine of Right with the Doctrine of Virtue he writes the following:

> The doctrine of right dealt only with the *formal* condition of outer freedom (the consistency of outer freedom with itself if its maxim were made universal law), that is, with **right**. But ethics goes beyond this and provides a *matter* (an object of free choice), an **end** of pure reason which it represents as an end that is also objectively necessary, that is, an end that, as far as human beings are concerned, it is a duty to have. (Ak. 6:380)

The distinction between the treatment of right and that of virtue involves two different elements. First, whilst the treatment of right is concerned only with *formal* conditions, the treatment of virtue concerns *matters* of choice or objects of choice. Second, the treatment of right is purely in relation to outer freedom but since the treatment of virtue is related to the activity of choice of objects for the will it must include within its province inner freedom or the setting of ends. This concentration on ends is constitutive of the treatment of virtue. It marks Kant's ethics as teleological.

However, if Kant is necessarily concerned with purposes when he sets out his treatment of ethics it is particular types of purpose he will be concentrating on, purposes that it is a duty to have. Ends that are also duties are the province of the account of virtue and this is why Kant describes ethics as 'the system of the *ends* of pure practical reason' (Ak. 6:381). In making this statement Kant is clear that the treatment of moral philosophy in his critical works is no more than a propaedeutic to the discussion of ethics proper, a discussion conducted necessarily in terms of ends. This does not of course mean that ends are treated as a pre-existent given to which the categorical imperative is now expected to adapt. It is in the Doctrine of Right that there was such an adaptation of the principles of morality to ends, with an allowance for ends to be selected according to whatever principle one wished as long as they in execution conformed to a general rule of conduct. But with ethics it is quite otherwise as in ethics 'the *concept of duty* will lead to ends and will have to establish *maxims* with respect to ends we *ought* to set ourselves' (Ak. 6:382). So the categorical imperative has to enable us to think of how to connect the concept of duty with that of an end in general.

The connection is made through the notion of ends that are also duties. Kant suggests that there are two ends or general purposes that can be adopted and, since the adoption of them is a duty, should be adopted. They are the perfection of oneself and the happiness of others. Since the distinction between perfection and happiness is accordant with the two elements of the *summum bonum* it is not a surprise that Kant should present these two as involved with ends that are duties. The adoption of one's own happiness as an end that is a duty is not entirely removed from consideration as there are circumstances in which neglect of one's happiness positively promotes ends that are dissonant with duty, conditions such as misery and destitution. Hence there are general reasons for being concerned with one's happiness in relation to moral ends but the adoption of one's happiness as an end is not something that one has to be (morally) constrained to do.[1]

The perfection of others is something I cannot promote as this perfection is clearly in accordance with autonomy and I am not able to make someone else autonomous. Since these principles of perfection and happiness are the ends we can adopt and that we also should adopt we need to gain further insight into how Kant specifies their content and the manner in which he relates them to the categorical imperative and the formulations of the *Groundwork*. In discussing perfection Kant rejects a theoretical understanding of it in terms of totality and explicitly adopts a teleological understanding of perfection as 'the harmony of a thing's properties with an *end*' (Ak. 6:386). Kant gives both a general explication of this notion and specific instantiations of it. The general explication is that this duty of making oneself perfect 'can consist only in *cultivating* one's *faculties*' meaning talents (as in the third example in the second section of the *Groundwork*) and cultivating one's will 'so as to satisfy all the requirements of duty' (Ak. 6:387). The specification of this general explication of the concept of perfecting oneself refers to two specific duties: raising oneself from animality to humanity (which clearly involves becoming involved with one's own autonomy at the expense of inclinations) and cultivating the will up to the purest disposition so that the law itself operates as our incentive and this disposition would be 'inner morally practical perfection' (Ak. 6:387).

The specification of the duty of perfecting oneself is however still clearly itself very general and requires further treatment. Before it can be given it, however, it is necessary to look at the framework in which Kant will separate out the two forms of specification. Prior to this it is first necessary to look at Kant's treatment of the duty of promoting the happiness of others. With regard to this Kant is brief as this notion is necessarily indeterminate given the different matters involved for others in terms of their happiness and he merely specifies the limits of this end in terms of my right to refuse others things which they may think will make them happy but which I do not, a limitation evidently related to a prohibition on satisfying ends of others which directly or indirectly compromise the moral standing of these others.

The categorical imperative is related to these two ends as in ethical consideration it is not actions themselves that are the object of the moral law; rather it is the maxims of actions that are tested by the relation to the test of universality. So, it is the basis on which particular choices of actions are decided, that is itself brought into view and this basis is what is tested. This produces as its consequence an interesting development in Kant's thinking. Whilst often characterized as a rigorist in moral terms, both by himself and others, Kant now makes clear the limits of this characterization:

> If the law can prescribe only the maxim of actions, not actions themselves, this is a sign that it leaves a playroom (*latitudo*) for free choice in following (complying with) the law, that is, that the law cannot specify precisely in what way one is to act and how much one is to do by the action for an end that is also a duty. (Ak. 6:390)

This key notion of 'playroom' or 'latitude' indicates that ethical duties have a type of obligation which is, in Kant's own terms, 'wide'. The question of the nature of this 'playroom' and the limits of it have bedevilled attempts to interpret the Doctrine of Virtue (in ways that I will specify below).

This is not the only problem however with Kant's description of the nature of duties of virtue. Subsequently, Kant connects this notion of a 'wide' duty to that of perfect and imperfect duties in the following manner:

> The wider the duty ... the more imperfect is a man's obligation to action; as he, nevertheless, brings closer to *narrow* duty (duties of right) the maxim of complying with wide duty (in his disposition), so much the more perfect is his virtuous action. (Ak. 6:390)

Not only is this statement itself rather opaque, it is made even more so by Kant's statement that imperfect duties are duties of virtue, a statement seemingly in contradiction to the treatment in the Doctrine of Virtue of such matters as perfect duties to oneself and perfect duties to others. The relationship between wide and narrow obligation would be straightforward if narrow obligation simply meant a duty of right and wide obligation a duty of virtue. The reason for supposing this is precisely Kant's treatment of duties of virtue as being imperfect duties, but this leaves high and dry the treatment of perfect duties to oneself and others, duties which seem then not to fit the Doctrine of Virtue at all. I will look at the various attempts that have been made in the literature to disentangle these strands below.

Before looking at the statement of this problem in the secondary literature, the prime problem of the justification of the architectonic of the Doctrine of Virtue, I will first mention the other significant elements of the material prefatory to it. A duty of virtue concerns matter, that is, ends. One of the prime ends given is described as simultaneously teleological and perfectionist. This is entirely in accord with the treatment I have provided thus far of the practical philosophy in general, but dissonant with many treatments of it that are still influential, so it is worth emphasizing again that when Kant sets out the part of his practical philosophy that he regards as providing in a strict sense his ethics (that is, the discreet and continuous application of the principles of his moral philosophy to judgment) one of the prime ways he does so is through the notion of ends, and one of the key ends involved states a perfectionist principle.

Furthermore, in stating the supreme principle of the doctrine of virtue, the principle that sets out the construal of the categorical imperative in relation to ethics strictly speaking he gives the following formula: 'act in accordance with a maxim of *ends* that it can be a universal law for everyone to have' (Ak. 6:395). This is not surprising given what has preceded the giving of this formula but it flies directly in the face of any attempt to construe Kant's ethics in a deontological fashion.[2]

Another point of interest is given in the way Kant distinguishes this supreme principle of virtue from the supreme principle of right. Since the supreme principle of right is no more than a formal statement of the concept of freedom as such Kant describes it as analytic. By contrast, the supreme principle of virtue 'goes beyond the concept of outer freedom and connects with it, in accordance with universal laws, an *end* that it makes a *duty*' (Ak. 6:396). Since the formal principle of freedom was given as abstracting from any end, the provision of an end is a synthetic move, indicating that the supreme principle of virtue is a synthetic a priori principle.

Finally, the account of emotions in the Doctrine of Virtue, an account that I will treat at some length below involves once more recourse to what I termed in the account I gave of *Religion within the Limits of Reason Alone* a transcendental philosophical anthropology. Kant here coins a new term for this: 'anthroponomy' (Ak. 6:406), intended to mark the importance of viewing humanity and human feeling not from the standpoint of an empirically derived study of affects, but rather through a determination of inclination by the law.

This review of the material prefatory to the Doctrine of Virtue has been sufficient to highlight the central questions that need to be addressed in interpreting the work. These questions include a detailed description of the principles underlying the division of the Doctrine of Virtue. Kant divides the elements of the doctrine of virtue into two parts, one part dealing with duties to oneself and the other with duties to others, but each part is subdivided in terms of perfect and imperfect duties. The nature of the reason for inclusion of perfect duties in the Doctrine of Virtue needs to be addressed, as does the rationale for the inclusion of the particular duties given. Another problem concerns the scope of the 'playroom' Kant allows to wide duties. The treatment of anthroponomy seems decisive in Kant's treatment of duties to others as this is divided between duties of respect and duties of love. Hence, a further account of the use of a vocabulary of feeling to describe non-pathological relations needs to be given. I also wish to pose by way of conclusion a problem about this anthroponomy, albeit a problem of a different type to that advanced in the critical literature on Kant's ethics.

Perfect and imperfect duties and the architectonic of the Doctrine of Virtue

In addressing the question of how Kant understands the distinction between perfect and imperfect duty in the Doctrine of Virtue and considering how the use of this distinction provides the architectonic division of the work I wish to address two sets of supplementary materials. First, I will review the use Kant makes of the terms 'perfect' and 'imperfect' duty in his *Lectures on Ethics* and in the *Groundwork*. Second, I will review the attempts made in the secondary literature on the Doctrine of Virtue to provide an account of the use of this distinction within this work. After reviewing both Kant's earlier uses of these terms and the dispute about their use in the secondary literature, I will provide my own account of how they operate within the Doctrine of Virtue itself. Providing the context of Kant's previous use of this distinction is important in terms both of showing that the contrast is not a novel one made in the Doctrine of Virtue and also in assessing whether Kant's use of the distinction demonstrates a development in his thinking. Reviewing the secondary material on this distinction within the Doctrine of Virtue itself, however, is of interest for assessing the degree to which previous treatments of the work have demonstrated a grasp of the nature and reason for the distinction and its prime operative role within the work. In the 1785 lecture notes from Mrongrovius we find numerous references to the distinction. The first use of it aligns it to the distinction between contradiction in conception and contradiction in willing found in the *Groundwork*, a work published the same year as these lecture notes were taken (Ak. 29:610). On this construal imperfect duties concern areas where if a maxim were adopted it would not fail the conception of a world being produced in accordance with, but would violate conditions of, volition within such a world whereas perfect duties are those the opposite of which cannot even be conceived without contradiction. Kant after introducing this distinction here divides morality itself in terms of it (Ak. 29:610).

Kant subsequently relates the distinction between perfect and imperfect duties to the difference between juridical and ethical duties suggesting that perfect duties are juridical and imperfect duties ethical (Ak. 29:618). This alignment is also supported by a statement in the lectures recorded by Vigilantius in 1793 where Kant aligns perfect obligations with the ability to coerce someone to perform them whilst imperfect obligations relate only to one's own moral principles (Ak. 27:528). Vigilantius also records Kant as stating that whilst all laws of right are strict, ethical duties are wide (Ak. 27:536). In the *Groundwork*, Kant, in introducing the examples of duties following the typic of the categorical imperative, stated that the duties were divided between perfect and imperfect duties although the division between these would be reserved for the writing of the *Metaphysics of Morals*. However, in a footnote Kant added: 'I understand here by a perfect duty one that admits no exception in favour of inclination, and then I have not merely external but also internal *perfect duties'* (Ak. 4:421n). Whilst this statement from the *Groundwork* suggests a recognition of the notion of perfect duties to oneself, the reference to duties that admit no exception in favour of inclination is *prima facie* puzzling as would one not expect from Kant the view that no duties could have such exception? I will return to this question in due course.

Leaving aside the puzzling aspect of the statement from the *Groundwork* it would appear from these materials prior to the writing of the Doctrine of Virtue that Kant intended the distinction between perfect and imperfect virtue to match that between narrow and wide obligation and in turn to map this latter on to the difference between duties of right and duties of virtue. This neat synchrony, however, would make no sense of the inclusion of perfect duties within the framework of the Doctrine of Virtue. This is also the conclusion of Mary

Gregor, who in her pioneering study of the Doctrine of Virtue, expressed astonishment at the degree of attention Kant gave within it to perfect duties to oneself. Her solution to the question of the place of such duties within the Doctrine of Virtue is ingenious:

> They are ... derived from the first principle of all duty prior to its differentiation into the special first principle of juridical duty and that of ethical duty, and they therefore belong neither to jurisprudence nor to ethics but rather to 'moral philosophy in general'.[3]

Gregor's solution is to derive perfect duties to oneself directly from the categorical imperative rather than from the supreme principle of virtue and this is the reason for suggesting that they do not belong within the province of ethics strictly speaking. However, in addition to the fact that this requires her to postulate a notion of 'moral philosophy in general' that Kant does not himself employ, her account is made all the more cumbersome by adopting a different solution to the account of perfect duties to oneself from the description of perfect duties to others. Whereas the former belong to moral philosophy in general on Gregor's account the latter are duties of virtue. This asymmetry between the two forms of perfect duty in addition to the postulation of a categorial distinction unused by Kant himself lends Gregor's attempt to deal with this area a baroque character.

Onora Nell (now O'Neill) parts company from Gregor and suggests a different solution to the problem of accounting for the presence of perfect duties within the province of the Doctrine of Virtue. Nell favours distinguishing between two different senses of the distinction between narrow and wide duties. Nell suggests that all duties that focus on omission rather than commission are narrow in requirement:

> That they are narrow in one sense Kant indicates by calling all these duties 'limiting' or 'negative' and even 'narrow', contrasting these with ethical duties of commission which are 'widening' or 'positive' as well as 'wide'. But both sorts of duty are always classified as duties of virtue: they are both duties of wide obligation since they all fall under one or another obligatory end and can only be shown to be duties by applying the first principle of the doctrine of virtue ... 'Ethical duties of omission' though narrow in requirement meet sufficient conditions for being duties of virtue: they can be derived only by applying the Formula of Universal Law to maxims of ends, i.e., from the first principle of the doctrine of virtue.[4]

Nell's argument provides an important corrective to Gregor. Unlike Gregor, Nell does not see it as a difficulty that there are duties of virtue that are narrow in requirement as such duties still have to be derived from the supreme principle of virtue. The mode of this derivation is something that needs to be examined in order to see whether it really is the case that these duties are based upon the supreme principle of virtue.

Whilst Nell is confident in her assumption that the problem identified by Gregor can be cleared up, the confusion around the architectonic of the Doctrine of Virtue is well captured by the following statement made by Walter Schaller:

> The contrast between perfect and imperfect duties does not so much get replaced by the distinction between juridical duties and duties of virtue as supplement it, thereby threatening to thwart anyone endeavouring to classify – systematically and coherently – the moral duties catalogued by Kant in the *Metaphysics of Morals*.[5]

The distinction between perfect and imperfect duties is carried out within the Doctrine of Virtue and is not just as a device to separate the duties of virtue from the duties of right. It is now time to attempt to clear up the confusion that has been generated around the use of this distinction within the Doctrine of Virtue, a distinction central to the organization of material within it.

Somewhat surprisingly none of the authors just discussed, in attempting to clarify this question, refers to Kant's treatment of the division of duties to oneself on two parallel but distinct lines as set out in the fourth section of the work. In this section we will discover an additional complication of the question, which will assist in settling the dispute concerning the place of perfect duties to oneself within the work. Indeed, it is just after presenting an initial justification of the very notion of duties to oneself as such that Kant provides the additional complication that I wish to discuss. In justifying the notion of duties to oneself Kant imagines an objection to this notion on the basis that I cannot bind myself and be both the one who lays down the rule and the one to whom it applies. This objection is cast in the form of an antinomy, but is one that Kant solves with great ease by reminding us of the distinction between our sensible being and our intelligible being and locating the act of law-giving within the intelligible. The point of rehearsing this just prior to setting out a justification of the division of the work will shortly become clear.

The additional complication introduced in the fourth section of the work is to state that there are two distinct ways of understanding the division of duties that is about to be presented, an objective manner and a subjective manner. The objective division is presented in terms of a distinction between formal and material elements of duty:

> The first of these [formal] are *limiting* (negative) duties; the second, *widening* (positive duties to oneself). Negative duties *forbid* a human being to act contrary to the **end** of his nature and so have to do merely with his moral *self-preservation*; positive duties, which *command* him to make a certain object of choice his end, concern his *perfecting* of himself. Both of them belong to virtue, either as duties of omission (*sustine et abstine*) or as duties of commission (*viribus concessis utere*), but both belong under it as duties of virtue. (Ak. 6:419)

So Kant is clear about the place of perfect duties to oneself. He does not, as Gregor suggests, derive them from the categorical imperative directly and include them within the province of something called 'moral philosophy in general', but rather directly justifies them in terms of the supreme principle of virtue but does so in relation to the notion of duties that are active and concern the moral growth of the agent. Such duties are also described by Kant as belonging to the moral 'prosperity' of the agent or to the moral 'cultivation' of him in order for perfecting to be possible. On this basis he also presents this objective division in terms of subordinate general principles that are derived from the supreme principle of virtue. This is stated in the following manner:

> The first principle of duty to oneself lies in the dictum 'live in conformity with nature' (*naturae convenienter vive*), that is, *preserve* yourself in the perfection of your nature; the second, in the saying '*make yourself more perfect* than mere nature has made you' (*perfice te ut finem, perfice te ut medium*). (Ak. 6:419)

These duties that accord to the 'objective' division of the duties of virtue indicate the general maxim underlying all of them. These general maxims in turn should be viewed as ways of instantiating the supreme principle of virtue. Hence, if the supreme principle of virtue concerns the adoption of ends and this adoption of ends that is added to the moral law itself produced a new synthetic a priori principle, we can view this principle in turn as requiring and enabling a further instantiation that allows the moral law to come close not merely to intuition but also to application in cases.

There is still an important question about the nature of this new division that needs to be addressed, namely why would Kant divide duties of virtue into formal and material when he has already stated that these duties are themselves all material as requiring the supreme principle of virtue? – a principle that in its reference to ends incorporates a matter and is hence not merely formal. This complication indicates that whilst duties of virtue all concern ends they do so in two distinct ways. Narrow duties of virtue, which Kant has termed formal and might more properly be termed formal instantiations of a material principle, involve a limit upon ends that orders them in terms of what renders them permissible ends to be adopted. Hence such duties are akin to the duties of right in effectively requiring us to limit ourselves in relation to that which accords with humanity in us, or to put it in terms familiar from the *Groundwork*, they require reference to the notion of ourselves as ends-in-themselves. Hence the lapidary statement copied from the Stoics of living in accord with our nature should be rendered more comprehensively as do not adopt any ends that conflict with the fact that you are yourself an end-in-itself.

Such duties are hence ones that aim at maintaining, as Kant puts it, the moral 'health' of the actor and do so in terms of corrective limits that are set in accord with that which gives the actor agency in the first place. By contrast the duties Kant terms material are more fully presentable as duties not to limit permissible ends but rather duties to expand the range of ends that the moral agent sets herself. In describing this expansive notion of a wide type of duty Kant is thus connecting the teleological supreme principle of virtue with a perfectionist maxim as expressed in the second duty to oneself, which entails that the duties of perfecting oneself are themselves to be understood as being imperfect duties.

This 'objective' division of the material of the Doctrine of Virtue relates to the distinction between perfect and imperfect duties in the following way. If conceived of as allowing no exception in terms of actions then perfect duties are one and all duties of right as the lectures Kant gave occasionally suggest. But if perfect duties are conceived of more broadly not as disallowing latitude *per se* but as severely limiting its scope, then there are perfect duties that are also duties of virtue. Such are described in the notion of 'formal' duties or duties that involve limitation of adoption of ends by specifying the type of ends that have to be regarded as impermissible. By contrast, the notion of imperfect duty involves the notion of 'material' duties or duties that aim at ensuring that the moral agent does not merely protect the conditions of their agency but actively cultivates this agency such that it develops. Such duties are hence in accord with the supreme principle of morality itself, the principle of autonomy. Perfect duties to oneself and others are located under this division and derived from the supreme principle of virtue via the second duty to oneself.

There is, however, yet another way in which Kant explains the division of the Doctrine of Virtue. Whilst the 'objective' manner just examined can be seen as settling the understanding of the scope of duties in relation to the manner in which the categorical imperative is related to either the principle of humanity (via a subordinate principle derived from the supreme principle of virtue) or from the supreme principle of morality itself the second division is termed 'subjective' as it involves a necessary relationship to the distinction between humanity understood in terms of animality and humanity understood in terms of morality alone. It hence bears on the relationship between philosophical anthropology *simpliciter* and the transcendental version of it, anthroponomy. Kant hence describes this division as that between treating the human being's duties to oneself in terms of animal being or in terms of pure moral being. The former are set out in a manner closely accordant with the division given in *Religion within the Limits of Reason Alone*:

> There are impulses of nature having to do with man's **animality**. Through them nature aims at a) his self-preservation, b) the preservation of the species, and c) the preservation of his capacity to enjoy life, though still on the animal level only. – The vices that are here opposed to his duty to himself are *murdering himself*, the unnatural use of his *sexual inclination*, and such *excessive consumption of food and drink* as weakens his capacity for making purposive use of his powers. (Ak. 6:420)

Whilst this description of duties to oneself as an animal being has difficulties that I wish to postpone until later it is clear that the basis of them is given as a 'formal' one if we understand that in the terms of the 'objective' division. These duties concern the phenomenal basis for the possibility of the moral health of the subject and are hence limiting, concerned only with putting out of bounds ends we might be tempted to adopt. The basis of them is hence to safeguard the possibility of agency.

Since the duties to oneself as an animal being are in fact 'formal' duties subjectively represented we would expect that the duties to oneself as a purely moral being are 'material' duties subjectively represented. However, whilst Kant does reintroduce in concluding the discussion of duties to oneself the imperfect duty of perfecting oneself, in treating duties to oneself merely as a moral being he focuses primarily on duties that are once again formal. In introducing the notion of duties to oneself as a purely moral being he states they consist in: 'what is *formal* in the consistency of the maxims of his will with the *dignity* of humanity in his person' (Ak. 6:420). In posing such duties in this way Kant presents the relation between the categorical imperative and the formula of humanity that we have come to recognize as involved in narrow duties that are aimed at restricting the range of ends to the realm of the permissible. The discussion given in the introduction to the account of duties to oneself accords with this:

> It consists, therefore, in a prohibition against depriving himself of the *prerogative* of a moral being, that of acting in accordance with principles, that is, inner freedom, and so making himself a plaything of the mere inclinations and hence a thing. – The vices contrary to this duty are **lying**, **avarice**, and **false humility** (servility). These adopt principles that are directly contrary to his character as a moral being (in terms of its very form), that is, to inner freedom, the innate dignity of a human being, which is tantamount to saying that they make it one's basic principle to have no basic principle and hence no character, that is, to throw oneself away and make oneself an object of contempt. – The virtue that is opposed to all these vices could be called *love of honour* ... (Ak. 6:420)

The prime requirement of the duty to oneself considered as a moral being is hence a negative, limiting one. This is why the treatment of the vices contrary to this duty is the main discussion that follows its statement as a duty. Duties to oneself considered as a purely moral being are thus almost entirely 'formal' duties, like the duties to oneself considered as an animal being. But the convergence between them is not exact as duties to oneself considered as a moral being include the imperfect duty of cultivating one's perfection in the form of encouraging the love of honour, a part of anthroponomy.

We can now understand the division of duties to oneself in a number of distinct but overlapping ways. There are perfect and imperfect duties to oneself. The perfect duties to oneself outnumber considerably the imperfect duties to oneself however and contrary to Mary Gregor's view, Kant does provide a clear justification for the extensive treatment within the work of perfect duties to oneself, a treatment that locates them as derived from the supreme principle of virtue via subordinate maxims. Perfect duties to oneself can be seen to be formal as they are narrow in range and to encompass the whole of the duties to oneself as an animal being and the vast majority of the duties to oneself as a purely moral being. Imperfect duties to oneself which are material duties concern only duties to oneself considered as a purely moral being and also only a small proportion of these. The discussion of the rationale for thinking that duties to oneself even can be said to exist should now be clear as without such a treatment the supreme principle of morality would not be given application to the discussion of cases. Furthermore, unless there are duties to oneself there would be a problem as to how one's own agency could be grasped in terms of the conditions that permit its survival and flourishing. Hence a general justification of the very possibility of duties to oneself was requisite before this discussion could be undertaken and the justification in reminding us of the distinction between our phenomenal and noumenal self enables the duties in question to take the form they do in a subjective presentation.

Before turning from architectonic considerations to the discussion of the nature of the latitude involved in duties of virtue it is worth concluding this survey of the division of the Doctrine of Virtue with a comparison of the treatment of the division of duties to oneself with the division of duties to others. One reason for expanding the discussion to include this comparison is that there are perfect duties to others as well as to oneself. The other major reason is that inclusion of it permits an overall justification of the architectonic of the Doctrine of Virtue.[6]

Duties to others involve only duties to human beings. This is contingent in the sense that any other finite rational being that we were in contact with would also involve us in the same ethical relation but since such relations do not exist there is only one example of a finite rational being. Sub-rational beings are not included within the province of duties to others as they do not themselves possess the characteristics of moral agents although Kant is clear that treatment of such beings does involve indirect duties aimed at preserving the sense of our own humanity. Super-rational beings have been treated extensively in *Religion within the Limits* and are simply discounted from further consideration here.

The division of this area is set out in terms that involve the resources of anthroponomy directly. Since duties to others concern only moral beings, we would be right to expect the relationship between our own agency and those of others to be of central concern here:

The chief division can be that into duties to others by performing which you also put others under obligation and duties to others the observance of which does not result in obligation on the part of others. – Performing the first is *meritorious* (in relation to others); but performing the second is fulfilling a duty *that is owed*. – Love and *respect* are the feelings that accompany the carrying out of these duties. They can be considered separately (each by itself) and can also exist separately.... But they are basically always united by the law into one duty, only in such a way that now one duty and now the other is the subject's principle, with the other joined to it as accessory. (Ak. 6:449)

The first way of explaining the division of duties to others concerns the notion of obligation in relation to indebtedness. Whilst a duty that puts another under obligation makes them indebted to you, a duty that does not put them under obligation is one that you owe others. Hence both types of relation to others involve a form of indebtedness, either on the part of the agent or on the part of others. This might be thought of as the 'objective' manner of dividing duties to others with the duties that are owed to others then being placed as the 'formal' duties that are of narrower requirement whilst the duties that put others into my debt are imperfect duties that have a material character.

This first division is then supplemented by a 'subjective' division in terms of reference to the domain of anthroponomy, with the introduction of the pure feelings of love and respect. This division is different from the subjective division of duties to oneself as here we are dealing entirely with pure feelings and thus solidly on the ground of anthroponomy and do not include data from philosophical anthropology *simpliciter*. Respect is correlated with the narrower duties that I owe it to others to perform. On this basis respect is the pure feeling that encourages me to respect the humanity of others considered in terms of the moral health of others. Love, considered as a pure feeling, by contrast encourages an active attitude on my part that relates to others in terms of the conditions of the moral prosperity of these others and it is this active concern for others that places them in my debt.

On this construal we would therefore expect duties of respect to be primarily negative and duties of love to be positive. This is confirmed by Kant's treatment of the duties in question. Duties of love are summarized under the subordinate maxim of *benevolence*, which involves pleasure in the perfection of others. Duties of respect, by contrast, are placed under the subordinate maxim of 'limiting our self-esteem by the dignity of humanity in another person' and thus involve a limitation on our permissible ends. Since duties of respect involve a limitation on our permissible ends they bear important relation to the majority of the duties to oneself. Duties of love by contrast are perfectionist in nature. That duties of respect are narrow and duties of love wide is a natural consequence of all this (Ak. 6:450).

Hence, duties of love for others are imperfect duties that involve care for the moral prosperity of others, or promotion of the moral perfection of others. Duties of respect by contrast are perfect duties that concern a relation to others that secures the conditions of the moral well-being of others. Duties of respect are what permit it to be said that moral relations exist between us and are hence akin to the social contract in the doctrine of right whereas duties of love aim at creating a moral community that has the same solidity as the political community. Since duties of respect are derived from the supreme principle of virtue via the subordinate maxim of limitation of my permissible ends in relation to the ends of others considered as moral they involve the relation between the categorical imperative and the formula of humanity we have seen to be constantly required for narrow duties. By contrast, duties of love are derived from the supreme principle of virtue by a subordinate maxim that combines the supreme principle of autonomy with a perfectionist principle, as we have noted is required for a wide duty.

We have thus now got in place an account of the principles underlying the division of both parts of the Doctrine of Virtue. Despite the bewildering number of terms Kant uses to mark the divisions of the work we have found the appropriate form to cast these divisions into, a form that allows for recognition of the place of perfect duties as duties of virtue, explains the extensive account of perfect duties to oneself and allows for a correlation between the division of duties to oneself and duties to others. In so doing it is to be hoped that the difficulties expressed by Mary Gregor that led her to adopt such an ingenious notion as that of 'moral philosophy in general' have been resolved in a manner that requires recourse to no such notion.

The nature and scope of latitude in perfect and imperfect duties: Kantian casuistry

Whilst the account of the architectonic thus gives reasons for a certain convergence with Onora Nell there are still some grounds for disquiet with her view. For example she writes: 'Perfect duties cannot consist only of duties of narrow obligation, for then they would all be duties of justice' (Nell, *op. cit.*, pp. 48–9). This suggests that on Nell's view there is only one pattern of narrow obligation, which is the one provided by duties of right. However, this is not in accord with Kant's presentation. I wish now to consider the nature of the latitude that Kant thinks is given to duties of virtue, distinguishing thereby the type of latitude that is permissible in relation to perfect duties both from duties of right and from imperfect duties.

Whilst it has been recognized by commentators on the Doctrine of Virtue that the notion of latitude has to be examined and explicated if Kant's account is to be grasped the attention has thus far concentrated mainly on the treatment of imperfect duties.[7] This concentration is unfortunate as it fails to ensure that the treatment of perfect duties is distinguished from duties of right as Nell rightly requires should be the case and it furthermore ensures that the nature of application of duties of virtue is restrictively examined. Since our treatment thus far of the architectonic of the Doctrine of Virtue has suggested reasons for thinking that despite the different terms utilised in the two parts of the work the division of duties follows a broadly similar pattern it should be possible to understand the distinction of either one of the parts through an examination of only one of them.

Accordingly, I will restrict my examination of this section to the distinction of latitude between the duties of love and the duties of respect. We discovered the prime duty of love to be benevolence and Kant subsequently aligns this duty with what he terms 'the ethical law of perfection' that he takes from the Gospels, namely that we should love our neighbour as ourselves. Benevolence was one of the examples used in the second section of the *Groundwork* and the question of its latitude has been treated previously though not with the intention of distinguishing its latitude from that of a perfect duty to others.[8] Rather than discussing Kant's justification of the notion that benevolence is indeed a duty, a justification that expands upon the account given in the *Groundwork*, I want here merely to set out an account of the latitude involved in its application in cases by contrast with the latitude involved in a perfect duty, a duty of respect.

Since duties of respect are negative in form it will be necessary to view one of the vices contrary to respect to others in order to be able to see the character of narrow or perfect duty. All the vices contrary to respect can be summarized in general according to Kant as expressing a maxim of contempt towards others. It is hence in general plausible to construe the duty of respect as one that requires adoption of a standard that enables moral life to persist. As such it will be shown to have considerable similarity to a duty of right and the distinction between them will in some respects be less decisive than the distinction between the duty of respect and the duty of benevolence. I wish briefly to indicate the nature of latitude involved in these duties and contrast them with duties of right in order that the notion of latitude can be given a general statement of a kind that would permit further investigation and exploration of the Doctrine of Virtue.

There are three duties of love: duties of benevolence or beneficence, duties of gratitude and duties of sympathy. I will return to sympathy in my subsequent discussion of anthroponomy, but will leave gratitude aside. Beneficence is described by Kant as the action in accordance with a feeling of benevolence and is, like the other specific virtues discussed in the Doctrine of Virtue, treated to a very brief justification that is followed by a set of casuistical questions, questions not directly answered by Kant. In order to think about the nature of latitude for imperfect duties it will be necessary to state the principles by which these casuistical questions are governed as only through the understanding of them can we reach an understanding of how Kant thinks latitude is to be grasped as operative.

In the introduction to the Doctrine of Right, Kant makes intriguing remarks about the nature of casuistry. Since ethics involves imperfect duties in all its applications by contrast to duties of right it involves latitude which 'unavoidably leads to questions that call upon judgment to decide how a maxim is to be applied in particular cases, and indeed in such a way that judgment provides another (subordinate) maxim' (Ak. 6:411). We have noted that the organization of the Doctrine of Virtue is itself given by the application of the supreme principle of virtue to the account of particular duties via a subordinate set of maxims. If these maxims in their turn require further maxims to meet cases then we will be led to casuistry, a procedure that Kant specifies as a practice 'in how *to seek* truth' (Ak. 6:411). Since casuistry is a form of judgment, and since the form of judgment in question concerns not the ability to discover something but rather the adoption of a procedure that enables discovery itself to be possible, it bears a remarkable similarity to reflective judgment. Kant described such a form of judgment in the second 'Introduction' to the *Critique of Judgment* in the following way: 'if only the particular is given and judgment has to find the universal for it, then this power is merely *reflective*' (Ak. 5:179). In such a procedure one does not merely apply a rule to a particular, rather one tries to find the rule for the particular. Similarly, with casuistry on a Kantian construal, one attempts to locate the subordinate maxim that allows the particular case to be classified under the general maxim in question. So casuistry has to enable us to locate the type of subordinate maxim that is involved and the manner thereby in which we can determine the scope of the general maxim that this subordinate one is applying.

Since a prime principle of reflective judgment was teleological it is perhaps not surprising that a similarity between reflective judgment and casuistry should be notable. Having made this connection and noting once again the teleological basis of the whole Doctrine of Virtue as given in the supreme principle of virtue it should be possible to locate the casuistical practice and therewith the degree of latitude involved in a duty in terms of a consideration of the nature of ends and the form under which their limitation is considered. Thomas Hill indicates one way in which this should be considered when he writes: 'in promoting an end prescribed by an imperfect duty, one must not do anything prohibited by a perfect duty'.[9] The degree of application of an imperfect duty has to be constrained by the prior requirements of a perfect duty. But in what do the requirements of perfect duties consist? Towards others in eschewing maxims of contempt and towards oneself overwhelmingly it is necessary to preserve the state of one's moral health. Since both involve a relationship to the principles of humanity and autonomy we can say confidently that there must be two clear subordinate maxims in the application of a maxim of beneficence: respect for the others concerned whom one is helping, a respect that ensures that the autonomy of the other is at least not compromised and at best promoted by one's action and protection of one's own moral health in not endangering the possibility of one's future moral well-being.

These subordinate maxims are indeed what we find referred to in Kant's casuistical questions. In addressing the question how far one should expend one's resources in practicing beneficence he states: 'Surely not to the extent that he himself would finally come to need the beneficence of others' (Ak. 6:454). Since we are aware of the standing temptation to vice that arises in situations of poverty and deprivation it would be a violation of a perfect duty to oneself to reduce oneself to destitution in the promotion of the well-being of others. This is sufficient to mark a clear limit on the practice of beneficence. This limit arises from the priority of the perfect duty over the imperfect duty and the nature of this priority is arrived at casuistically by finding the subordinate maxims that must guide the application of a maxim of beneficence.

Another limit to beneficence that again arises from conflict between perfect and imperfect duties is found in the case of someone who paternalistically looks after someone in order to present them with goods that are in accordance with the giver's conception of happiness. The interesting thing about this example is the reason Kant has to fill it out quite as much as he does. Would not the reference to paternalistic action itself be sufficient? No, as the principle of such paternalism has to be disclosed for the problem with it to be revealed. The nature of paternalism is that it substitutes one's own preference for that of another.[10] It is this principle that violates the autonomy of the other and hence presents a clear limit to the practice of beneficence. As Kant puts it: 'I cannot do good to anyone in accordance with *my* concepts of happiness (except to young children and the insane), thinking to benefit him by forcing a gift upon him; rather, I can benefit him only in accordance with *his* concepts of happiness' (Ak. 6:454).

Whilst these casuistical questions are brief and touch only on a couple of points they are nonetheless instructive. It is clear that the limitations upon beneficence concern the prime limits that are instantiated in perfect duties as these limitations govern the whole realm of ethical action. This demonstrates the correctness of Hill's point about the regulation of imperfect duty by perfect duty. In so doing, however, it relates both types of duty back to the supreme principle of virtue and enables the process of latitude to be grasped in relation to permissible purposes. Permissible purposes follow the rule of universalizability and in so doing instantiate the supreme principle of morality, the principle of autonomy. Permissible purposes hence either safeguard or promote the autonomy of others or myself. The limits of beneficence are thus sketched in terms of the application of it to cases via a further appeal to that which grounds permissive purposive behaviour in general. This enables an appeal to the coherence and mutual interconnection of purposes to perform a guard round the area of ethical action (as the notion of purposiveness is in general terms revealed to operate in the Third Critique as that which enables the connection of an aesthetic reflection with a reflection on nature that enables unity of both in a principle).

If we turn by contrast to the treatment of duties of respect, we find at the very opening of Kant's discussion of this area an indication of the latitude involved in this perfect duty. Kant writes:

> *Moderation* in one's demands generally, that is, willing restriction of one's self-love in view of the self-love of others, is called *modesty*. Lack of *such moderation* (lack of modesty) as regards one's worthiness to be *loved* by others is called *egotism* (*philautia*). But lack of modesty in one's claims to be **respected** by others is *self-conceit* (*arrogantia*). The *respect* that I have for others or that another can require from me (*observantia aliis praestanda*) is therefore recognition of a *dignity* (*dig-*

nitas) in other human beings, that is, of a worth that has no price, no
equivalent for which the object evaluated (*aestimii*) could be
exchanged. (Ak. 6:462)

Two things are immediately important about this description of the latitude involved in duties of respect. First, it is presented not, as in the
case of beneficence, at the end of the account of the virtue but at the
beginning. Second, it is not presented in a casuistical form. The reason
for the non-casuistical form is not explainable by the fact that we are
dealing here with a perfect duty however as perfect duties to oneself are
followed by casuistical questions.

In introducing this discussion Kant immediately connects the
account of respect due to others with the respect others owe to oneself.
Hence, it is immediately asserted that there is a relationship that needs
to be observed between perfect duties to others and the perfect duty
that reciprocally follows in what others owe to one. The description of
modesty as a self-limitation indicates that the respect due others is
something that prevents the respect one requires from them to be conditioned by them. This mutuality about the notion of respect is what
designates the problem on my own side to come from denial of the
equality that the virtue in question demands. This equality is one that
over-rides the distinctions involved in such virtues as beneficence.[11]
Disdain for such equality of condition is expression of contempt for
others and this is the vice contrary to the virtue of respect.

That there is latitude involved in such a perfect duty is what is requisite for it to be contrasted as a duty of virtue and hence in some sense
as an imperfect duty with the duties of right. There is latitude in the
sense that the respect I am due is conditioned by the respect I show.
This mutuality is grounded squarely on the equality of dignity that
comes from a shared rationality. But whilst others respond to me in a
way that enables me to come to adopt the necessary self-limitation of
self-love that enables my practice of the virtue of respect I also have to
be active in inducing in others the same attitude. But there is no basis
for denying all respect even to one who demonstrates none himself as
even such an agent has the qualities within them that enable respect to
be given and this attitude conditions the nature of punishments, preventing those that would degrade humanity itself (Ak. 6:463).

How does this degree of latitude differ from that of a duty of right and
on what basis does Kant here omit casuistical treatment? Kant states that
failure in the duty of respect 'infringes upon one's lawful claim' (Ak.
6.464) meaning by this that it directly violates the supreme principle of

morality to fail to note the autonomy of others. This is what causes Kant to label such failure a true vice and a wrong (by contrast with duties of love as failure to perform them does not do anyone a wrong but merely fails to do them a good). This should enable us to locate the nature of narrow duties of virtue in order to see what it is about them that leads Kant to treat them as 'narrow' in relation to other duties of virtue whereas they are 'wide' with respect to duties of right. With regard to other duties of virtue the duties labelled within the terms of the Doctrine of Virtue 'perfect' are narrow in that they define the conditions of living within a moral world in the first place. Violation of such virtues is violation of the laws of the moral world itself and points us to a moral state of nature. This is the reason why Kant can label such violations 'wrong' and bring them into proximity with duties of right. The distinction between such virtues and duties of right is clearly given in general terms in that the latter concern conditions only of external freedom. However in terms of the notion of 'narrowness' this distinction between internal and external freedom has to be understood in the following way: duties of right present the minimal conditions for there being exercise of freedom *per se* in a form that permits the settlement and growth of any group of people. Such a use of freedom is a prerequisite for there being any practice of virtue. Hence obedience to the supreme principle of right is lexically prior to obedience to the supreme principle of virtue.

Not only is this the case but also deviation from the supreme principle of right directly and overtly contravenes the capacity for free action of others. By contrast, deviation from 'narrow' principles of virtue does detract from the ethical conditions of all but does not in itself undermine the minimal moral conditions as specified in duties of right. Lack of respect for another is not equivalent to stealing from them even though the latter action manifests an attitude of the prior sort. Action in accordance with a maxim of contempt for others can be lawful and yet such action is clearly a wrong and as such an action that contravenes the conditions of ethical life.

There is hence no latitude involved in duties of right as such duties safeguard the conditions under which virtue is itself possible even though one can act in accordance with conditions of right and do wrong. The wrong that is thus done is violation of the 'narrow' conditions of virtue, that is, denial of respect. Such denial cannot be lightly undertaken and such denial is not itself permissible but in saying it is not permissible one does not thereby remove latitude from judgments of respect. It is a matter of judgment in cases when someone is arrogant for example. Whereas Kant's description of this vice has great precision in indicating that action in accord with such a maxim is a demand that others hold themselves worthless in comparison to oneself there are certainly occasions in which people have precedence over their natural equals. Such occasions are not themselves manifestations of disrespect but could rather be ceremonial recognitions of respect due achievements. But since the exaltation of even talent is something that has to be held within limits it would be correct to think that there are degrees of allowance for such events or prece- dence's. This is how latitude is present within even a 'narrow' duty of virtue, a latitude not present in a duty of right where outward action is regulated in accordance with a maxim that may not be held by those to whom it is applied but the application of which creates the possibility of a moral world and this moral world is the ground on which ethical action and ethical dispositions can flourish.

A final question remains as to why Kant did not include casuistical questions in regard to respect although he does this with regard to per- fect duties to oneself. The reason is that with regard to perfect duties to oneself it is necessary to be on one's guard with regard to oneself whereas with others the centrality of respect is the basis of moral rela- tions with them in any sense or degree. To the extent therefore that one is able to watch over oneself with regard to perfect duties to oneself there is a basis for thinking that the duty of respect for others will not need special attention of the kind at work in casuistry, this is the reason why Kant can set out the latitude involved in this duty directly whereas elsewhere the procedure of casuistical questions has to prompt us indi- rectly to reflection upon subordinate maxims.

Anthroponomy: Kant's account of pure feeling

A familiar accusation raised against Kant's treatment of ethics is that it does not provide any account of emotions. Since this is regarded as a fault the nature of the 'fault' in question is worth considering. It seems prima- rily to reside in uneasiness about the capacity of a moral agent to operate with sensitivity to cases requiring it if there is no development of some form of 'moral feeling'.[12] In response to this challenge I wish therefore to point out and draw out the degree of use Kant makes of the notion of pure feeling, a notion prominent in the account of duties to others, an account even divided between duties of love and duties of respect.

We have already noted the extensive development of a transcenden- tal philosophical anthropology in *Religion within the Limits of Reason Alone*. The development of this extensive form of moral psychology fol- lowed the discussion within the Second Critique of an 'aesthetic' of practical reason. This treatment is carried further still in the Doctrine of Virtue. In describing the disposition of inner morally practical perfection Kant writes:

> Since it is a feeling of the effect that the lawgiving will within the human being exercises on his capacity to act in accordance with his will, it is called *moral feeling*, a special *sense* (*sensu moralis*), as it were ... it is a moral perfection, by which one makes one's object every particular end that is also a duty. (Ak. 6:387)

Kant's discussion of this notion is a well-kept secret amongst Kantian scholars and philosophers.[13] This discussion does not contradict his repeated denials that inclination can have any place in determining moral maxims as it is not included as a pathological feeling but as a pure feeling. The place of such a pure feeling within Kant's account is directly continuous with the description of moral psychology provided within *Religion within the Limits of Reason Alone*. Just as within the earlier work Kant described the propensity to evil as 'radical' so also moral feeling is an original possession (Ak. 6:399).

As it is an original possession the obligation with regard to moral feeling is to *cultivate* it. 'This comes about by its being shown how it is set apart from any pathological stimulus and is induced most intensely in its purity by a merely rational representation' (Ak. 6:400). This setting apart of moral feeling from any pathological stimulus is what enables it to be classed as a *moral* feeling and this setting apart was described both in the Second Critique and in *Religion within the Limits of Reason Alone*. The means by which the moral feeling is placed within us can no more be described than could the origin of evil but the means by which moral feeling can be cultivated is open to description, it is through the development of conscience in order to 'sharpen one's attentiveness to the voice of the inner judge, and to use every means to obtain a hearing for it' (Ak. 6:401).

The development of conscience is the key to the understanding of practical feeling. Cultivating moral feeling through sharp development of our conscience requires an aesthetic of morals states Kant, echoing the view of the Second Critique. Such an aesthetic of morals is a subjective presentation of the metaphysics of morals 'in which the feelings that accompany the constraining power of the moral law (e.g., disgust, horror, etc., which make moral aversion sensible) make its efficacy felt, in order to get the better of *merely* sensible incitements' (Ak. 6:406). The appeal to such a range of feelings is an indication of the degree to which

Kant found it possible to expand anthroponomy. The method of expansion of practical feeling is characteristically through use of a method of vivid presentation that follows the pattern of the typic as when Kant describes virtue as something that possesses one rather than being something one possesses. This personification is an aesthetic device, the same device utilized in the schematism of analogy of *Religion within the Limits of Reason Alone.*

Alongside the use of devices that awaken disquiet and are patterned on a schematism of analogy there is also the appeal to the key notion of honour as involving the 'final end' of the existence of the moral agent. Honour is here understood again purely, that is, as a form of practical wisdom that presents humanity in accord with the ideal of moral perfection. To have honour in this sense is to have the courage of virtue (Ak. 6:405). We can connect these terms also to the division of duties towards others in terms of duties of love and duties of respect. Respect is the prime element of practical feeling as it is the wonder at autonomy's existence. Respect is connected to love in the sense that love is the development of an active respect for others that promotes the well-being of them. As such, practical love is simply active respect but such active respect is the development of a relation to others that permits the horizon of moral history that Kant outlined in *Religion within the Limits of Reason Alone* and the *Conflict of the Faculties.*

Since practical feeling develops a central aesthetic element of Kant's practical philosophy the general failure to acknowledge it is evidence of a lack of vision in relation to the resources of transcendental philosophy. If all emotion is pathological then there exists no non-empiricist account of emotion. What Kant's treatment of anthroponomy shows is that an alternative to empiricist treatments of feeling does exist and resides in the setting out of pure feelings, feelings that are related to and based upon the moral law itself. These feelings show an emotional life that is not thereby impure or empirical but rather grounded on the finest aspects of humanity as captured in Kant's transcendental vision. The description and development of them is central to challenging empiricist accounts of volition and motivation as through such an account it becomes possible to describe a moral psychology that is able to describe the character of moral agency and in describing it to allow for moral education, moral development and moral history. This is the reason for Kant's inclusion of an 'ascetics' in the doctrine of method of the Doctrine of Virtue and the casuistical questions are also included as a way of awakening practical judgment, a judgment that requires sensitivity for its application, hence a moral feeling.

The intimate importance of this notion for the setting of the Doctrine of Virtue can be seen with the discussion that closes the account of duties towards others, an account of friendship as a union of respect and love. This discussion of moral friendship locates the attitude involved as a perfect relationship that 'actually exists here and there' (Ak. 6:472). Whilst Kant describes the relationship involved as one that is delicate the union of these two pure feelings together marks an acme of the treatment of anthroponomy. Within pure moral friendship a relation to another is set out that is emblematic of the moral community Kant would point us towards, a society of friends. Whilst this indicates that feeling is of prime importance in Kant's treatment of virtue it is necessary constantly to be aware of this as a practical feeling as the inconstancy and lack of moral focus of pathological feeling is still precisely ruled out.

It is worth mentioning in concluding this account of anthroponomy a reservation that has been raised as to the capacity of such an account to reply to the objections of those who wish for a fuller account of feeling from Kant. This concerns his treatment of one of the duties of love, the duty of sympathetic feeling. The offending passage is the following one:

> It was a sublime way of thinking that the Stoic ascribed to his wise man when he had him say 'I wish for a friend, not that he might help *me* in poverty, sickness, imprisonment, etc., but rather that I might stand by *him* and rescue a human being'. But the same wise man, when he could not rescue his friend, said to himself, 'what is it to me?' In other words, he rejected compassion. (Ak. 6:457)

In this example Kant seems both to endorse the sympathetic feeling expressed in the first citation from the Stoic and also to distinguish this, with approval, from the notion of compassion, a notion the same Stoic is shown to reject. The citation is, in general terms, thought to indicate that for all Kant's professed concern with the development of sensitivity in terms of moral feeling the type of feeling he wishes for is one that is not suitable for human relations.[14]

Kant in his treatment of sympathetic feeling distinguishes this feeling as a moral feeling from the receptivity given through nature to sympathetic joy and sadness. Hence he is intending to mark a demarcation in the treatment of the duty of love that is the duty to develop sympathetic feeling between the moral element of sympathy and the purely pathological element as evidenced in the compassion expressed towards the suffering of others independently of the adoption of any maxim to act towards others in such a manner that the development of mutuality within humanity is directly helped through being placed on a moral footing. This is what distinguishes the two statements of the Stoic as the rejection of compassion is the rejection of action in accordance with a maxim based on pathological reaction. What Kant concurs here with the Stoic about is the rejection of the notion that there could be a *duty* to have a compassionate relation to others, not least because it would be akin to stating 'an insulting kind of beneficence, since it expresses the kind of benevolence one has toward someone unworthy, called *pity*; and this has no place in people's relations with one another, since they are not to make a display of their worthiness to be happy' (Ak. 6:457).

This further discussion makes clear that this duty of love is once more given a limitation in relation to the perfect duty towards others, the duty of respect for their autonomy. It is in fact an expression of respect for these others that is here intended in rejecting an intrusiveness that cannot offer help but only display a fine feeling. The peculiarity of this however is that after making this statement Kant goes on to state that there is an indirect duty to cultivate the feeling of compassion as a means to developing sympathy based on moral principles and he uses this as a means of urging visits to places where the poor live (Ak. 6:457). Since the distinction in kind between sympathetic feeling as a pure feeling and compassion as a pathological response has just been made clear this is odd as now Kant uses the compassionate feelings in a form of typic that suggests an element of moral education can be allotted to them. If this is the case, however, it becomes less clear why one should endorse the Stoic's attitude, an attitude we have located as based on attentiveness to respect for others.

The casuistical questions that follow the treatment of sympathetic feeling concern gratitude as much as sympathetic feeling and it is the problems with gratitude that are mainly here highlighted in terms of how in rendering someone a service for which there is reason to expect gratitude a relation of inequality is created, a relation that creates resentment. This helps a little with the question of sympathetic feeling however as clearly if there is a problem with expressing sympathetic feeling to one who has given one help there is likewise a difficulty in giving help. The difficulty in giving help is creating a situation in which the one helped becomes a dependent and in this way loses their autonomy. This is what the Stoic is warning against and this is the nature of the problem with action on a maxim of pity. However, whilst this problem is real, this does not prevent it from being the case that the development of sympathetic feeling is a duty. The reason it is a duty is clearly because it is a form of moral feeling that promotes mutuality of concern and development. The provision of guard-rails around this virtue is delicate for the same reason that the union of love and respect in moral friendship is delicate. Just as friendship can be compromised through too active a stance of beneficence being adopted by one friend towards the other so the sympathetic feeling can be compromised by undercutting either the conditions of agency of the other or by providing me with an attitude that does not promote mutuality but merely gives occasion for insulting displays of concern that offer no help.

Whilst the difficulties with this example would be worthy of an extensive treatment the nature of the problem that Kant here touches on would not be avoided by one who based their account of moral concern on pathological feeling. Under such an account there could be much greater reason for concern given that a proliferation of action in accordance with maxims of pity is wont to produce very disturbing results and it is such an appeal that would lie at the heart of the alternative account to Kant's.

A problem with perfect duties to oneself: masturbation and *crimina carnis*

The importance and scope of Kant's notion of anthroponomy does not prevent enquiry into the treatment he gives to pathological relations. Whilst I have expressed reasons for thinking providing a morality based on inclination would mark the reverse of an improvement on Kant's account there are in my view aspects of Kant's treatment of sensible relations that provoke disquiet. The area in which my disquiet is concentrated is with regard to one of the perfect duties to oneself, a duty to oneself considered as an animal being. It is presented as 'article II' of the treatment of such duties and is headlined 'On Defiling Oneself by Lust'. Developing the account of natural ends provided within *Religion within the Limits of Reason Alone* Kant uses the resources of the typic to discuss a purposive notion of human bodily capacities. This discussion is related to the justification of marriage right in the Doctrine of Right and concerns, as befits a perfect duty, a limiting law. Practising the virtue of modesty in relation to the topic under discussion, Kant is very circumspect about what he is here treating, but it is clearly masturbation, a 'vice' on Kant's construal and one he connects intimately with homosexuality when he writes:

> Lust is called *unnatural* if one is aroused to it not by a real object but by his imagining it, so that he himself creates one, contrapurposively; for in this way imagination brings forth a desire contrary to

nature's end, and indeed to an end even more important than that of love of life itself, since it aims at the preservation of the whole species and not only of the individual. (Ak. 6:425)

Before directly treating this account in terms of how it is presented in the Doctrine of Virtue I wish to connect it both to earlier lectures on ethics and also to other resources within the work that give it buttress.

In the lectures from Vigilantius of 1793, Kant is reported as stating that the first right and duty of man in his own person is never to treat himself as a thing (Ak. 27:601). In the lectures from Collins from 1784–5 Kant includes a discussion of *crimina carnis* that lumps together masturbation, homosexuality and bestiality. Leaving aside bestiality, it is worth looking at the reasons given here for regarding masturbation and homosexuality as vices. Of the former Kant states, as in the Doctrine of Virtue, that it involves a misuse of the sexual impulse that conflicts not merely with the ends of humanity but even with animal nature. The treatment of homosexuality here is strictly parallel as this is regarded as contrary to the ends of humanity as it does not preserve the species (Ak. 27:391).

Within the Doctrine of Virtue Kant attempts to provide a proof for this conviction but admits it is not easy to provide one that is rational (Ak. 6:425). The attempt he makes is as follows:

> The *ground of proof* is ... that by it [unnatural lust] the human being surrenders his personality (throwing it away), since he uses himself merely as a means to satisfy an animal impulse. (Ak. 6:425)

This involves a comparison of this 'vice' to suicide in the sense that the consideration of it shows that it involves a denial of the principles of moral life. However, a difficulty arises when the casuistical questions are presented. Kant here discusses the question whether sexual activity that does not take procreation into account is permissible and mentions women who are sterile or even who feel an aversion to intercourse. With the latter example Kant comes close to making an allowance for the practice of 'self-defilement' in terms of allowing the permissive law of exception in terms of prevention of a greater violation that may ensure through unfaithfulness.

The allowance of sexual relations within marriage that are not capable of procreation weakens the argument that states that it is only in accordance with a purpose thought of as nature's in accordance with a typic that provides a basis for allowance of sexuality. But since marriage right is in any case a duty of right it is more apropos that Kant conceives of the possibility of exception in cases where this may be the only release for one of the parties involved. This permissive rule suggests a degree of latitude that is surprising for a perfect duty.

There are further problems. The exposition of this duty in accordance with the typic is no longer plausible in an age in which the procreation of the species no longer requires intercourse between two individuals due to the availability of artificial means of enabling conception. In such circumstances the typic's use can be seen to be illegitimate and to be based on taking a contingent end for procreation for a necessary end. With the removal of this support for the argument it is worth asking on what the argument is truly based: the typic or a statement that permits its use as support?[15] If we remove the typic there is still an element of Kant's argument in place, which concerns the treatment, involved in masturbation of oneself as a thing. It is worth pointing out that it is only with reference to masturbation that this applies, not with regard to the treatment of homosexuality. But whilst the treatment of oneself as a thing is against the central rules of duties to oneself, it is plausible to conceive of a contract between the noumenal self and the phenomenal self that permits the use of aspects of the phenomenal self for the purposes of temporary pathological pleasure under a restrictive rule that does not permit ends that run directly contrary to those of morality itself.

The importance of such a contractual settlement being entirely self-given is that it would permit a use of oneself as a means and yet also an end in itself, a mutuality impossible when one trades one's body with another. An objection to this would be that the restrictive rule would have to prevent this action, the very action it is intended to permit. The reason for thinking this can rest only on the ground that to treat oneself in terms of pathological demands is precisely to fail to treat oneself morally. However Kant's permissive rule in relation to the marriage relation indicates that this is far from a compelling argument as it fails to relate to the duty to oneself that is involved in ensuring one's happiness, let alone the question of whether certain actions are permissible, as Kant suggests here in his casuistical question, if they prevent worse from taking place. Furthermore, there is no solid ground for the view that this form of self-relation permits the analogy with suicide drawn by Kant.

This analogy is really justified only by the typic as the action in accord with an impulse if regulated in a contract given to oneself would cease to have the unsettling effects Kant regards it as having. Thus the argument in general terms does not meet the requirements of a perfect duty as its degree of latitude even in Kant's own terms is far too wide, the use of the typic is illegitimate, the analogy with suicide ruled out both by the failure of the typic and the permissive rule that Kant himself appears prepared to countenance and which ensures that the 'vice' in question cannot be characterized in the strong terms Kant uses. Put together these arguments seriously weaken Kant's position and suggest that at best the discussion of this question should be included under imperfect duties to oneself, not least the central perfectionist model of taking virtue as one's central inclination. Even within such a purview, however, a restrictive permission from a basis in self-given contract that gave strict grounds of permission and abstention is conceivable, plausible and surely more reasonable. The disquiet I have over Kant's treatment of this question does alert one to the potential for a degree of attention to the role and limits of imagination in Kant's work as it was the provision of an imaginary object in the practice of masturbation that seemed to provide Kant with his first ground for disapproval, a ground however out of key with the extensive allowance given to the purely pathological element of compassion.

In resting my treatment of the Doctrine of Virtue here I am conscious of a large number of discussions within it of considerable interest that have not yet been addressed. I will now attempt to set the discussions of the Doctrine of Virtue into closer relation to the discussions of the Doctrine of Right in order to provide a unitary conception of Kant's practical doctrine and to relate this to the key notions of his critique of morality.

8
The Final Ends of Practical Philosophy

In this chapter I wish to address two questions that are of ultimate significance for Kant's practical philosophy. First, I will discuss the question of how the two halves of the *Metaphysics of Morals* combine in order to demonstrate the unity of this work. The importance of this is not merely textual as unless the two halves of the work unite there will be a fundamental failure of relation in the discussion of right by comparison with the discussion of virtue. Such a failure would ensure that Kant's concluding statement in practical philosophy demonstrated a failure of scope in this philosophy and an inability to coherently unite discrete treatments. Second, I will address the relationship between Kant's doctrinal practical philosophy and his critique of morality. This relationship is one scarcely touched on within the commentaries on Kant's practical philosophy undertaken within the Anglo-American world to date. But the significance of it is crucial in replying to critics of Kant's practical philosophy. The criticisms of Kant's practical philosophy that are current, from Hegelian inspired work to the more recent concentration on an ethics of virtue, practically all depend on the view that Kant's critique of morality is tantamount to the whole of his practical philosophy. Whilst the investigation of Kant's practical doctrine is itself sufficient to demonstrate the untruth of this widely adopted assumption, a demonstration of the way that the critique of morality actually does relate to the practical doctrine, a demonstration that shows the unity between these two parts of Kant's programme, will present the nature of Kant's work in an overall framework that should prove decisive for future response to his practical programme.

The ambition of such an attempt within the scope of one chapter is certainly large. It will, naturally, not be possible however to include within the scope of this discussion all the types of consideration that could be advanced in terms of assessing Kant's practical philosophy.[1] What will be attempted though is a statement of the general principles that guide the unitary conception of Kant's practical philosophy and the statement of such principles in terms of how they cross the divide between right and virtue and, even more fundamentally, between critique and doctrine to demonstrate the terrain of future engagement with Kant's legacy, a terrain insufficiently mapped within contemporary work.[2]

Peace and the Doctrine of Right

In beginning to treat the question of the unity of the *Metaphysics of Morals* I will look first at the concluding topic of the Doctrine of Right. The final section of the Doctrine of Right prior to the conclusion of the work concerns cosmopolitan right and, as we will see, the conclusion of the Doctrine of Right makes clear that this topic is not to be regarded as merely one amongst others but has a peculiarly important status. The nature of this status is what I will seek to illuminate before turning to a central question about the Doctrine of Virtue that I wish to relate to this topic.

In introducing the topic of cosmopolitan right Kant speaks of the original community of land that all nations could be said to have possessed. Whilst this original community did not lead to a rightful community of possession it is the basis of commerce between peoples. Whilst Kant proceeds with ruminations about settlement of land the key question that promoted in presenting the notion of cosmopolitan right is in terms of a right to visit foreign countries with a view to establishing relations that promote peace. This is subsequently returned to in the conclusion of the work when Kant states that pure practical reason states: '*there is to be no war*' (Ak. 6:354). This statement emerges from consideration of a problem about the division of land between settled nations. The problem is that this division whilst emerging from the constitution of rightful states creates between these states a new state of nature. Since this state of nature operates between states the resort to violent means of settling disputes, the means we call by the collective name 'war', has the same status as the use of violence within any state of nature. That is, it may be the provisional manner necessary to defend a rightful claim but without a body to establish rightful claims between disputants it must remain in some doubt which side of the dispute actually can claim their action is grounded on right. Hence in the absence of such an authority the violent resolution of disputes is as plausibly capable of creating unjust conclusions as just ones. Thus war is far from being a good way in which to establish rightful claims.

Due to these considerations Kant speaks of the quest for perpetual peace and the form of constitution most likely to promote it as something that it is a duty to work towards.[3] It is at this point that Kant raises the status of the question concerning perpetual peace:

> It can be said that establishing universal and lasting peace constitutes not merely a part of the doctrine of right but rather the entire final end of the doctrine of right within the limits of mere reason; for the condition of peace is alone that condition in which what is mine and what is yours for a multitude of human beings is secured under *laws* living in proximity to one another, hence those who are united under a constitution; but the rule for this constitution, as a norm for others, cannot be derived from the experience of those who have hitherto found it most to their advantage; it must, rather, be derived a priori by reason from the ideal of a rightful association of human beings under public laws as such. (Ak. 6:355)

Kant also speaks, in the very last line of the conclusion of the work of perpetual peace as the 'highest political good'. This highest political good, the final end of the doctrine of right, is the basis under which property can finally be secured. Without perpetual peace the basis of right is constantly under threat as the state of nature persists, at least between states. With the persistence of the state of nature we have a persistence of uncertainty and the constant possibility of disruption of relations.

Thus the construction of perpetual peace has the same basis as the original contract that brought about rightful conditions. It is a condition that we can all rightfully be expected to join in constituting. There is, however, one central difference between perpetual peace and the original contract that established states of right. This is that in the case of perpetual peace we are dealing not with the obligations that can rightly be expected of individuals but rather those that can be requested of states. Such a request is made thus to a body that itself is the embodiment of right and hence there can be no possibility, as there was with individuals constituting a state of right, of force being used to bring about perpetual peace. The absence of this possibility ensures that the conditions for the establishment of perpetual peace have rather to be sought within the nature of the state itself or deduced from this nature.

Rather than pursue the question further at this point however Kant abruptly terminates the discussion and closes the Doctrine of Right. The conclusion has stated that perpetual peace is the final end of the doctrine of right but has not then provided a very extensive discussion of this final end. How is this to be understood? It could be argued that Kant is here referring the reader back to his earlier statement *Perpetual Peace: A Philosophical Sketch* but this would be an odd conclusion as that work is cast in critical form and it is as the final end of the Doctrine of Right that we wish to consider Kant's notion of perpetual peace. Within the earlier work however Kant did address the problem of the transition from a state of nature between states to the establishment of perpetual peace by the proposal of a federation between the states (Ak. 8:835–6). As in the Doctrine of Right itself however, Kant appeals in this earlier work to the notion of commerce as productive of peace as when he writes that: 'the *power of money* may well be the most reliable of all the powers (means) subordinate to that of a state' (Ak. 8:368) and that money is a power that promotes peace. If money is in fact a power that promotes peace then it is not merely the means in which trade is prosecuted but rather since it regulates the laws of such trade something akin to the sovereign power within such trade. In other words, money is the institution that approximates most closely to the law of cosmopolitan right, the law of promoting peace through allowing exchange between peoples. Money brings about the exchange and regulates its manner. If money is thus conceivable on this basis as a prime institution of right it would seem to have a role in the development of historical relations that is akin to that of providence in a traditional scheme and it is the context of a discussion of the rational guarantee of perpetual peace, a guarantee that Kant *terms* providence, that this discussion is presented. I will now turn to the manner in which Kant limits the province of the Doctrine of Virtue in order to prepare for the first way of presenting the unity of the *Metaphysics of Morals*.

The limits of virtue

Kant concludes the Doctrine of Virtue quite differently from the way in which he concludes the Doctrine of Right. Whilst the latter culminates in a suggestion that there is a final end of right, the former concludes instead with a description of the limits of conceiving duties of virtue. The reason for this difference can be left aside until we have treated the nature of Kant's account of the limits of virtue.

In concluding the account of virtue Kant turns to the topic of duties to God. In so doing Kant distinguishes between the formal aspect of religion and the material aspect of it. The formal aspect of religion concerns the area described in *Religion within the Limits of Reason Alone*, namely duties considered as divine commands, which is the way the schematism of analogy presents our duties to us in intuitive form. By contrast, the material aspect of religion concerns particular special services said to be necessary that we perform for God. Such duties however would not emerge from pure reason but must be dependent on some empirically attested revelation. The use of revelation in the place of reason would ensure that such duties could form no part of a philosophical morality, as it has no grounding in philosophically demonstrable cognition. Hence, if religion considered materially involves us in duties to God, then such duties are beyond the boundaries of virtue.

This contrast between formal and material aspects of religion is in a sense indicative of Kant's special use of history. It is by applying religious notions to the comprehension of history in the process of setting out a schematism of analogy that we derive the fullest use of religious terms within Kant's philosophy. But such a use of terms necessarily takes the terms used beyond the level of religion purely considered and into an application that is dependent not on revelation but on reason.[4] The manner in which this is worked out, and the limits to the possibility of being able to work it out, are given a novel treatment in the conclusion of the Doctrine of Virtue.

> All moral relations of rational beings, which involve a principle of the harmony of the will of one with that of another, can be reduced to *love* and *respect*; and, insofar as this principle is practical, in the case of love the basis for determining one's will can be reduced to another's *end*, and in the case of respect, to another's *right*. (Ak. 6:488)

If the relation of respect involves recognizing right then we can see the basis in anthroponomy for the concept of right. Contrastively, the notion of love as something connected to the relation to ends of others, implies a teleological grounding for pure ethical feeling. This distinction needs now to be related to the involvement of humans with God.

The *summum bonum*, the ultimate good guaranteed by God, includes happiness within its terms. God's love for human beings should be expressed in relation to the ultimate ends of humans and since these ultimate ends are unified in the conception of the *summum bonum*, indicate a necessary concern on God's behalf for human happiness. Whilst the notion of love is expansive, the notion contrastive to it is limitative and sets the basis for allowable ends. This limitative basis has another name in addition to right, justice. Justice in terms of God's relation to human beings involves however, states Kant, 'extravagant principles' that cannot be brought into accord with experience. In saying this Kant does not neglect to set these principles out. Rather the extravagant nature of this treatment is presented according to the usual procedure of a schematism of analogy, in this case presenting punitive justice as personified in the intuitive form of God. Justice is thus presented in a manner akin to a *fate*.[5]

After a series of vivid sketches conforming to this presentation of justice, including reference to the expiatory blood of Christ, Kant writes of this type of use of the schematism of analogy that it:

> Conforms, indeed, with the *formal aspect* of this principle [justice], but it conflicts with the *material aspect* of it, the *end*, which is always the *happiness* of human beings. – For, in view of the eventual multitude of criminals who keep the register of their guilt running on and on, punitive justice would make the *end* of creation consist not in the creator's *love* (as one must yet think it to be) but rather in the strict observance of his *right* (it would make God's right itself, located in his *glory*, the end). But since the latter (justice) is only the condition limiting the former (benevolence), this seems to contradict principles of practical reason, by which the creation of a world must have been omitted if it would have produced a result so contrary to the intention of its author, which can have only love for its basis. (Ak. 6:490–1)

On the basis of this conclusion Kant suggests that the question of the moral relation between God and us is altogether incomprehensible and hence beyond the bounds of ethics. Therefore, it is only the relations of rational beings to each other in the form of our relations between ourselves that can be treated within the scope of ethics.

This limitation of what can be presented within the realm of ethics itself has two consequences, both of which I wish to explore a little further. The first is that the description given by Kant of the scope of providence within *Perpetual Peace* is one that must be regarded as outside the scope of ethics and with this goes outside the scope of ethics the whole treatment of history *per se* even though this treatment appears to conform to the *formal* aspect of religion as Kant defines it in the conclusion of the Doctrine of Virtue. Looking again at the division of religion into formal and material aspects we should remind ourselves of the fact that the application of religious terms to history in accordance with a rational use of the schematism of analogy in fact expands on the concept of duty itself and thus involves more than the formal aspect of religion as the formal aspect is merely a way of rendering duty intuitive. But to treat history in accordance with concepts of practical philosophy is not merely to make duty intuitive, it is to combine duty with the schematism of analogy in order to enlarge the scope of comprehension of application of morally practical principles into an analogue of cognition, thus forming moral history as a distinct enquiry.

The enquiry that is moral history is hence outside the bounds of ethics *per se* as ethics *per se* cannot make use of its terms in setting out principles of duty although this limitation of ethics can lead us to the meeting point in a sense of ethics and right. The way in which this meeting point is approachable can be seen from the second consequence of Kant's limitation of the sphere of virtue. The second consequence is that the positive effect of this limitation is to draw our attention to our duties towards one another as the whole basis of ethics. A final suggestion as to where these duties point us should help to lead us towards the sought unity of principle that enables the *Metaphysics of Morals* to be comprehended as a work that coheres.

Moral friendship and social virtue

In the discussion of anthroponomy in the previous chapter I mentioned the account of friendship as being the acme of Kant's notion of practical feeling. I will now treat this account of friendship as the basis for building a bridge between the treatment of virtue and the treatment of right. Friendship is treated in the same manner as the relation of humans to God, that is, as involving the same combination of practical feelings, love and respect. Whereas the practical relation to God has a clear limit when considered from the province of duties of virtue the notion of this union of the highest practical feelings in a relation to another person is an ideal. The adoption of this ideal is one that points us towards the possibility of achieving the *summum bonum* as it makes us deserving of happiness (Ak. 6:469).

Since friendship involves an equality between those relating to each other and since this equality involves a combination of feelings that pull the friends together on the one hand whilst giving distance between them on the other it is a relation that is fraught with difficulties. These difficulties concern the nature of dignity itself as respect involves showing the other that their autonomy is not compromised by one's relation to them whilst love connects one to the other in a harmony of ends. The basis of friendship fundamentally involves the social necessity of speech and communication (Ak. 6:472–3). The use of these means is the manner in which rational contact with others is constituted. Hence friendship arises from a need to involve oneself in public reason.

If friendship can be connected with the demands of public reason it can also, as a sought goal with another, promote the relation to others in general that is termed philanthropy. Philanthropy is the relation to the group of others as such in terms of pursuit of the happiness of others, the principle that underpins all the duties to others and provides them with their basic principle. Hence if the pursuit of friendship promotes in one the disposition towards the pure moral feeling that underpins all duties to others it is the basis of the essential ethical attitude, certainly so in terms of all wide duties.

Since the notion of philanthropy points one towards a social relation with others on a foundation of ethics it also suggests a notion that, whilst not explicitly mentioned by Kant, emerges naturally from his treatment, a society of friends. In the discussion of moral community in *Religion within the Limits of Reason Alone* Kant wrote of a 'system of well-disposed human beings in which and through the unity of which alone, the highest moral good can come to pass' (Ak. 6:97–8). This highest moral good emerges from the conversion of political community into ethical community. The basis for such a conversion can be found in anthroponomy and this conversion permits the unity in our relations of the highest forms of practical feeling, a unity not conceivable within the conception of our relation to God. Hence, if the kingdom of heaven is not cognisable on the grounds of Kant's practical philosophy in terms of a picture of heaven itself it is presentable in terms of a final goal of history in accordance with the schematism of analogy. Thus one way in which we can picture the unity of the *Metaphysics of Morals* is through the combination of the highest political good, perpetual peace, with the highest moral good, friendship. This is not however the only way and I will now turn to a different way in which the work can be shown to cohere.

Freedom and the unity of the *Metaphysics of Morals*

A different, though not clearly incompatible, treatment of the unity of the *Metaphysics of Morals*, is suggested in the following statement made by Mary Gregor: 'If all moral laws are derived from the supreme principle of morality, the cardinal concept of Kant's jurisprudence, as well as that of his ethics, must be that of moral autonomy' (Gregor, *op. cit.*, p. 63). Whilst the notion of autonomy itself is one that I do not wish to focus on just yet, the implicit suggestion of this quote is that what unifies Kant's treatments of right and virtue has to do with the notion of freedom. Since Kant claims that there is only one innate right and this is the right to freedom and since the operative concept of the whole doctrine of right is external freedom there is no doubting the importance of the notion of freedom in Kant's account of right.

Whilst the account of freedom in the Doctrine of Right is presented explicitly and immediately, Kant subsequently presents it as part of an analytic treatment, as the notion of freedom itself implies external action under some sort of rule. By contrast, the Doctrine of Virtue begins not from freedom but from the concept of duty but presents this concept as concerning the internal determination of the will and hence as involving self-constraint (Ak. 6:380). Since this notion of self-constraint is one that is set out in terms of the ability of the self to be governed by pure practical reason this requires a reference to the *ends* of reason and it is this reference that makes the supreme principle of virtue a synthetic principle. The introduction of this synthetic principle allows for the notion of duties to oneself, a cardinal notion in the explication of virtue. Since this notion explicitly requires setting out concepts of moral personality it leads ineluctably to the notion of anthroponomy. This notion is by contrast nowhere deployed in the Doctrine of Right and it this that makes the province of the Doctrine of Virtue wider than the Doctrine of Right and allows Kant to present all duties of right as indirect duties of virtue.

It is when we have the notion of inner freedom presented positively as an operative concept, that is, when we have the doctrine of virtue, that we are possession of the full notion of autonomy. By contrast, in the treatment of right, we only think freedom as a limit concept, that is, on the model of a necessary notion that has only a negative force. Since this marks the difference between right and virtue we can say that the Doctrine of Right has only a negative notion of freedom, the Doctrine of Virtue a positive one (although even within the Doctrine of Virtue many duties are presented in the form of ones that ensure only moral health, not moral prosperity).

This relationship shows that it is within the doctrine of virtue that the connection is made back with the account of right ensuring that the notion of right is given a second level of justification. This double form of justification of the Doctrine of Right incorporates it into a wider setting of moral description and this wider setting also helps to further establish that the account of right is indeed a part of moral philosophy (and even, though only indirectly, part of ethics *per se*). There are frequent complaints about the limits Kant's account places on political thinking. Howard

Williams, for example, argues that whilst Kant's notion of right is intended to encourage individual freedom and hence to be neutral between the choices made by people it involves a notion of liberty that 'itself implies a view of society and how individuals should order their lives'.[6]

This criticism dovetails with suggestions that Kant's alignment of right with the notion of property is indicative of an inbuilt prejudice towards the form freedom must take, a prejudice that is revealed, for example, in the very form of contractarian argument, an argument that assumes the position of agents on a model of what is occasionally termed 'methodological individualism'.[7] The force of this objection is often unclear. It seems to reside in a twofold problem: on the one hand, Kant's account of right is presented as one that does not involve a positive choice of the good whilst on the other it involves substantive commitments to certain specific 'basic goods'. This criticism can then be conjoined with a disagreement about what should be given the status of 'basic goods' with suggestions contrary to the ones of a commitment to individualism advanced as more congruent with a notion of, to use the fashionable phrase, 'human flourishing'.[8]

The question of whether Kant's predilection for autonomy is too narrow in ignoring other possible positive goods or simplistic in being presented as overarchingly preferable to other goods is one I will leave aside for a moment. Attending instead to the question of covert assumptions in the structure of Kant's thinking I will, in answering this charge, proceed to demonstrate the interdependence of Kant's account of external freedom with his notion of virtue in order to prepare the way for a more extensive account of virtue.

The argument that there is a covert assumption in Kant's account of right that involves a more substantive commitment in political terms than Kant might be thought to be officially committed to seems to me to rest on certain confusions. That Kant's account of right depends on a negative conception of freedom is taken by many to indicate that it is officially presented as substantively neutral between conceptions of the good. Kant does indeed argue, as we have seen, that in terms of strict right, it is not possible to suggest that one can demand that the universal principle of right actually be adopted as anyone's motive in acting in accordance with it. This does hence entail that in terms of the rationale that is given by anyone who operates in accordance with this principle there is no basis, strictly within the notion of right itself, to require *any* given motive for so acting as preferable. In this sense the doctrine of right is supported by a methodological principle that operates on a basis that seems not, on Pogge's construal, to be 'comprehensive'.

If it is merely a matter of the rationales of individuals alone then there is a ground for saying that Kant's universal principle of right is given in a form that suggests neutrality between different versions of the good. However, Kant's critics allege that this neutrality is bogus as the negative notion of freedom that is the basis of the Doctrine of Right has a substantive element, as is clear from its close connection with notions of property and concomitant with this, a form of social arrangement that is based on a substantial material inequality.

That Kant's position does involve an acceptance of these material consequences does not seem to me to be contentious. Does the structure of his thought in leading so clearly to this conclusion involve hidden presuppositions that damage the claim to neutrality between notions of the good? There are two senses in which we could understand this claim to neutrality. Either, what is intended by it is that individuals are left to determine their own rationales for acting in accordance with the universal principle of right or the society that is ordered by this principle is declared to be in itself constitutively neutral between conceptions of the good. If the latter is Kant's claim then we have a clear problem as the society that is governed in its contractual form by the universal principle of right does constrain people to act in terms of a conception of the good in the sense that this society guarantees through its negative notion of freedom a construal of right in terms of the double conception of restraint and restrictive use of resources in the sense of property ownership being guaranteed. Hence if the notion of neutrality is presented as one of societal indifference to social goodness then there is a clear difficulty as the universal principle of the society constrains action in such a way that property-holding is seen as a significant good that requires the organization of constraint and the form of the state to be built around it. Therefore if the scope of the notion of neutrality is said to hold at this level then Kant is placed into an insoluble contradictory bind of holding forth unreserved freedom of conception of the good at the same time as covertly preferring one way of life to another.

There are, however, a number of reasons to assume that this cannot be the sense or scope of the claim of neutrality in Kant's conception. Were this to be the level at which the claim of neutrality held then there would in fact be a peculiarity in attributing to him a notion of methodological individualism in the first place as it would seem that the rationale of his doctrine is based on setting a constraint at the level of the society rather than from his conception of individuals as the basic core of society. The social form constituted through the notion of the

Doctrine of Right has at its heart a commitment to freedom as the one and only innate right. As such, the social whole is not claimed to have neutrality in terms of conceptions of the good. The social whole rather is constituted around a commitment to the notion of what is good, a notion that entirely accords with the whole of Kant's moral philosophy and suggests the 'comprehensiveness' of Kant's account of right. What enables this commitment to a social good that is held to be the basic form of the society as a whole is a methodological neutrality as to what is held to be able to motivate individuals to act in accordance with the universal principle of right. In terms of right there is no problem with instrumental reasoning guiding action in accordance with the universal principle of right. If the reason a shopkeeper, for example, does not over-charge any of his customers, including those unable to know that he has done so such as small children, is because he reasons that only by acting thus can he ensure that he will keep his trade and be best able to com-pete with others but has no interest in or even scorn for the universal principle of right, then he is still acting as rightly as one who actively chose the principle of right as their maxim when regulating their trade.

The level of claimed neutrality is hence at the level of individual maxim formation. Since there are allowed a multitude of rationales for acting in accordance with the principle of right there is neutrality between the notions of goodness held by individuals even though it remains certainly true that the social whole of which they are part is formulated in accordance with a particular substantive conception of the good. This has consequences. For example, someone who holds religious convictions that are not grounded either in part or in entirety on pure practical reason has a conception of the good that is at variance with that which constitutes the society of right. This does mean that the ability of such a person to impose their will on others in terms for example of 'moral' doctrines that have no basis in pure practical reason is severely limited and against the spirit of their views they are forced to 'privatize' their religion. Hence such people can rightly claim that they belong to a society that has a substantive conception of the good with which they do not agree and which they may attempt to influence in terms of polit-ical and religious lobbying. Whilst it follows, therefore, that Kant's account of right is comprehensive as it involves a commitment to the centrality of autonomy and pure practical reason this commitment is not, at the level of right, directly binding on the maxims of individuals and is hence neutral between different rationales for acting in accord-ance with the universal principle of right. That Kant's account does involve a positive and substantive conception of the good is in fact a

central burden of my entire argument. If the Doctrine of Right is interpreted as including such a substantive conception only at the level of the
social whole, not at the level of the individual and hence as forming no
more than the limits of allowable action but not the maxims on which
people operate, then it can be seen that this element of moral philosophy is constitutively negative whilst still remaining comprehensive.

Autonomy, humanity and eschatology

Since the force of the objection that Kant's account of right involves a
presupposition in favour of an ultimate conception of the good really
resides in an argument about what constitutes the good and as to
whether Kant has really circumscribed this conception correctly it is
now worth stepping back to evaluate again how this conception was
arrived at in order to relate the *Groundwork* to the *Metaphysics of Morals*.
It is often overlooked that the *Groundwork* begins with a declaration
about the nature of the good: 'It is impossible to think of anything at
all in the world, or indeed even beyond it, that could be considered
good without limitation except a **good will**' (Ak. 4:393). Given that the
Groundwork is, unfortunately, the work of Kant's practical philosophy
most widely studied, lack of attention to this statement is surprising.
Kant here, in the opening sentence of the first section of the work,
declares a view on what constitutes the good. The notion of the 'good
will' is arguably the central conception of the whole of the first section
of the *Groundwork*. Kant clearly states that the notion of a good will is
equivalent to a 'pure and good will' hence that this conception is the
same in content as the notion of autonomy that the second section of
the work reveals to be the supreme principle of morality.

The focus on the categorical imperative in much work on the
Groundwork has led to a neglect of the supreme principle of morality
although this principle is in fact equivalent to a substantive and positive conception of the good, as stated by Kant at the opening of the
work. In explaining the notion of the good will in the first section Kant
equates the status of the will, in a manner anticipating the accounts of
Religion within the Limits of Reason Alone and the Doctrine of Virtue, with
character (Ak. 4:393). The will is set out by Kant as the manner of volition or the form of choice that guides our maxims. If our choice is to
base our maxims on pure practical reason then we have a will that is
good in itself and indeed the highest good (Ak. 4:397). Hence the will is
nothing else than practical reason as Kant states in the second part of
the *Groundwork* (Ak. 4:412).

If the first part of the *Groundwork* is based on setting out the connection between the good will and duty in order to show, on the basis of commonly available concepts, the basis for appealing to the notion of a pure disposition in morality, then the point of the second part of the *Groundwork* is to provide a preliminary conception of a metaphysics of morals, a conception more limited in scope than given in the *Metaphysics of Morals* itself but centrally in harmony with it. The point at which Kant turns to the notion of metaphysics in the second part of the *Groundwork* is when examining the connection between rationality and morality. It is to try to show an intrinsic connection between these notions that Kant resorts to metaphysics. The manner in which the connection is made is formulated initially in the striking statement that: *'rational nature exists as an end in itself'* (Ak. 4:428). The basis for this claim is not initially evident unless we remember the argument that has preceded it for the view of the absolute goodness of the good will. In that claim was contained the notion of the will as the capacity to set ends for oneself in a pure manner, that is, independently of sensible inclination. Since the argument of the first part of the work gave grounds for thinking of this as the only good that is unconditional we should in reflecting on this startling claim of the second part of the *Groundwork* recall it. If the will is identical to practical reason then to have a reason that relates to volition is to be in possession of that which would have absolute value. Hence, given the linkage between volition and rationality in the notion of practical reason, we have to conclude that the value of rationality cannot be sought in something that is extrinsic to it (in the form of something it could relate to instrumentally only) as it must rather lie in what would make it pure.

This is what leads Kant to move from a negative conception of humanity as given in the end-in-itself formula where humanity is viewed as limited in action in relation to others who also possess rationality to the positive conception of it that is subsequently formulated as autonomy or as a being who, through the will, gives 'the law to itself' (Ak. 4:431). Thus rationality is thought of as an *'independently existing* end' that is not reliant on any other end or as an end-in-itself that gives the law to itself. This status of pure practical reason as the one self-given end marks it out as distinct from all instrumental ends and enables Kant to distinguish between teleology as an account of nature from morals as a doctrine that can be thought of as a pattern for the ends of all nature, hence eschatologically (Ak. 4:437$_n$). The final ends of all nature are given in that which is the absolute good and the principle of autonomy is hence worth citing once more before reflecting once again on its relation to the *Metaphysics of Morals* and the reasons for preferring it as a supreme principle to the communitarian alternatives:

> Autonomy of the will is the property of the will by which it is a law to itself (independently of any property of the objects of volition). The principle of autonomy is, therefore: *to choose only in such a way that the maxims of your choice are also included as universal law in the same volition.* (Ak. 4:440)[9]

The principle hence provides the condition of autonomous action, which is to act in such a way, that the maxims of our action are explicitly conceived of as universal laws in the volition of choosing them. This constitutive limit on our action requires therefore that ethical action is such that it cannot allow disseverance between the adoption of the action and its consistent relation to that which is the end of all nature itself. Hence Kant's ultimate conception of ethics is clearly eschatological.

Mary Gregor makes the connection between this conception of the supreme principle of morality and the account of virtue provided in the *Metaphysics of Morals* in the following manner:

> The freedom from contradiction which he requires in a universalised maxim is ... a teleological consistency between our maxim and our objective, rational ends. Thus in Kant's own account of suicide it is not the self-defeating character of the maxim that makes it immoral. It is rather the fact that, in acting on a maxim of arbitrarily destroying our capacity for free or moral action, we are in contradiction with our objective end as free or moral agents, and so in contradiction with ourselves. (Gregor, *op. cit.*, p. 203)

This notion of a teleological relationship between the maxim and the end in itself that is given to us independently in the form of our rationality is one that accords fundamentally with the thrust of my account. Kant's system of ethical connections in the Doctrine of Virtue is a teleological one that relies upon an ultimate and fundamental notion of the good-in-itself, a good that is equivalent to and provides the orientation for, the end of nature itself and is hence eschatological.

The two parts of the *Metaphysics of Morals* correspond roughly though far from perfectly to the distinction between two senses of the notion of the 'end-in-itself'. The first sense of this is given in the formula of humanity as a limit upon all action, do not act in such a way that you treat an end in itself as a means unless you also relate to it as an end in itself. This negative construal of the notion of the end in itself as limitative on action broadly corresponds to the negative conception of action set out in the universal principle of right as this principle specifies the conditions under which action is allowable. The conditions of allowable action involve constraint on the use of one's freedom in accordance with allowing others the use of their freedom and hence in accordance with an implicit recognition of the status of these others as possessing the same eschatological quality as oneself. Since the universal principle of right is not set as a guidance for maxims however it diverges from the principle of humanity as an end in itself but the presentation of the former as a guidance for maxims is only provisional en route to the provision of the principle of humanity itself.

By contrast, the Doctrine of Virtue in being governed by the notion of internal law-giving follows the principle of autonomy in its basic conception although many of the duties set out can be and are justified only on the grounds of the principle of humanity. These duties are ethical equivalents to the doctrine of right as they allow the possibility of the autonomy of others and this allowance is what makes such duties comparatively strict whilst the wider duties are those which truly allow others to prosper and hence require the adoption of maxims for others that are perfect in form, just as the principle of autonomy itself is.

The criticism that Kant's notion of autonomy is not the only candidate for the place of the good is clearly right if intended only to indicate that other such accounts exist. If intended as an argument in favour of other doctrines than Kant's however, it requires rather more to be added, as it is clear that the rationale behind Kant's notion of autonomy is grounded on a system. The conception of communitarianism considered in the most general terms as the argument in favour of traditional communal virtues that have served us well over time is indistinguishable from conservatism despite the leftist background of many adherents of this doctrine. If the notion of the social good is taken to be prior to the notion of that which forms the grounds for thinking of what would enable each taken separately to morally prosper this can be granted but only in the sense that a state of right is the indispensable condition for the possibility of virtuous action having any stability and lasting effect. If it is to be claimed that virtue is a set of practices that need teaching and cannot be left entirely in the hands of separate persons or group of persons to be formed then it is possible to refer to Kant's treatments of moral education, including the account given in the Doctrine of Virtue, as indications that this is recognized by him. If the appeal to moral education is intended however to render virtue itself dependent on external enforcement then this would seem to render Kant's critics close to the model of Robespierre, a model often invoked against him.[10] A republic of virtue can be brought about only from the universal agreement to leave the moral state of nature, an agreement unlike that to leave the political state of nature, that cannot be enforced. The attempt to enforce such agreement seems however to be the impetus behind the authoritarian impulses of communitarians, an impetus that is perhaps the basic ground to their opposition to the notion of autonomy.[11]

From critique to doctrine: the categorical imperative and the nature of freedom

The connection between the *Groundwork* and the *Metaphysics of Morals* can be shown in terms of the relationship between the supreme principle of morality and the supreme principles of right and virtue. The connection between these principles reinforces the argument for seeing the *Metaphysics of Morals* as unified around the notion of freedom and helps to present a rationale for Kant's presentation of autonomy as the supreme principle of morality. However, this presentation seems to sideline the notion that is most prominently associated with Kant in most contemporary writing on his practical philosophy, the categorical imperative. In thinking of the connection between the categorical imperative and the *Metaphysics of Morals* I wish to return again to the unity of Kant's practical philosophy demonstrating the movement from his critique of morality to his presentation of a positive metaphysics of morals.

As noted in Chapter 3 above there has been considerable controversy about the relationship between the 'formulas' of the *Groundwork* and their relationship. I will now turn to setting out not an account of the formulas distinct from the account given there but a further reason for thinking that the account Kant gives of the categorical imperative in the *Groundwork* is an integral part of his critique of morality and then connecting this project of critique to the doctrinal treatment of morality. At the conclusion of the first part of the *Groundwork* Kant presents the categorical imperative for the first time though without here naming it as such. The context of this presentation is within the attempt to demonstrate, using the principles of ordinary moral thought, that the good will is the only absolute good. Whilst the presentation of the imperative at this time is given within the account of ordinary moral thought the formulation of it is not very different from that of the second section of the work. In the first part Kant gives the formula as: *'I ought never to act except in such a way that I could also will that my maxim should become a universal law'* (Ak. 4:402), whereas in the second section it is given as: *'act only in accordance with that maxim through which you can at the same time will that it become a universal law'* (Ak. 4:421). The difference between the two is that in the first the conditions under which I 'ought' to act are specified whilst in the second the law is itself simply stated. In the first case therefore the formula is expressed in terms of what I should do, hence in a form that directly appeals to me whereas the second simply gives the form of the law itself.

Both formulas, however, specify the same, which is that action should be conducted in accordance with a maxim that I will not merely for myself but universally. This is connected back to the notion of the good will by the statement that what is good in acting in accordance with the categorical imperative consists in 'the disposition', hence in the quality of the will (Ak. 4:416). Since to act in accordance with the categorical imperative is to act in a manner that requires one possesses a good will then evidently action in accordance with this principle is action in accordance with pure practical reason. Stating things this way indicates the intrinsic connection between the categorical imperative and the principle of autonomy, a connection clear in the statements of the two. Both state essentially the same, that is, that the conditions of autonomous action are to have a pure disposition which disposition has to adopt maxims on the basis of their universality.

Whilst the *Groundwork* sets out to demonstrate what the supreme principle of morality is, the Second Critique sets out reasons for thinking that practical reason can be conceived of purely. This distinction between the works gives them distinctive architectonics but no essential differences in argument. As in the *Groundwork*, so in the Second Critique, the categorical imperative is presented as the guide to comprehending morality and the statement of it in the latter work again differs little from the former work (Ak. 5:30). Whereas the earlier work also started by dealing with the good will as it wished to demonstrate on the basis of the concepts of ordinary morality the case for thinking of a good that is unlimited the later work instead begins on a quest for the law in order to establish in accordance with it what the unlimited good has to be. These distinctions in presentation should not, however, be taken to be differences of substantive import as the fundamental principles are the same in both as indicated by the stress in both on the notion of autonomy.

If the role of the categorical imperative is to set out the criterion of universality then the importance of this notion is intertwined with the separation of the moral principle from heteronomous ones. The notion of law as such is expressed for Kant in terms of a necessary universality and what enables the moral law to have this character is its basis in autonomy. Heteronomous principles effectively lack universality and, since they are grounded on something external to practical reason itself, they are not *based* on rationality. The distinction between the moral principle and the principles of heteronomy therefore is that the former is self-grounded and this self-grounding is connected to universality as it rests upon the quality of all rational beings as such whilst the ends given independently of pure practical reason itself are all contingent.

The critique of morality is one that is intended therefore to present the nature of freedom as something that effectively flows from the self-disclosed character of reason itself. The effect of this critique is thus to divide the possible grounds for describing morality into those that arise extrinsically to reason and those that are self-grounded. If the notion of a self-giving of law is granted then with it comes the categorical imperative although in another sense the possibility of thinking one will act in accordance with the categorical imperative is sufficient to think the conditions of freedom. This dual connection is presented from two different angles in the *Groundwork* and the Second Critique as the former has the task of demonstrating the possibility and necessity of a metaphysics of morals on the basis of common conceptions of morality whilst the latter wishes, beginning from the notion of practical reason in general, to demonstrate the case for a pure form of practical reason.

If the primary task of the critique of morality is hence to justify the notion of pure morality through the description of the law of such morality and to connect this law to the nature of the being to whom it is meant to apply then this indicates that the nature of critique is intended merely to demonstrate that moral thinking is possible. The critical works thus describe the conditions under which such thinking is possible and this requires visiting a number of topics from those of the *Groundwork* to those of the *Conflict of Faculties*. But what is not discussed in these works is the manner of application of the moral law save through the necessity of use of the typic. The typic is first introduced in the second section of the *Groundwork* in the presentation of the universal law as a law of nature but much more extensively presented in the Second Critique and *Religion within the Limits of Reason Alone*.

The use of the typic in these works allows a preliminary notion of an aesthetic of morals to be provided, a notion that allows Kant's moral psychology to be given general rules, rules that are more completely set out in the anthroponomy of the Doctrine of Virtue.

Aside from the examples discussed in the second part of the *Groundwork*, the application of the moral law to the consideration of actions or maxims is not set out in any detail in the critical works. The turn from critique to doctrine is the turn from the disclosure of the possibility of thinking morally to the manner in which this thinking has to be conducted in relation to situations. This involves setting out the minimal conditions of morality in terms of the notion of right as conditions that specify the manner in which a moral life can have its material possibility given. These minimal conditions are then expanded into the system of duties Kant promised in the *Groundwork* he would derive from the categorical imperative (Ak. 4:421).

The connection between the categorical imperative and the universal principle of right is not difficult to see. The universal principle of right is couched in universal forms and defines right action as that which can coexist with 'everyone's freedom in accordance with a universal law' (Ak. 6:230). Since freedom is the basis of right it is not surprising to learn that the only innate right is the right to freedom. By contrast the supreme principle of virtue is stated as acting in accordance with 'a maxim of *ends* that it can be a universal law for everyone to have' (Ak. 6:395), a positive conception of freedom that is defined in terms of purposes. The teleological nature of this formula specifies the type of test that Mary Gregor mentions and it relates maxims to the basic end in itself, rationality as the capacity to set ends.

The supreme principles given in the *Metaphysics of Morals* relate fairly directly to the categorical imperative of which they are in fact specifications. The elaboration of the duties as flowing from them has no great difficulties with regard to the Doctrine of Right in terms of relating these duties back to the nature of the categorical imperative itself. The duties of right all have the character of preserving the capacity to act in accordance with the categorical imperative or in other terms conditions that do not inhibit ethical action are provided by this principle. The principle of virtue by contrast specifies the conditions under which the kingdom of ends can be established as something that prospers. It is time now to turn to looking at how the notion of casuistry used in the Doctrine of Virtue relates to the typic as set out in the earlier works in order to begin to think about the way the moral world is mapped by these procedures.

Casuistry and practical schematism

In the previous chapter I explicated the procedure of casuistry in the Doctrine of Virtue with a dual purpose: to explain the way in which anthroponomy is structured in relation to duties of virtue and to give an account of the form of latitude in perfect and imperfect duties. In returning again to look at the topic of casuistry I want this time to relate the use of a casuistical method in the Doctrine of Virtue to the extensive use of schematism elsewhere in Kant's practical works. Since casuistry is a use of judgment it is appropriate to relate the use of it not merely to reflective judgment as was done in the previous chapter but also to the type of judgment that schematism effects.

In order to set out for a final expansive consideration the account of practical schematism and to consider its relationship with casuistry it is helpful to remind ourselves of the roles of schematism in theoretical philosophy, at least as specified in the First Critique. The account of the schematism in the First Critique is introduced as dealing with 'the sensible conditions under which alone pure concepts of the understanding can be employed' (A136/B175) and follows immediately after the demonstration *that* pure concepts of the understanding can be said to apply to intuition in the Transcendental Deduction. The schema is introduced as performing the function of showing *how* these pure concepts of understanding relate to intuition. This takes place by demonstrating that the pure concepts of the understanding are restricted in terms of their application to the formal conditions of sensibility. This account is given in two different and distinct forms. First, the schema of the concepts is set out as applicable to each of them taken separately and hence as an operation carried out on a given particular concept through the provision of its conditions of restriction and realization. This element of the section of the work entitled the schematism is the majority of it. But there is also mentioned in conclusion of this section a broader notion of schematism when Kant describes sensibility in general as realizing the understanding at the same time as it restricts it (A147/B187). This suggests that if schematism can be presented in terms of application to particular pure concepts of the conditions of formal intuition, then it can, in addition, be regarded as a manner in which the faculty of pure concepts is itself determined *in toto* by sensibility.

There is, however, another use of schematism in the First Critique. This is what I would term the 'final end' schema and it is presented in the chapter on the architectonic of pure reason not in the chapter devoted to schematism. In this penultimate chapter Kant is discussing the necessity of system as 'the rational concept of the form of a whole' (A832/B860). In formulating such a rational concept we have need of this third type of schema which is described as 'an essential manifoldness and order of the parts determined *a priori* from the principle of the end' (A833/B861). Here the parts arise from 'a single supreme and inner end, which first makes possible the whole' (A833–4/B861–2). With this type of schema we can see the dependence of the organization of a whole enquiry on a part that makes it possible and is supreme. This is the type of schema that is deployed in practical philosophy.

In practical philosophy we have, it appears, no reference to intuition and hence no strict parallel to the two versions of a restriction and realization schema. However, whilst there is no direct dependence on intuition in practical philosophy it is impossible to operate without recourse to the use of analogy and what I wish to make clear now is how the use of analogy relates to the notion of the final end schema in order to prepare to connect this notion with Kant's practice of casuistical questioning in the Doctrine of Virtue. The first time Kant appeals to a practice of analogical presentation in practical philosophy is in the second part of the *Groundwork* with the introduction of the intuitive presentation of the categorical imperative 'as if' it were a law of nature (Ak. 4:421). At this point, however, Kant does not reflect upon this procedure but merely presents it. In the Second Critique by contrast Kant closes the second chapter of the Analytic with a description of what he terms the 'typic of pure practical judgment', a description which puts forth the presentation of an action as produced by a law of nature, the same example used in the *Groundwork* (Ak. 5:69). On this occasion, however, the rule underlying this analogical procedure is supplied as being a schema 'of a law itself' by which Kant means that: 'in cases where causality from freedom is to appraised it makes that *law of nature* merely the type of a *law of freedom*' (Ak. 5:70). This analogical procedure should in fact be seen as constitutive of the very notion of the categorical imperative itself as the law that is formulated within this imperative is only conceivable to us on the same grounds as a law of nature, that is, as universally applicable and necessary. Kant terms this '*rationalism* of judgment' as here we have only a pure law connected with action.

How does this notion of a typic relate to the final end schema described towards the close of the First Critique? Whilst the final end schema is a way of thinking how a system must be organized, that is, in accord with a supreme inner end that is responsible for the presentation of the parts having a necessary form, the typic supplies the condition under which a pure law is presentable and hence organizes the sensible in accordance with an intelligible principle. On the basis therefore of the typic we can see what shape moral psychology must take and this shape is thus constructed in accordance with this inner supreme end in *Religion within the Limits of Reason Alone* and in the Doctrine of Virtue. What *Religion within the Limits of Reason Alone* terms a 'schematism of analogy' is no more than an application of the typic to the province of conception of moral character, a conception later considerably enriched in the anthroponomy of the Doctrine of Virtue. In both cases we must begin from the law and present the law under the conditions of a law of nature and thereby we will have an *a priori* account of moral character, precisely as we do in fact have it given in these works.

Thus effectively we can now equate the final end schema with the typic or schema of analogy. The operation of the former is the inner principle of the organization of the latter but the latter is the necessary way the former must be exhibited. If this is so, then despite the lack of appeal to the transcendental imagination in practical philosophy this faculty is replaced in effect by something akin in principle in terms of the necessity of appeal to something that makes vivid and intuitive the pure concepts of morality. Here, however, due to the schema in question being a final end schema, the pure feelings that are thus set out in the description of Kant's moral psychology are not given a role as primarily determinative of motivation though they do have an indirect relationship to it as over time the habit of virtue would make the feelings automatic and this indeed is presented by Kant as a necessary process for the inculcation of virtue, as when he describes the processes of moral education and the notion of ethical ascetics (Ak. 6:480–6).

In looking a little further at the nature of Kant's anthroponomy I will return now to the topic of casuistry to connect it with the account thus given of the use of practical schematism. Casuistry is introduced by Kant as something that is '*woven into ethics* in a *fragmentary* way, not systematically ... and is added to ethics only by way of scholia to the system' (Ak. 6:411). Hence the fragmentary character of casuistry entails that it is not governed by the same rule of judgment as practical schematism, it is not a final end that organizes the whole but rather something that is partially introduced. In describing moral education Kant adds that casuistical questions help to add to the *interest* in morality by ensuring that one *loves* it (Ak. 6:484).

Thus the place of casuistry is closely linked to the role of anthroponomy and it is not fortuitous that we find them connected together as just as the development of habits in accordance with virtue helps to make virtue a basic response of the pure feelings so the practice of casu-istical questioning is one of these habits, one that arises particularly in relation to the operation of the pure feelings. If the point of the typic is hence to present the necessary intuitive form of the moral law the point of casuistry is to help the pure feelings it allows interrogation of to develop under the process of self-cognition.

Pure feeling can now be seen to be a product of the law as given under the process of practical schematization and to develop under the impact of casuistry. Since pure feeling is a product of the processes of morality then the personality that is related to by the moral law is itself a pro-duct of this law. This is why Kant refers in *Religion within the Limits of Reason Alone* to rebirth, revolution and moral progress as conditions of there being any discussion of moral psychology. Whilst this suggests that there is pure feeling because there is morality, it would nonetheless follow that the development of the capacity to be receptive to the law, a capacity that has to be original, also has to proceed to be the way in which the law can come to find a home in certain characters. Since there is no room however for a permanent good conscience on Kant's picture no such home can be regarded as durable and so if there is con-stant revolution and rebirth within each one of us it may also be the case that there is no durable basis for moral progress in history. In turn-ing to this question in conclusion I wish to raise the question of the effect the shift from critique to doctrine has on the ability of Kant's practical philosophy to enable us to envisage the prospects for the trans-formation of historical conditions in the light of the demands of the eschatological moral principle.

Practical eschatology and the limits of Kant's practical philosophy

Within Kant's critical works there are four types of enquiry into a notion of practical eschatology. The obvious place where such a type of enquiry can be stated to be presented is in Kant's works on religion where we have a rational presentation of both the notions of the kingdom of God and of radical evil. The first approximation to this is given in *The Final End of All Things* but a much fuller account is given in *Religion within the Limits of Reason Alone*. A second form of practical eschatology organizes the works on the philosophy of history. In these works a notion of progress is set out that attempts to explicate the conditions of realization of the ideals of morality. This takes place within *The Idea for A Universal History* and also in the section of the

Conflict of the Faculties entitled 'An Old Question Raised Anew: Is the Human Race Constantly Progressing?'[12] The third place in which we can discern a thought of practical eschatology is in the account of a final end of for the political in the notion of perpetual peace as set out in *Perpetual Peace* and the Doctrine of Right. Perhaps the most all-embracing notion of practical eschatology however is that based upon the notions of humanity as an end in itself and the principle of autonomy, the principles set out in the *Groundwork* and the Second Critique and which guide the Doctrine of Virtue. This involves a thinking of end *qua* end and is strictly eschatological. It gives the ultimate sense to the critique of morality.

Only the third and fourth enquiries are given both doctrinal and critical treatment. This is why the first suggestion I made about the unity of the *Metaphysics of Morals* concerned the two forms of the highest good, perpetual peace and the social promise of friendship. The thought of eschatology that emerges from the notions of rational religion clearly is integrally linked to the enquiries into historical development and yet Kant nowhere brings these notions together in a work that attempts to disclose the basis of rational hope in terms of a coherent and systematic treatment. This lack of a systematic work on rational eschatology that discloses the doctrinal equivalents of the notions of hope presented within the works on history and those on religion leaves us with a sense of a missing link in Kant's practical philosophy.

Whilst the connection of anthroponomy to the moral psychology of *Religion within the Limits of Reason Alone* is clear there is a constitutive ban at the close of the Doctrine of Virtue into enquiring further about the nature of God's intervention into history and a disquieting failure to unite the notion of God's justice with his love. The Doctrine of Right is constitutively separated from the philosophy of history despite the presence in the marginalia of the work of the extraordinary references to the executions of Charles I and Louis XIV discussed in Chapter 5 above. There thus appears to be an account of right that does not and cannot relate to the prospects for historical progress and an account of virtue that does not and cannot relate to conceptions of theodicy. The status of Kant's practical eschatology thus emerges as constitutively limited to conditions that prevent the full horizon of action being visible either with regard to the historical prospects for moral progress or with regard to the ultimate horizons that are partially suggested by the appeal to the notion of the *summum bonum*. Since Kant's conception of practical eschatology thus has more scope in his critical treatment than his doctrinal one it becomes clear that there are definitive limits to the application of the principles of practical philosophy to intuitive conditions.

These limits of practical philosophy are not the familiar ones of a limit of cognition such as are referred to by Kant at the conclusion of the *Groundwork* when he refers to the 'incomprehensibility' of the moral imperative (Ak. 4:463). Whilst the nature of moral psychology is revealed to us only through the illumination of the moral law itself it would appear that in relation to historical conditions there are two openings that are both partial whilst both appearing necessary for Kant's account. On the one hand, we require some account of how it is that the state of nature has been superseded which gives us confidence that we will not relapse into it easily and this is what prompts Kant to discuss the philosophy of history in which he presents an ambiguous guarantee of moral progress due to the role of the power of money in promoting peace. But this account of history never reaches beyond a sketch and even this sketch appears flawed as the guarantee of conflict appears necessary given that it has prompted, in its way, a competition between peoples that has been productive, a competition that even leads Kant in the Third Critique to describe war as 'sublime' (Ak. 5:262–3). On the other hand, the appeal to God's action is given a rational formulation in terms of a providential guarantee in *Religion within the Limits of Reason Alone* whilst the nature of this guarantee is one we are prevented from comprehensively uniting with a vision of his love by the conclusion of the Doctrine of Virtue.

These points in Kant's practical philosophy concern matters that are of some importance to the prospects for the departure from the moral state of nature that Kant presents in *Religion within the Limits of Reason Alone* and hints at in the Doctrine of Virtue. Without the superseding of the moral state of nature we remain in a condition of injustice, one that Kant is occasionally acutely aware of as when he writes in the Doctrine of Virtue that having the resources to practice beneficence is 'a result of certain human beings being favoured through the injustice of the government, which introduces an inequality of wealth that makes others need their beneficence' (Ak. 6:454). The criticism that Kant's account of right requires constitutive inequality whilst correct does not prevent Kant from being aware of the savage consequences of such inequality.

The nature of Kant's ultimate practical position thus emerges as one that inevitably appears unsatisfactory. The nature of rational hope remains constitutively underdetermined and without the prospects for stating more about the possibilities of progress or the nature of the rela tionship to the divine It appears that we are faced with an inability to recover the ground that was lost when modernity was formed through exclusion of supernatural principles.[13] Whilst Kant's doctrinal practical philosophy allows a much richer account of culture than his critical philosophy it does not significantly alter the wide gap between eschatological expectation and actuality. Within the scope of this gap and constrained by it in terms of a social disposition that inevitably forecloses individual aspiration to a social context of monetary success rather than an eschatological horizon there remains the task, beyond the range of Kantian thinking, of a different manner of grasping the relationship between history, eschatology and ethics, a manner that might allow the prospect of something else to emerge than a final constitutive limit, a limit that suggests in principle a final failure on Kant's part to develop distinctive principles for a practical doctrine of history.

Notes

Introduction

1 The ancestry of this view can be traced to Hegel (1821) *Elements of A Philosophy of Right* (1991 trans. by H.B. Nisbet, Cambridge University Press: Cambridge). Other classic sources of this position include Friedrich Nietzsche (1887) *On the Genealogy of Morals* (1967 trans. by Walter Kaufmann, Vintage Books: New York), Second Essay; Henry Sidgwick (1874) *The Methods of Ethics* (Macmillan & Co: London) and Max Scheler (1913–16) *Formalism in Ethics And Non-Formal Ethics of Values: A New Attempt toward the Foundation of an Ethical Personalism* (1973 trans. by M.S. Frings and R.L. Funk, Northwestern University Press: Evanston). Contemporary treatments that converge with this traditional account are legion but perhaps one of the most influential has been Bernard Williams (1981) *Moral Luck: Philosophical Papers 1973–1980* (Cambridge University Press: Cambridge), first three chapters. Williams has added to the traditional charges a further one of 'abstracting from the identity of persons', a charge which enables him to somewhat surprisingly conflate 'Kantian ethics' as he characterizes it with the utilitarianism found in a work such as R.M. Hare (1981) *Moral Thinking: Its Levels, Method and Point* (Clarendon Press: Oxford). For one of the earliest and most influential presentations of ethical theory as divided between deontological and teleological accounts see W.D. Ross (1930) *The Right and the Good* (Clarendon Press: Oxford), a work well worth comparison with the popular account presented earlier by J.H. Muirhead (1892) *The Elements of Ethics* (John Murray: London). For popular accounts that follow the line presented by Ross see the classic account by P.H. Nowell-Smith (1954) *Ethics* (Penguin: Harmondsworth and Baltimore) and compare this with the standard account presented for A-level students by Anthony Harrison-Barbet (1990) *Mastering Philosophy* (Macmillan: Basingstoke). The popular works indicate the view retailed to generations of undergraduates. For a representative account of the problems raised about Kant and emotion see Justin Oakley (1992) *Morality and the Emotions* (Routledge: London and New York), Chapter 3.

2 This is the view presented for example by A.R.C. Duncan (1957) *Practical Reason and Morality: A Study of Immanuel Kant's 'Foundations for the Metaphysics of Morals'* (Thomas Nelson & Sons: London). For a response to this work see T.C. Williams (1968) *The Concept of the Categorical Imperative: A Study of the Place of the Categorical Imperative in Kant's Ethical Theory* (Clarendon Press: Oxford).

3 This is the account provided for example by Sir David Ross (1954) *Kant's Ethical Theory: A Commentary on the Groundwork of the Metaphysics of Morals* (Clarendon Press: Oxford).

4 The major exception to my claim to treat 'all' Kant's major works on practical philosophy is that I do not here treat *Perpetual Peace*, a work treated at length in G. Banham (2002) 'Kant's Critique of Right' *Kantian Review*, Vol. 6.

5   This is clear from the titles of the works in question, see for example the previously cited works of Duncan and Ross and see also Patrick Hutchings (1972) *Kant on Absolute Value: A Critical Examination of Certain Key Concepts in Kant's* Groundwork of the Metaphysics of Morals *and of His Ontology of Personal Values* (George Allen & Unwin: London), Robert Paul Woolf (1973) *The Autonomy of Reason: A Commentary on Kant's Groundwork of the Metaphysics of Morals* (Harper & Row: New York). Other works that appear more general are in fact no more than studies of the *Groundwork*, such as for example Bruce Aune (1979) *Kant's Theory of Morals* (Princeton University Press: Princeton) and P.C. Lo (1987) *Treating Persons As Ends: An Essay on Kant's Moral Philosophy* (University Press of America: Lanham, New York and London). Lo's book is distinctive in treating Kant's ethics as teleological.

6   For an attempt to assess this comparison see Christine Korsgaard (1986) 'Aristotle and Kant on the Source of Value' *Ethics* 96. It is worth comparing this account with that given by Robert Louden (1986) 'Kant's Virtue Ethics' *Philosophy* 61.

7   This has recently begun to change as is witnessed by the pioneering work of J. B. Schneewind (1998) *The Invention of Autonomy* (Cambridge University Press: Cambridge). Schneewind concentrates primarily on treating the currents prior to Kant and attempts to culminate with an account of Kant, an account which fails to have the range sufficient to really give the kind of richness of treatment that would be requisite to respond to previous unbalanced presentations. For a different account that is arguably richer see Howard Caygill (1989) *Art of Judgment* (Basil Blackwell: Oxford).

8   Compare for example the widely different treatments provided by Paul Arthur Schlipp (1938) *Kant's Pre-Critical Ethics* (Northwestern University Press: Evanston and Chicago) and Keith Ward (1972) *The Development of Kant's View of Ethics* (Basil Blackwell: Oxford).

9   Thus Keith Ward for example writes: 'if Kant's ethics is formalistic, it is a formalism which means to take full account of all natural and moral purposes, and of the essential ends of humanity, perfection and happiness' (Ward, *ibid.*, p. 129).

10   For many years this text received little attention, but for a pioneering treatment of it see John R. Silber (1960) 'The Ethical Significance of Kant's *Religion*' in Greene and Hudson (eds. and trans.) (1960) *Religion within the Limits of Reason Alone* (Harper Torchbooks: New York). This translation has now been superseded but Silber's essay is of historical importance. A more recent but still isolated account is provided by Allen Wood (1970) *Kant's Moral Religion* (Cornell University Press: Ithaca & London).

11   Yirmiahu Yovel (1980) *Kant and the Philosophy of History* (Princeton University Press: Princeton) remains the only serious book-length study of Kant's account of history presented to English-speaking audiences. This work is however primarily critical and despite possessing many fine qualities does not engage with the eschatological focus of Kant's treatment.

12   Dick Howard (1988) *The Politics of Critique* (University of Minnesota Press: Minneapolis), p. 89.

13   Mary Gregor (1963) *Laws of Freedom: A Study of Kant's Method of Applying the Categorical Imperative in the Metaphysik der Sitten* (Basil Blackwell: Oxford)

indicates both in its title and in its procedure a broad allegiance to this view of the distinction between the critical works and the doctrinal ones.

14 Hannah Arendt (1982) *Lectures on Kant's Political Philosophy* (ed. and trans. by Ronald Beiner, Harvester Press: Brighton) not only confines Kant's political philosophy to the horizons of the Third Critique but also interprets this latter in terms only of the *Critique of Aesthetic Judgment*, entirely leaving aside the *Critique of Teleological Judgment*. For a response to this account that locates the political significance that the Third Critique does have through a unitary reading of the whole work see Gary Banham (2000) *Kant and the Ends of Aesthetics* (Macmillan and St. Martin's Press: London and New York), especially Chapter 10. Recent works on Kant's political philosophy include George Armstong Kelly (1969) *Idealism, Politics and History: Sources of Hegelian Thought* (Cambridge University Press: Cambridge), Patrick Riley (1983) *Kant's Political Philosophy* (Rowman and Littlefield: Totona) and Howard Williams (1983) *Kant's Political Philosophy* (Basil Blackwell: Oxford).

15 For a representative display of such new work see Paul Guyer (ed.) (1998) *Kant's Groundwork of the Metaphysics of Morals: Critical Essays* (Rowman & Littlefield: Lanham, New York and Oxford).

16 With regard to Guyer himself see for example the essays collected in P. Guyer (1993) *Kant and the Experience of Freedom: Essays on Aesthetics and Morality* (Cambridge University Press: Cambridge) which whilst having the salutary effect of connecting practical philosophy with aesthetics does not include any treatment of Kant's doctrinal works. This is only partially rectified in Paul Guyer (2000) *Kant on Freedom, Law and Happiness* (Cambridge University Press: Cambridge) where there is one essay, out of a total of twelve, devoted to the Doctrine of Virtue. Recently a major collection has appeared that focuses exclusively on the *Metaphysics of Morals*. Cf. M. Timmons (ed.) (2002) *Kant's Metaphysics of Morals: Interpretative Essays* (Oxford University Press: Oxford). This work appeared as the present one was being completed and hence I have not been able to address it as yet as fully as I would like but I should add that seven of the essays within it where previously published in the supplement of Vol XXXVI of the *Southern Journal of Philosophy* (1997) and are discussed in this form in Chapters 6 and 7 below. I had advance sight of the essay by Kenneth Westphal from this volume which I mention in Chapter 6 below. I intend on another occasion to respond to the aspects of the collection that are not dealt with here.

17 For Rawls' own classic essay on the topic of the "categorical imperative procedure" see John Rawls (1989) "Themes in Kant's Moral Philosophy" in Ronald Beiner and William James Booth (eds.) (1993) *Kant & Political Philosophy: The Contemporary Legacy* (Yale University Press: New Haven and London).

Chapter 1

1 Citations here, and throughout if this corresponds to an English translation, from the Akademie edition. This work is included in D. Walford and R. Meerbote (eds. and trans.) *Theoretical Philosophy, 1755–1770* (Cambridge University Press: Cambridge).

2 For a fuller account see Howard Caygill (1989) *Art of Judgement* (Blackwell: Oxford), Chapter 3.

3 For an extensive account of Mendelssohn's essay, see Paul Guyer (1991) 'Mendelssohn and Kant: One Source of the Critical Philosophy' in P. Guyer (2000) *Kant on Freedom, Law, and Happiness* (Cambridge University Press: Cambridge). Kant's essay is translated in Walford and Meerbote, *op. cit.*

4 For an an extensive account of the British 'common sense' school of ethical philosophy, see H. Caygill, *op. cit.* Chapter 2.

5 Immanuel Kant (1764) *Observations on the Feeling of the Beautiful and the Sublime* (1973 translation by John T. Goldthwaite, University of California Press: Los Angeles).

6 For a discussion of these remarks, see Richard L. Velkley (1993) 'The Crisis of the End of Reason in Kant's Philosophy and the *Remarks* of 1764–1765' in Ronald Beiner and William James Booth (eds.) (1993) *Kant & Political Philosophy* (Yale University Press: New Haven and London).

7 Immanuel Kant (1766) *Dreams of A Spirit-Seer Elucidated by Dreams of Metaphysics* (trans. 1992) in Walford and Meerbote, *op. cit.*

8 Immanuel Kant (1770) *On the Form and Principles of the Sensible and Intelligible World* (trans. 1992) in Walford and Meerbote, *op. cit.*

9 But for a contrary reading of the Inaugural Dissertation which asserts its importance in Kant's practical development see M. Kuehn (1995) 'The Moral Dimension of Kant's *Inaugural Dissertation*: A New Perspective on the 'Great Light' of 1769?' in Hoke Robinson (ed.) (1995) *Proceedings of the Eighth International Kant Congress*, Vol. 1, Part 2 (Marquette University Press: Milwaukee).

10 For an account of reflections dating from the 1770s that have a practical interest see Paul Guyer (1989) 'The Unity of Reason' in P. Guyer (2000) *op. cit.* and for a discussion of Kant's lectures and reflections on anthropology see G. Felicitas Munzel (1999) *Kant's Conception of Moral Character: The 'Critical' Link of Morality, Anthropology, and Reflective Judgment* (University of Chicago Press: Chicago and London).

11 Immanuel Kant (1803) *On Education* (1899 trans. by Annette Churton, Kegan Paul, Trench, Trübner & Co. Ltd: London), p. 14. All references to this translation hereafter cited as Churton.

12 Immanuel Kant (1798) *Anthropology from a Pragmatic Point of View* (trans. by V.L. Dowdell, Southern Illinois University Press: Carbondale Edwardsville).

13 For account of the sets of notes and their provenance see the 'Introduction' by J.B. Schneewind to P. Heath and J.B. Schneewind (eds.) (1997) *Emmanuel Kant: Lectures on Ethics* (trans. by P. Heath, Cambridge University Press).

14 *Ibid.*, p. xiv.

15 Here I am following the Cambridge translation in departing from Collin's order in order to integrate material from Mrongovius.

Chapter 2

1 For a statement and short defence of the arguments and results of the Transcendental Aesthetic see G. Banham (2000) *Kant and the Ends of Aesthetics* (Macmillan & St. Martin's Press: London and New York), Chapter 1.

2 Lewis White Beck (1960) *A Commentary on Kant's Critique of Practical Reason* (University of Chicago Press: Chicago and London), p. 192.

3 For a similar suggestion motivated by a reading of the antinomy of teleological judgment see George Schrader (1953–54) 'The Status of Teleological Judgments In the Critical Philosophy' *Kant-Studien* 45.

4 For an attempt at a solution of this kind see John D. McFarland (1970) *Kant's Concept of Teleology* (University of Edinburgh Press: Edinburgh).

5 For a fuller account of the antinomy of teleological judgment and criticism of the various attempts at comprehending it see G. Banham, *op. cit.*, Chapter 8.

6 Werner Pluhar (1987) 'Translator's Introduction' to his translation of the *Critique of Judgment* (Hackett Publishing Company: Indianapolis/Cambridge), p. cv_{n106}.

7 See Henry Allison (1990) *Kant's Theory of Freedom* (Cambridge University Press: Cambridge and New York), p. 76, for a brief attempt at dealing with this objection, an attempt which fails, however, to see the true nature of this objection. See also G. Banham *op. cit.*, Chapter 8 for an account of Pluhar which is more responsive to the nature of his account of the antinomy of teleological judgment.

8 Robert E. Butts (1984) *Kant and the Double Government Methodology* (D. Reidel Publishing Company: Boston), pp. 261–3 by contrast follows the path of arguing for a regulative status for all the categories, a suggestion also mooted by Beck. Pluhar *op. cit.*, p. cvi_{n107} raises a number of problems with this solution.

9 Ottfried Höffe's account of the Second Analogy seems to me entirely right. As he writes:

> The principle of causality is a rule for spelling out appearances in their temporal succession so that they can be read as determinate objects and objective experiences. Whoever wishes to know nature is required to view all events as effects and to investigate their underlying causes. What the causes are in each particular case can be discovered only empirically (cf. B 165). Every determinate causal relation, even the form of rules of cause and effect, is due to experience and to the scientific theory of experience—not to transcendental necessity. Not only the mathematical side of the modern science of nature but also its character as an empirical investigation of causes receives from Kant a philosophical justification. The transcendental critique of reason does not put shackles onto the science of nature but liberates it to carry out an ongoing process of research.

> Ottfried Höffe (1992) *Immanuel Kant* (1994 trans. by Marshall Farrier, State University of New York Press: Albany), p. 104.

10 The analogies are described as 'constitutive of experience' (A664/B692) but here Kant is making a very specific contrast between concepts and ideas and this does not effect the point of the distinction between mathematical and dynamical as this distinction is here in fact restated by Kant.

11 Bernard Carnois (1973) *The Coherence of Kant's Doctrine of Freedom* (1987 trans. by David Booth, The University of Chicago Press: Chicago and London), p. 30.

12 It is noteworthy when one considers that the point of the Fourth Antinomy is to present a problem about the relationship between necessity and contingency and that the problem of contingency is also at the heart of the antinomy of teleological judgment that discussion has not centred on the question of the relationship between these antinomies rather than on the relationship between the Third Antinomy and the antinomy of teleological judgment.

Chapter 3

1 There are now a number of translations of the *Groundwork* which all have merit, but the one I will be citing throughout is by Mary Gregor, which is included in her contribution to the Cambridge Edition of the works of Immanuel Kant. Immanuel Kant, *Practical Philosophy* (1996 trans. by M. Gregor, Cambridge University Press: Cambridge).

2 James Ellington in his 'Introduction' to his translation of the *Groundwork* writes: 'For those familiar with Kant's system of theoretic philosophy there is an obvious analogy between the function of the categorical imperative in morals and the function of the transcendental unity of apperception in speculative thought which Kant claims in the *Critique of Pure Reason* (B134 note).' J.W. Ellington, 'Introduction' to Immanuel Kant, *Grounding for the Metaphysics of Morals with On A Supposed Right to Lie Because of Philanthropic Concerns* (1981 trans. by J.W. Ellington, Hackett Publishing Company: Indianpolis and Cambridge), p. v.

3 Since Kant is so often represented as opposed to teleological ethics it is very important to emphasise this point and to suggest therewith reasons for questioning the identification of teleological ethics with utilitarianism and consequentialism.

4 Perhaps surprisingly it is rarely noted that these are the categories of quantity discussed by Kant in the 'metaphysical deduction' of the First Critique (A80/B106).

5 H.J. Paton (1947) *The Categorical Imperative: A Study In Kant's Moral Philosophy* (University of Pennsylvania Press: Philadelphia).

6 Philip Stratton-Lake (1993) 'Formulating Categorical Imperatives' *Kant-Studien* 84:3.

7 Paul Guyer (1995) 'The Possibility of the Categorical Imperative' in Paul Guyer (ed.) (1998) *Kant's Groundwork of the Metaphysics of Morals: Critical Essays* (Rowman & Littlefield Publishers, Inc: Lanham and Oxford).

8 John Rawls (2000) *Lectures on the History of Moral Philosophy* (ed. by Barbara Herman, Harvard University Press: Cambridge, Mass and London), p. 167.

9 For some of the other leading statements of the 'problem' of multiple formulations see: A.R.C. Duncan (1957) *Practical Reason and Morality: A Study of Immanuel Kant's 'Foundations for the Metaphysics of Morals'* (Nelson: Edinburgh), Judith Baker (1988) 'Counting Categorical Imperatives' *Kant-Studien* 79:4, Sir David Ross (1954) *Kant's Ethical Theory: A Commentary on the Groundwork of the Metaphysics of Morals* (Clarendon Press: Oxford), A.T. Nuyen (1993) 'Counting the Formulas of the Categorical Imperative: One Plus Three Makes Four' *History of Philosophy Quarterly* 10, and Bernard Rollin (1976) 'There Is Only One Categorical Imperative' *Kant-Studien* 67.

There is also a fair number of articles concentrating on one of the formulations and promoting one above the others. For examples of these arguments see Christine M. Korsgaard (1996) *Creating the Kingdom of Ends* (Cambridge University Press: Cambridge), Allen Wood (1995) 'Humanity As An End In Itself' in Guyer (ed.) *op. cit.*, Rawls *op. cit.*, Chapters I–IV of the Kant section.

10 At the close of his translation of the second section of the *Groundwork* James Ellington writes: 'The ensuing Third Section is difficult to grasp. Kant expressed himself more clearly regarding the topics discussed there in the *Critique of Practical Reason*, Part I, Book I ('Analytic of Pure Practical Reason').' Ellington, *op. cit.*, p. 48.

11 Dieter Henrich (1975) 'The Deduction of the Moral Law: The Reasons for the Obscurity of the Final Section of Kant's Groundwork of the Metaphysics of Morals' in P. Guyer (ed.) *op. cit.*, translated by P. Guyer, p. 311. Guyer's translation of this essay only renders part of it into English and the original is found in A. Schwann (ed.) (1975) *Denken in Schatten des Nihilismus* (Wissenschatfliche Buchgesellschaft: Darmstadt), pp. 55–110.

12 Karl Ameriks (1982) *Kant's Theory of Mind: An Analysis of the Paralogisms of Pure Reason* (Clarendon Press: Oxford).

13 Henry Allison (1990) *Kant's Theory of Freedom* (Cambridge University Press: Cambridge).

14 I would not wish to suggest that no one else has challenged this general assumption of the failure of the argument of *Groundwork* III. There is an important precedent for my account here in a series of articles by Michael McCarthy: M. McCarthy (1979) 'Kant's Application of the Analytic/Synthetic Distinction to Imperatives' *Dialogue* 18, M. McCarthy (1982) 'Kant's Rejection of the Argument of *Groundwork* III' *Kant-Studien* 73:2, M. McCarthy (1985) 'The Objection of Circularity in *Groundwork* III' *Kant-Studien* 76:1. McCarthy's arguments are directed mainly against the interpretations of Paton and Ross but do not entirely correspond to my account of the argument and have been replied to by Allison. Whilst Allison's responses to McCarthy are far from compelling it seemed to me appropriate to restate the defence of the argument of *Groundwork* III in an independent fashion. Another defence of the argument of *Groundwork* III is presented in Onora O'Neill (1989) *Constructions of Reason: Explorations of Kant's Practical Philosophy* (Cambridge University Press: Cambridge), Chapter 3.

Chapter 4

1 Lewis White Beck (1960) *A Commentary on Kant's Critique of Practical Reason* (The University of Chicago Press: Chicago), p. 172.

2 Henry Allison (1990) *Kant's Theory of Freedom* (Cambridge University Press: Cambridge), p. 238.

3 Lewis White Beck, *op. cit.* Chapter 1 provides a discussion of the various plans Kant had for writing works on practical philosophy but his reason for why the Second Critique was written is problematic as he concentrates on only two topics that he takes to justify it: the treatment of the unity of reason and the discussion of the relationship between the supreme principle of morality and humanity as provided in the chapter on the 'drives' (*Triebfeder*)

(Beck, *op. cit.*, p. 15). Whilst the former topic was not treated in the *Groundwork*, the latter topic was given some attention there and neither seems sufficient in themselves for the writing of the new work.

4   Michael McCarthy (1982) 'Kant's Rejection of the Argument of Groundwork III' *Kant-Studien* 73:2, p. 187.

5   Jean-Luc Nancy (1988) *The Experience of Freedom* (1993 trans. by B. McDonald, Stanford University Press: Stanford), Section 3 draws attention to this passage and suggests that this placing of freedom as a 'fact' whilst not as new in Kant's work as many suggest, does indicate the impossibility of avoiding subreption in the categories of practical reason. For a related view see Howard Caygill (1995) *A Kant Dictionary* (Blackwell: Oxford), entry on 'fact'.

6   For a different approach to this problem, compare Bernard Carnois (1973) *The Coherence of Kant's Doctrine of Freedom* (1987 trans. by D. Booth, University of Chicago Press: Chicago), pp. 64–8.

7   Lewis White Beck is once again in the vanguard of Kant's critics setting the tone for the majority of subsequent commentary when he writes: 'Kant's usual high-quality workmanship is not much evident in the discussion of the antinomy [of practical reason]'. Beck, *op. cit.*, p. 246. John Silber (1959) 'Kant's Conception of the Highest Good As Immanent and Transcendent' *Philosophical Review* 68 presented an alternative picture to Beck and Silber directly replies to Beck in his 1963 article 'The Importance of the Highest Good In Kant's Ethics' *Ethics* 73. A response to these works was presented which gave reasons against Silber's interpretation: Jeffrie G. Murphy (1965) 'The Highest Good As Content For Kant's Ethical Formalism: Beck *versus* Silber' *Kant-Studien* 56. There have been two recent defences of Kant against the approaches of Murphy and Beck: Steven G. Smith (1984) 'Worthiness to be Happy and Kant's Concept of the Highest Good' *Kant-Studien* 75:2 and Manfred Kuehn (1985) 'Kant's Transcendental Deduction of God's Existence as a Postulate of Pure Practical Reason' *Kant-Studien* 76:2. These recent defences are, however, not representative of the mainstream opinion and involve difficulties of their own. Rather than attempt to engage with these defences of Kant I will concentrate instead on the mainstream criticisms.

8   Hegel's account of the postulates has been reprised recently by Thomas Auxter (1982) *Kant's Moral Teleology* (Mercer University Press: Macon), Chapter 6. Auxter's arguments are however considerably less interesting than Hegel's so it would seem preferable to refer directly to Hegel. The account that I will be citing is given in Hegel (1807) *The Phenomenology of Spirit* (1974 trans. by A.V. Miller: Oxford University Press), citations by paragraph number rather than page.

Chapter 5

1   For a further account of this see Gary Banham (2000) *Kant and the Ends of Aesthetics* (Macmillan: London and St. Martin's Press: New York), Chapter 8.

2   I have throughout used the translation by George di Giovanni, although I do not accept his reasons for altering the English title of the work and have not followed him in this alteration.

3   It is noteworthy in the account of propagation that Kant slips between the desire for offspring and the sexual drive as if there were no genuine difference between them, a slip that colours his attitude to sexual mores in the Doctrine of Virtue in ways that distort his own account as we will see in discussing his notion of 'defiling oneself by lust' (Ak. 6:424–6). The fascinating nature of his casuistical questions will however also give us reasons for thinking that his own account here is one that his systematic treatment undercuts.

4   This is precisely what makes the following statement of Gordon Michalson so peculiar: 'Kant can no more explain the 'fall' than could Augustine, his long-windedness on the matter notwithstanding.' Gordon E. Michalson, Jr (1990) *Fallen Freedom: Kant on Radical Evil and Moral Regeneration* (Cambridge University Press: Cambridge), p. 65. As will become swiftly clear, Kant's alleged 'long-windedness' has seemed to many authors the reverse, a concision that they have rushed to fill in. Michalson's desire for an 'explanation' of the 'fall' beyond the figurative account I will be describing suggests a complete failure to grasp the nature of the realm of freedom.

5   Leo Strauss sets out in a number of places the contention that a fundamental philosophical anthropology (or, as we would have it in Kantian terms, a transcendental philosophical anthropology) always determines humanity as evil and that this is the root of the need for politics. Cf. for an important statement of this view Leo Strauss (1932) 'Comments on Carl Schmitt's *Der Begriff Des Politischen*' in Carl Schmitt (1927) *The Concept of the Political* (1976 trans. by George Schwab, Rutgers University Press: New Brunswick and New Jersey). The connection of this claim with some of Kant's political observations will be noted in our account of the Doctrine of Right.

6   These examples are then supplemented in a footnote by reference to a perpetual war between the Arathapescaw Indians and the Dog Rib Indians. The examples are mainly taken from the travel books that Kant spent an inordinate amount of time reading. It is worth comparing the examples given with Nietzsche's similar move when in *The Birth of Tragedy* he refers to the 'practical pessimism' of the Fiji Islanders in section 15 of that work. Friedrich Nietzsche (1872) *The Birth of Tragedy* (1967 translation by Walter Kaufmann: Vintage Books, New York).

7   'Philosophical chiliasm' is the topic of *Towards Perpetual Peace: A Philosophical Project* (1795). For my account of *Perpetual Peace*, see G. Banham (2002) 'Kant's Critique of Right' *Kantian Review*, Vol. 6.

8   Elsewhere, however, Kant himself does succumb to the temptation of the view that evil is merely a privation, a view generally known as the *privatio boni* view. In his *Lectures on the Philosophical Doctrine of Religion* Kant states: 'evil in the world can be regarded as *incompleteness in the development of the germ toward the good*. Evil has *no special* germ; for it is *mere negation* and consists only in the *limitation of the good*. It is nothing beyond this, other than incompleteness in the development of the germ to the good out of uncultivatedness' (Ak. 28:1078). This statement occurs in the context of dismissing the Manichean view that the evil principle is equivalent to the good one in strength and basis and is a clearly less developed view than given in *Religion within the Limits of Reason Alone* as

Kant also states in these lectures that evil 'arises as a *by-product*, since the human being has to struggle with his own limits, with his animal instincts' (Ak. 28:1078). Since this statement seems to be equivalent to the Stoic view explicitly repudiated in the passage of the *Religion* I have been foregrounding in that it equates evil with 'bestial vice' and the failure to struggle against it then it would appear that Kant is here criticizing the view that he presented in the lectures.

9 The two references to this notion also involve appeals to Scripture and the type of interpretation of Scripture at work within these references (as also with other references to Scripture within the *Religion*) do themselves need some comment and will be given such in a treatment of Kant's Biblical hermeneutics below.

10 The *locus modernus* for the thought of evil in relation to the Final Solution is Hannah Arendt (1963) *Eichmann in Jerusalem: A Report on the Banality of Evil* (Viking: New York). Given that evil arises on Kantian terms from the same free ground as good and since it is taken in the *Religion* to be so clearly positive as to be figured in the image of an 'evil spirit' it would *not* be Kantian to suggest that evil is 'banal'.

11 Perhaps the subtlest of such accounts is provided in J.F. Lyotard (1983) *The Differend: Phrases in Dispute* (1988 translation by Georges Van Den Abbeele, Manchester University Press: Manchester). For a partial response to this account which indicates some of the difficulties presented for thinking the position of Jews and Judaism within political thinking and philosophy see Gary Banham (1996) 'The Terror of the Law: Judaism and International Institutions' in J. Brannigan, R. Robbins and J. Wolfreys (eds.) (1996) *Applying: To Derrida* (Macmillan Press: London and St. Martin's Press: New York).

12 For example the discussion of evil in J-L. Nancy (1988) *The Experience of Freedom* (1993 translation by Bridget McDonald, Stanford University Press: Standford) draws on Schelling and Heidegger rather more than on Kant.

13 Alenka Zupančič (2000) *Ethics of the Real: Kant, Lacan* (Verso: London and New York), p. 100.

14 Joan Copjec (1996) 'Introduction: Evil in the Time of the Finite World' in J. Copjec (ed.) (1996) *Radical Evil* (Verso: London and New York), p. xvi.

15 There is, however, a precedent for making a connection between these writers albeit mainly for the purposes of explicating Benjamin. For an account of Benjamin that sees him as responding very precisely to Kant see Howard Caygill (1998) *Walter Benjamin: The Colour of Experience* (Routledge: London and New York), particularly Chapter 1. Caygill's account does not however focus on the matters I will be visiting here.

16 Walter Benjamin (1928) *The Origin of German Tragic Drama* (1977 translation by John Osborne, Verso: London and New York), p. 230. The translation of the title is somewhat inaccurate as the German term *Trauerspiel* literally means 'mourning play' and the reference to 'mourning' is in fact important in Benjamin's discussion for reasons which should become apparent. I will therefore refer to Benjamin's work henceforth as the *Trauerspiel* study.

17 This oscillation in fact occurred within the life of the father of modern world-denying pessimism, Schopenhauer. Whilst theoretically committed to pessimism and the denial of the inclinations he patterned his life as one in

which his favourite pleasures had regular recurrence and hence was a practical hedonist and theoretical pessimist.

18 This is the nature of nihilism. For a characterization of it that attempts to connect it to the loss in modern representation of teleological thinking that I am building on here but which involves other elements than I will be setting out here see Gary Banham and Charlie Blake (2000) 'Introduction' to G. Banham and C. Blake (eds.) (2000) *Evil Spirits: Nihilism and the Fate of Modernity* (Manchester University Press: Manchester).

19 This is the problem with Zupančič's suggestion that logically Kant's argument in favour of the postulate of the immortality of the soul should really lead to an argument for the immortality of the body. Whilst this suggestion does point to the problem of viewing the struggle that is involved in virtue as being purely a struggle with the inclinations, a representation that Kant at times is guilty of, it is clear that his discussion of the struggle must involve more than this as otherwise he would not be capable of viewing evil, as he does in the pages of the *Religion*, as a positive power. Zupančič's suggestion of an immortality of the body is part of the hedonistic strain of the Satanic consciousness. The 'synthesis' of this consciousness that Benjamin points to however indicates that the unification of this consciousness cannot be based on such a view. I follow here Benjamin as this is the direction that this consciousness will move in once the illusory nature of this 'progress' is acknowledged.

20 For an argument to this effect with the discernment by contrast of tendencies that are moving back in a Kantian direction, see Gary Banham (2000) 'Teleology, Transcendental Reflection and Artificial Life' *Tekhnema: Journal of Philosophy and Technology* Issue 6.

21 Jacob Rogozinski (1996) 'It Makes Us Wrong: Kant and Radical Evil' in Copjec, *op. cit.*, makes this suggestion.

22 Such might, for example, be said to be the rationale behind the common assumption amongst Gnostics of an illuminati or 'pure' group who are freed thereby from the law because of having in some sense incarnated its essence. This paradoxical but consistent heresy always has the effect of giving allowance for any depravity to those who are 'pure' an indication of the dialectic inherent in assurance of such 'purity'.

23 John E. Hare (1996) *The Moral Gap: Kantian Ethics, Human Limits and God's Assistance* (Clarendon Press: Oxford), pp. 63–4. Hare is, as he concedes, restating an objection from Michalson. Michalson presented it in the following manner: 'Notice to begin with how Kant begs his own question [concerning how someone with a corrupt disposition can become good again] by simply assuming that this transformation has already occurred' (Michalson, *op. cit.*, p. 94).

24 The discussion here also bears comparison with that carried out in Kant's *Idea for a Universal Human History From A Cosmopolitan Point of View*. For a discussion of this text see Gary Banham (2000) *Kant and the Ends of Aesthetics* (Macmillan: London and St. Martin's Press: New York), Chapter 10.

25 Given the history of the revolutionary wars this might seem a peculiar point. However, Kant's footnote here which makes clear that it does not follow that there could not be a republican constitution with a monarch still being in place indicates a distancing from some of the precise aspects of the revolution, a distancing in accord with the disturbance over the execution of the

monarch revealed in the Doctrine of Right. (Ak. 7:86n) The account of republican constitutions in *Perpetual Peace* also makes clear that they are judged peaceful due to the fact that within them it is the people themselves who make the decision for war, a decision they will not make lightly and that this is what is of the nature of the preference for such constitutions as war is, as Kant adds here in *The Conflict of the Faculties*, 'the source of all evil and the corruption of morals' (Ak. 7:86).

Chapter 6

1   I owe this point to Eckhart Förster (2000) *Kant's Final Synthesis: An Essay on the Opus Postumum* (Harvard University Press: Cambridge, Mass and London), p. 54. Since Förster's book concerns the place of the *Opus Postumum* it points up a parallel problem about theoretical philosophy to the one I am examining in this work about practical philosophy and it would be worth examining in some detail on another occasion the manner of Förster's treatment.

2   There is an additional systemic problem about the question of whether there is a critique of right that paves the way directly for the doctrine of right. Unfortunately, I am unable to respond to this problem within the confines of the investigation I have delimited in this particular book. I have treated it elsewhere. I can indicate that I do think there is a particular work that carries out a critique of right and that this work is *Perpetual Peace*. See G. Banham (2002) 'Kant's Critique of Right' *Kantian Review*, Vol. 6.

3   Thomas Pogge (1997) 'Is Kant's *Rechtslehre* Comprehensive?' *Southern Journal of Philosophy*, Volume XXXVI, Supplement, p. 175. The question in Pogge's title refers to another context for this discussion than is directly within the forefront of my attention here. The notion of 'comprehensive' views comes from John Rawls (1993) *Political Liberalism* (Harvard University Press: Cambridge, Mass. and London). In this work Rawls argues against basing political philosophy on moral philosophy due to the fact that modern societies are 'pluralist' in the sense that they contain distinct groups of people who have differing views of the good. Due to this a political position that is neutral between them is to be preferred to one that seems to favour any one of them and Rawls here suggests that metaphysical positions are basically the same as religious ones. The difficulties with this argument are connected to the view that it is required of us to adopt a broadly 'constructivist' view of morals that is based on non-controversial premises. Some constructivists argue that beginning from the categorical imperative will be sufficient for this and hence disagree with Rawls that Kant's moral philosophy is in any case a 'comprehensive' view, but such an argument has problems in explaining the relationship between the categorical imperative and the supreme principle of morality, namely autonomy. I do not wish to enter these debates here as they would take me too far from my purpose, only to assess whether Kant's view of right is constitutively independent of his system of moral philosophy in the way Pogge suggests.

4   Katrin Flikschuh (2000) *Kant and Modern Political Philosophy* (Cambridge University Press: Cambridge), pp. 111–12 and Chapter 4 *passim*. Whilst

Flikschuh provides an interesting and novel treatment of the account of possession and property in the Doctrine of Right on this basis there are real problems with the treatment of Kant's position in this work. Flikschuh is clear in the work that she does not intend to offer a scholarly reading of Kant and she takes this to be equivalent to sanctioning an abandonment of what the status of 'metaphysics' is in Kant despite her avowed aim in the book to defend the role of metaphysics in political thinking. Instead of setting out a Kantian account of what a 'metaphysics of morals' is therefore she relies on the notion of metaphysics given by Stephan Korner (1984) *Metaphysics: Its Structure and Function* (Cambridge University Press: Cambridge). This has the unfortunate effect of obscuring the connection between the Doctrine of Right and transcendental idealism ensuring therefore that Flikschuh's account is not an adequate reply to Pogge as she does not justify in Kantian terms the necessity of a 'comprehensive' theory. This problem with Flikschuh's work may well be indicative of the influence of the contemporary anti-metaphysical climate even on those who would oppose it.

5 Immediately after this second invocation of the categorical imperative Kant makes his famous distinction between *Willkür* and *Wille*. Roughly put the former is the fact that decisions are made by us whilst the latter is the basis of such decisions being made, our freedom itself. For a treatment of this distinction in relation to the argument of the Doctrine of Right see Lewis White Beck (1965) 'Kant's Two Conceptions of the Will in Their Political Context' in Ronald Beiner and William James Booth (eds.) (1993) *Kant & Political Philosophy: The Contemporary Legacy* (Yale University Press: New Haven and London).

6 Since the conditions of freedom's relationship to equality and independence as stated at Ak. 6:237–8 essentially reprises the division earlier given from Ulpian it is a matter of some regret that Kant bothered to invoke the authority of the Roman jurist (Ak. 6:237–8). The three types of duty set out here however in terms of the rights of humanity, the constrain on action involved in forbiddance of wrong and the authorization to form a civil society are key to the work, not least the first of these in terms of private right and the third in terms of public right.

7 Mary Gregor (1988) 'Kant's Theory of Property' *Review of Metaphysics* 41. She writes for instance: 'this concept of "humanity" seems not only to bear the weight of the *Doctrine of Right* but also to connect its first principle with the supreme principle of morality' (p. 766).

8 For discussions of this aspect of the problem see Thomas Mauthner (1981) 'Kant's Metaphysics of Morals: A Note on the Text' *Kant-Studien* 72 and Bernd Ludwig (1990) 'The Right of a State in Immanuel Kant's *Doctrine of Right*' *Journal of the History of Philosophy* 27:3. The latter article argues for a large number of changes in the traditional order of the text. Mary Gregor in her translator's introduction to the *Metaphysics of Morals* discusses Ludwig's suggestions and indicates which she has adopted. Whilst I have no wish to contribute to this discussion it is clear that the text was published in an unsatisfactory condition and this certainly appears to have distorted the presentation of the argument about possession and property

9 Flikschuh, *op. cit.*, Chapter 4.

10   Kenneth R. Westphal (2002) 'A Kantian Justification of Possession' in M. Timmons (ed.) (2002) *Kant's Metaphysics of Morals: Interpretative Essays* (Oxford University Press: Oxford and New York).

11   The key role of this part of the First Critique is now widely recognised in the wake of the treatment provided by Béatrice Longuenesse (1993) *Kant and the Capacity to Judge* (1998 trans. by Charles T. Wolfe, Princeton University Press: Princeton, NJ). The effect of this account on the question of how to interpret the Transcendental Deduction of the First Critique is something I wish to explore at considerable length elsewhere. For an account of how a table is utilized in the precise division of types of contract that Kant describes in the Doctrine of Right see Kenneth R. Westphal (1997) 'Is Kant's Table of Contracts Complete?' *The Southern Journal of Philosophy* Volume XXXVI, Supplement.

12   Kenneth Westphal's argument that Kant does not attempt to justify property rights is based on his point that property rights contain a multitude of specific rights and that deduction of them by an a priori method is implausible (Westphal 2001, p. 1). Whilst this argument of Westphal's is correct in its own terms what I intend by claiming that Kant's argument about possession is preliminary to his justification of property rights is that it is preliminary not to an attempt to justify all the cases that fall under the heading of property right but rather that it is preliminary to an attempt to justify property right as an overall category.

13   Hugo Grotius (1625) *The Law of War and Peace* (1925 translation by Francis Kelsey, Oxford University Press: Oxford), Book II, Chapter 2. For a different formulation of the relationship between this tradition and the course of Kant's argument than mine see Kenneth Baynes (1989) 'Kant on Property Rights and the Social Contract' *Monist* 72.

14   This is the clear sense in which Kenneth Westphal is right to claim that Kant does not give an argument for the right to property as he really only gives an argument for the civil condition, a condition that is the basis of property being a claim that is enforceable and hence real.

15   These difficulties concern the question of why Kant treats a contract as involving 'two *preparatory* and two *constitutive* acts of choice' (Ak. 6:272). This seems an unnecessarily elaborate account to modern eyes. For a treatment of the rationale for this in Kant's account and the relationship between it and the simpler notions of contract deployed in modern treatments see B. Sharon Byrd (1997) 'Kant's Theory of Contract' *The Southern Journal of Philosophy* Volume XXXVI, Supplement.

16   On these grounds Kant explicitly states that marriage right has to be conceived of as a contract 'made between two persons of opposite sex' (Ak. 6:279) without saying what would fail to accord with conditions of rationality in this contract being made between two members of the same sex. The explicit statement by Kant here that marriage right does not include reproduction as part of its remit, a declaration he has to make as otherwise it would ensure that childless couples had no right to their status as married, also ensures that there is no clear basis as to what the couple form should be. It is only in the Doctrine of Virtue that Kant deals with this question and as such I will discuss it below. The remarkable absence of discussion of this question in commentaries on Kant's account of domestic right contrasts

rather sharply with the plethora of objections to his account of the status of women within marriage right. Howard Caygill in his entry on 'sex' in *A Kant Dictionary* provides a wide-ranging response to this question and is a notable exception here.

17 This does again pose some problems for Kant's account however as the problem of physical incapacity needs to be tackled and in invoking a principle of application he has to distinguish between a condition of incapacity that precedes the assumed contract and one that post-dates it indicating that in the latter case the contract is not invalid despite the fact that it no longer conforms to '*lege*'. This difficulty indicates the problem of thinking through the principles of application, a problem we will see as constitutive of the Doctrine of Virtue but which does point to problems already in the Doctrine of Right.

18 Jean-Jacques Rousseau (1762) *The Social Contract* (1974 translation by Lowell Bair, Mentor and New American Library: New York and London), Book I, Chapter VI.

19 Women in general are excluded from the class of active citizens and the rationale for this exclusion could only be that women are not conceived of by Kant as having a possible independent economic existence and the supporting reason for this reading is the terms of Kant's justification of women's subordination within domestic right, a subordination framed to ensure that there is moral equality in marriage right all the same (Ak. 6:279). With regard to the question of citizenship this gets Kant into a real difficulty however as whilst on the one hand he claims that anyone should be able to work themselves up from the status of passive citizen to that of active (Ak. 6:315) this would seem not to extend to the case of any woman as all women have been excluded by him from the status of active citizenry.

20 This assumption is held for example by Katrin Flikschuh (*op. cit.* p. 152) but an argument against it that refers to the deployment of such arguments in the French and American revolutions is provided by Leo Strauss (1953) *Natural Right and History* (University of Chicago Press: Chicago) and in this connection two citations are worth giving from Strauss. First his statement on p. 2: 'To reject natural right is tantamount to saying that all right is positive right, and this means that what is right is determined exclusively by the legislators and the courts of the various countries' and the statement on p. 5: 'The contemporary rejection of natural rights leads to nihilism – nay, it is identical with nihilism'. Whilst Kant wishes to ensure that there is a clear distinction between positive right and natural right his account of sovereignty leads to the latter not being a real claim that can be enforced in the civil condition against the power that is supposed to be its guarantor. Hobbes, who posed this problem most forcefully, can thus claim to be the father of political nihilism, with Rousseau serving as his foremost descendant. See the accounts of both these thinkers in Strauss' work and with this note that the principal alternative to a Kantian account of politics need not be Hegelian but could well be conceived of in natural law terms.

21 Thomas W. Pogge (1988) 'Kant's Theory of Justice' *Kant-Studien* 79 interprets Kant's commitment to this view of sovereignty as based purely on a principle of consistency and as not entailed by the principle of universality. This would make the notion of sovereignty an example of a faulty principle of

application and would permit its rejection without compromising Kant's basis of departure.

22   This is the reason why Roger Sullivan, for example, presents Kant as an ancestor of modern-day libertarianism in his 'introduction' to Mary Gregor's translation of the *Metaphysics of Morals*. For a lengthy challenge to this account of Kant that clearly traces the history of reception of Kant that paved the way for this reading and the quite different readings provided by socialist writers see Alexander Kaufman (1999) *Welfare in the Kantian State* (Clarendon Press: Oxford) and for an account of socialist readings of Kant see Harry Van Der Linden (1988) *Kantian Ethics and Socialism* (Hackett Publishing Company: Indianapolis and Cambridge).

23   Some aspects of Kant's treatment are again peculiar reflecting further oddities in his principles of application. For example his statement that 'elderly unmarried people of both sexes' are in some way responsible for the production of foundlings and hence have a prima facie case for being specially obligated to pay taxes for their upkeep is one that it is difficult to find other than bizarre (Ak. 6:326–7).

24   In terms of contemporary political theory this question is a clear point of contention between John Rawls and libertarians such as Nozick.

25   Intriguingly, Kant makes no provision here for the notion of cautions. Since the principle of caution is to institute a type of relation between the criminal and the law where the latter is seen as a source of restraint that is tempered by considerations of circumstance perhaps Kant would have thought it outside the province of strict right and in any case susceptible to interpretation in terms that would violate the principle of equality (as tending to favour most those least in need of such education). It is part of the curious absence of considerations of education in terms of right in Kant's account and contrasts rather sharply with his commitment to moral education (Ak. 6:477–84). Since the latter is constitutively separate from a treatment of strict right it would be reasonable to expect an equivalent to it in terms of right and the absence of it makes Kant's treatment harsher than it need be.

26   There is again a curious omission here. The equivalent to the physical death caused by the murderer could be conceived of as a civil death, a death understood in terms of permanent imprisonment. This latter would involve permanent loss of rights however and this would suggest a person who is not treated as a person but merely as a means (for state purposes perhaps). This indicates the core of Kant's failure to consider such a notion. However, since the principle of equality has to be considered in such strict terms the jurisprudential system will suffer real difficulties in assessing the right response to some crimes.

27   That these are a somewhat incongruous pairing is indicative of another case of principles of application. Here the leniency indicated towards duelling contrasts sharply with an attitude towards illegitimate children that strikes the modern reader as barbaric (Ak. 6:336). The notion of a compassionate response to the mother's case is evidently not in keeping with strict right but the necessity of principles of application in any case indicates the need for the treatment of right to extend beyond the level of strict principles and to be accorded a regulative role in some detailed sense.

28 Leslie Mulholland (1990) *Kant's System of Rights* (Columbia University Press: New York), p. 278.

29 For a very similar claim, see Oliver Goldsmith (1766) *The Vicar of Wakefield* (Penguin Books: Harmondsworth, 1982 edition edited by Stephen Coote), Chapter 19 for a speech by Primrose arguing for the King as the defender of liberty.

Chapter 7

1 Kant suggests that there is no sense in which promoting my happiness is something I need be constrained to do but this ignores the cases of seriously disturbed people who wish for misery or have no positive wish for happiness. It also ignores the significant extent to which some who adopt the ends of others as primary for themselves may be led thereby to neglect their own needs.

2 For a description of the history of this construal and a posing of sharp problems with it see Barbara Herman (1993) *The Practice of Moral Judgment* (Harvard University Press: Cambridge, Mass and London), Chapter 10, 'Leaving Deontology Behind'.

3 Mary Gregor (1963) *Laws of Freedom: A Study of Kant's Method of Applying the Categorical Imperative in the Metaphysik der Sitten* (Basil Blackwell: Oxford), p. 116. This ingenious solution is further justified in the following manner: 'by removing from the term "Right" all that makes it properly juridical, we can also speak of the 'Right of humanity in our own person' as an "inner *ius*". By analogy with the definition of Law in the proper sense of the term, this inner *ius* might be described as the limitation of our inner exercise of freedom to the condition of its formal consistency with itself' (p. 118).

4 Onora Nell (1975) *Acting on Principle: An Essay On Kantian Ethics* (Columbia University Press: New York), p. 53.

5 Walter E. Schaller (1987) 'Kant's Architectonic of Duties' *Philosophy and Phenomenological Research* Vol. XLVIII, No. 2, p. 299.

6 Or at least of the doctrine of elements of the Doctrine of Virtue. I do not wish to discuss the doctrine of method that is included within the Doctrine of Virtue.

7 The clearest discussion thus far is provided by Marcia W. Baron (1995) *Kantian Ethics Almost Without Apology* (Cornell University Press: Ithaca and London), Chapter 3.

8 Barbara Herman, *op. cit.*, Chapter 3 considers the latitude involved in the duty of benevolence but whilst she is clear that the constraint upon it concerns a protection for my agency she does not attempt here to contrast the type of latitude she discerns this virtue to have from the type of latitude a perfect duty to others (a duty of respect) would have.

9 Thomas E. Hill, Jr. (1971) 'Kant On Imperfect Duty and Supererogation' *Kant-Studien* 62, p. 57.

10 There is a complication here due to the necessity of such substitution in cases where the other holds only impermissible ends as here it is a duty to refuse to help to meet such ends and to attempt to present permissible ends instead. In such a case of course there is a moral motive underlying the treatment not an account of happiness in terms of sensible conditions alone.

11   Though it is worth noting Kant's caustic remarks concerning the beneficence of the rich (Ak. 6:453 and Ak. 6:454).

12   This type of argument has been given many forms in recent years but for a description of it from a feminist angle see Sally Sedgwick (1990) 'Can Kant's Ethics Survive the Feminist Critique?' in Robin May Schott (ed.) (1997) *Feminist Interpretations of Immanuel Kant* (The Pennsylvania State University Press: University Park, Pennsylvania). The problem, however, with a number of the objections raised here is, as Sedgwick herself recognizes, that there is less distinctive to these feminist criticisms than might be thought as they often repeat familiar Hegelian lines of thought. There is also a considerable degree of reliance on objections to the use of the term 'autonomy' in terms that owe more to developmental psychology than to transcendental philosophy.

13   There is an extensive literature on Kant and the emotions and indeed on Kant's philosophical anthropology but one will look in vain through it for a treatment of pure feeling and hence of the place of moral feeling in Kant's ethics. For the kind of treatments that are standard in the contemporary literature see Nancy Sherman (1997) *Making A Necessity of Virtue: Aristotle and Kant on Virtue* (Cambridge University Press: Cambridge) and Paul Guyer (2000) 'Moral Worth, Virtue, and Merit' in Paul Guyer (2000) *Kant on Freedom, Law, and Happiness* (Cambridge University Press: Cambridge).

14   Marcia W. Baron, *op. cit.*, Chapter 6 treats this example at some length and her unease with Kant's statement motivates the 'almost' in her title.

15   Mary Gregor is quite clear that the argument is not based on the typic but rather thinks this offers supporting material to bring the discussion closer to intuition. (Gregor, *op. cit.*, pp. 139ff.). Gregor seems, however, to have no difficulties with Kant's views on these topics, any more than do any other contemporary commentators on the Doctrine of Virtue despite implications it has for the position of homosexuals.

Chapter 8

1   For example, it is not my intention to discuss further the degree to which Kant's application of his ethical system takes place in terms of describing a 'non-pure' ethics. This has been attempted by Robert B. Louden (2000) *Kant's Impure Ethics: From Rational Beings to Human Beings* (Oxford University Press: Oxford and New York).

2   The success of the interpretations of Kant presented by Rawls and Habermas in recent years is testimony to the failure of a fruitful and full engagement with the whole terrain of Kant's practical philosophy as both these thinkers, whatever their other merits, perform a substantial reduction in the scope of practical philosophy by comparison with Kant.

3   The constitution most capable of promoting perpetual peace is clearly republican and, broadly speaking, a republican regime corresponds to the requirements of public right. Kant's notion of a republican constitution being one that is most likely to promote peace has been related in recent years to the conduct of democratic regimes with the implicit suggestion that contemporary democracies are broadly equivalent to Kantian republics. See

Michael W. Doyle (1993) 'Liberalism and International Relations' in Ronald Beiner and William James Booth (eds.) (1993) *Kant & Political Philosophy* (Yale University Press: New Haven and London) and Sharon Anderson-Gold (2001) *Cosmopolitanism and Human Rights* (University of Wales Press: Cardiff). Anderson-Gold introduces a number of subtle emendations of the thesis that Kantian cosmopolitanism has quite the same range as contemporary international codes.

4   This is the reason for Yirmiahu Yovel's rejection of Kant's treatment of religion. See Yirmiahu Yovel (1980) *Kant and the Philosophy of History* (Princeton University Press: Princeton, NJ). However such a rejection has a very high price, namely the renunciation of rational guidance in consideration of religious terms, a price that Yovel agrees to pay. Others may be less willing.

5   This comparison has a long after life, influencing for example both Hegel and Nietzsche.

6   Howard Williams (1983) *Kant's Political Philosophy* (Basil Blackwell, Oxford), p. 73. This criticism is also voiced by William A. Galston (1993) 'What Is Living and What Is Dead In Kant's Practical Philosophy?' in R. Beiner and W. J. Booth (eds.) (1993) *Kant & Political Philosophy: The Contemporary Legacy* (Yale University Press: New Haven and London).

7   This criticism has often been used against the political philosophy of John Rawls and from there extended to Kant and it is arguable that it has helped to motivate the shifts in Rawls' positions from the original formulation of his theory. Jurgen Habermas has replied to attacks of this sort on his own theory in J. Habermas (1983) *Moral Consciousness and Communicative Action* (1990 trans. By C. Lenhardt and S.W. Nicolsen, Polity Press: Oxford) and has also engaged in a debate with Rawls the significance and scope of which I will review elsewhere.

8   This general position of 'communitarianism' claims an ancestry back to Aristotle with a suggestion of a necessary communal basis for humanity presented as an up-dated form of Aristotle's notion of the *zoon politikon*. The classic statement of this view is Alasdair MacIntyre (1984) *After Virtue* (University of Notre Dame Press: Notre Dame).

9   My emphasis. It is noteworthy how, in the many debates about the 'formulas' of the *Groundwork*, this one, the one in which Kant expressly and emphatically states the supreme principle that the work is written to discover, is consistently missed.

10 This comparison is mentioned by Bernard Williams (1976) 'Moral Luck' in Bernard Williams (1981) *Moral Luck: Philosophical Papers 1973–1980* (Cambridge University Press: Cambridge and New York), p. 38. Williams traces the ancestry of the comparison back to Heine but it is also used in Hegel (1807) *The Phenomenology of Spirit* (1975 trans. by A.V. Miller, Oxford University Press: Oxford and New York), section on the moral view of the world.

11 The work of Alasdair MacIntyre is an interesting case in point here as, originating in Marxism, it seems, for the time being to have culminated in Roman Catholicism. The movement between external forms of binding belief might be thought to suggest some fundamental difficulties with attempts to circumscribe the importance of the principle of autonomy.

12   For an account of the nature and lacunae of *Idea for A Universal History* see G. Banham (2000) *Kant and the Ends of Aesthetics* (Macmillan & St. Martin's Press: London and New York), Chapter 10.

13   For a fuller account of this story see G. Banham and C. Blake (2000) 'Introduction' to G. Banham and C. Blake (eds.) (2000) *Evil Spirits: Nihilism and the Fate of Modernity* (Manchester University Press: Manchester and New York).

Bibliography

Editions of Kant in German

The Academy Edition which was begun in 1902 by the Prussian Academy of Sciences, continued later by the German Academy of Sciences in Berlin and the Academy of Sciences in Göttingen is now the recognized standard edition. All citations refer to this wherever there is an English translation that includes its pagination. The major exception is in references to the First Critique as these follow standard A and B reference.

English translations of Kant

Cambridge University Press is now presenting Kant's works to an extensive and almost standard English translation and I have referred to these editions on a number of occasions. Amongst these are the following:

D. Walford and R. Meerbote (eds.) (1992) *Theoretical Philosophy: 1755–1770*
Paul Guyer and Allen Wood (eds.) (1997) *Critique of Pure Reason*
Mary Gregor (ed.) (1996) *Practical Philosophy*
Mary Gregor (ed.) (1996) *The Metaphysics of Morals*
George Giovanni and Allen Wood (eds.) (1996) *Religion and Rational Theology*
Peter Heath and J.B. Schneewind (eds.) (1997) *Lectures on Ethics*

Other translations consulted:

James W. Ellington (1981) *Grounding for the Metaphysics of Morals* (Hackett Publishing Company: Indianapolis and Cambridge)
Victor Lyle Dowdell (1978) *Anthropology From A Pragmatic Point of View* (Revised and edited by Hans H. Rudnick, 1996, Southern Illinois University Press: Carbondale and Edwardsville)
Lewis White Beck (1956) *The Critique of Practical Reason* (Library of Liberal Arts: New York and Oxford)
Werner S. Pluhar (1987) *Critique of Judgment* (Hackett Publishing Company: Indianapolis and Cambridge)
Werner S. Pluhar (1996) *Critique of Pure Reason* (Hackett Publishing Company: Indianapolis and Cambridge)
Norman Kemp-Smith (1929) *Critique of Pure Reason* (Macmillan Press: Basingstoke)
John T. Goldthwaite (1973) *Observations on the Feeling of the Beautiful and the Sublime* (University of California Press: Los Angeles)
Annette Churton (1899) *On Education* (Kegan Paul, Trench, Trubner & Co.: London)

Secondary sources

Allison, Henry (1990) *Kant's Theory of Freedom* (Cambridge University Press: Cambridge)

Ameriks, Karl (1982) *Kant's Theory of Mind: An Analysis of the Paralogisms of Pure Reason* (Clarendon Press: Oxford)

Anderson-Gold, Sharon (2001) *Cosmopolitanism and Human Rights* (University of Wales Press: Cardiff)

Arendt, Hannah (1963) *Eichmann in Jerusalem: A Report on the Banality of Evil* (Viking: New York)

Arendt, Hannah (1982) *Lectures on Kant's Political Philosophy* (ed. and trans. by Ronald Beiner, Harvester Press: Brighton)

Aune, Bruce (1979) *Kant's Theory of Morals* (Princeton University Press: Princeton, NJ)

Auxter, Thomas (1982) *Kant's Moral Teleology* (Mercer University Press: Macon)

Baker, Judith (1988) 'Counting Categorical Imperatives' *Kant-Studien* 79:4

Banham, Gary (1996) 'The Terror of the Law: Judaism and International Institutions' in J. Brannigan, R. Robbins and J. Wolfreys (eds.) (1996) *Applying: To Derrida* (Macmillan and St. Martin's Press: London and New York)

Banham, Gary (2000) 'Teleology, Transcendental Reflection and Artificial Life' *Tekhnehma: Journal of Philosophy and Technology* 6

Banham, Gary (2000) *Kant and the Ends of Aesthetics* (Macmillan and St. Martin's Press: London and New York)

Banham, Gary (2002) 'Kant's Critique of Right' *Kantian Review*, Vol. 6

Banham, Gary and Blake, Charlie (2000) 'Introduction' to G. Banham and C. Blake (eds.) (2000) *Evil Spirits: Nihilism and the Fate of Modernity* (Manchester University Press: Manchester)

Baron, Marcia W. (1995) *Kantian Ethics Almost Without Apology* (Cornell University Press: Ithaca and London)

Baynes, Kenneth (1989) 'Kant on Property Rights and the Social Contract' *Monist* 72

Beck, Lewis White (1960) *A Commentary on Kant's Critique of Practical Reason* (University of Chicago Press: Chicago and London)

Beck, Lewis White (1965) 'Kant's Two Conceptions of the Will in Their Political Context' in Beiner and Booth (eds.) (1993)

Benjamin, Walter (1928) *The Origin of German Tragic Drama* (1977 trans. by John Osborne, Verso: London and New York)

Butts, Robert E (1984) *Kant and the Double Government Methodology* (D. Reidel Publishing Company: Boston)

Byrd, B. Sharon (1997) 'Kant's Theory of Contract' *The Southern Journal of Philosophy* Volume XXXVI, Supplement

Carnois, Bernard (1973) *The Coherence of Kant's Doctrine of Freedom* (1987 trans. by David Booth, The University of Chicago Press: Chicago and London)

Caygill, Howard (1989) *Art of Judgment* (Basil Blackwell: Oxford)

Caygill, Howard (1995) *A Kant Dictionary* (Basil Blackwell: Oxford)

Caygill, Howard (1998) *Walter Benjamin: The Colour of Experience* (Routledge: London and New York)

Copjec, Joan (1996) 'Introduction: Evil in the Time of the Finite World' in Joan Copjec (ed.) (1996) *Radical Evil* (Verso: London and New York)

Doyle, Michael W. (1993) 'Liberalism and International Relations' in Beiner and Booth (eds.) (1993)

Duncan, A.R.C. (1957) *Practical Reason and Morality: A Study of Immanuel Kant's 'Foundations for the Metaphysics of Morals'* (Thomas Nelson & Sons: London)

Flikschuch, Katrin (2000) *Kant and Modern Political Philosophy* (Cambridge University Press: Cambridge)

Förster, Eckhart (2000) *Kant's Final Synthesis: An Essay on the Opus Postumum* (Harvard University Press: Cambridge, Mass. and London)

Galston, William A. (1993) 'What Is Living and What Is Dead in Kant's Practical Philosophy' in Beiner and Booth (eds.) (1993)

Goldsmith, Oliver (1766) *The Vicar of Wakefield* (Penguin Books, Harmondsdsworth)

Gregor, Mary (1963) *Laws of Freedom: A Study of Kant's Method of Applying the Categorical Imperative in the Metaphysik der Sitten* (Basil Blackwell: Oxford)

Gregor, Mary (1988) 'Kant's Theory of Property' *Review of Metaphysics* 41

Grotius, Hugo (1625) *The Law of War and Peace* (1925 trans. by Francis Kelsey, Oxford University Press: Oxford)

Guyer, Paul (1989) 'The Unity of Reason' in P. Guyer (2000)

Guyer, Paul (1991) 'Mendelssohn and Kant: One Source of the Critical Philosophy' in P. Guyer (2000) *Kant on Freedom, Law, and Happiness* (Cambridge University Press: Cambridge)

Guyer, Paul (1993) *Kant and the Experience of Freedom: Essays on Aesthetics and Morality* (Cambridge University Press: Cambridge)

Guyer, Paul (1995) 'The Possibility of the Categorical Imperative' in Paul Guyer (ed.) (1998)

Guyer, Paul (2000) 'Moral Worth, Virtue and Merit' in Paul Guyer (2000)

Guyer, Paul (ed.) (1998) *Kant's Groundwork of the Metaphysics of Morals: Critical Essays* (Rowman & Littefield: Lanham, New York and London)

Habermas, J. (1983) *Moral Consciousness and Communicative Action* (1990 trans. by C. Lenhardt and S.W. Nicolsen, Polity Press: Oxford)

Hare, John E. (1996) *The Moral Gap: Kantian Ethics, Human Limits and God's Assistance* (Clarendon Press: Oxford)

Hare, R.M. (1981) *Moral Thinking: Its Levels, Method and Point* (Clarendon Press: Oxford)

Harrison-Barbet, Anthony (1990) *Mastering Philosophy* (Macmillan: Basingstoke)

Hegel, G.W.F. (1807) *Phenomenology of Spirit* (1974 trans. by A.V. Miller, Oxford University Press: Oxford)

Hegel, G.W.F. (1821) *Elements of A Philosophy of Right* (1991 trans. by H.B. Nisbet, Cambridge University Press: Cambridge)

Henrich, Dieter (1975) 'The Deduction of the Moral Law: The Reasons For the Obscurity of the Final Section of Kant's *Groundwork of the Metaphysics of Morals*' in Paul Guyer (ed.) (1998)

Herman, Barbara (1993) *The Practice of Moral Judgment* (Harvard University Press: Cambridge, Mass. and London)

Hill, Thomas E. Jr. (1971) 'Kant on Imperfect Duty and Supererogation' *Kant-Studien* 62

Höffe, Ottfried (1992) *Immanuel Kant* (1994 trans. by Marshall Farrier, State University of New York Press: Albany)

Howard, Dick (1988) *The Politics of Critique* (University of Minnesota Press: Minneapolis)

Hutchings, Patrick (1972) *Kant on Absolute Value: A Critical Examination of Certain Key Concepts in Kant's* Groundwork of the Metaphysics of Morals *and of His Ontology of Personal Values* (George Allen & Unwin: London)

Kaufman, Alexander (1999) *Welfare in the Kantian State* (Clarendon Press: Oxford)

Kelly, George Armstrong (1969) *Idealism, Politics and History: Sources of Hegelian Thought* (Cambridge University Press: Cambridge)

Körner, Stephan (1984) *Metaphysics: Its Structure and Function* (Cambridge University Press: Cambridge)

Korsgaard, Christine M. (1986) 'Aristotle and Kant on the Source of Value' *Ethics* 96

Korsgaard, Christine M. (1996) *Creating the Kingdom of Ends* (Cambridge University Press: Cambridge)

Kuehn, M. (1995) 'The Moral Dimension of Kant's *Inaugural Dissertation*: A New Perspective on the "Great Light" of 1769?' in Hoke Robinson (ed.) (1995) *Proceedings of the Eighth International Kant Congress*, Vol. 1, Part 2 (Marquette University Press: Milwaukee)

Kuehn, Manfred (1985) 'Kant's Transcendental Deduction of God's Existence As A Postulate of Pure Practical Reason' *Kant-Studien* 76:2

Linden, Harry Van Der (1988) *Kantian Ethics and Socialism* (Hackett Publishing Company: Indianapolis and Cambridge)

Lo, P.C. (1987) *Treating Persons As Ends: An Essay On Kant's Moral Philosophy* (University Press of America: Lanham, New York and London)

Longuenesse, Béatrice (1993) *Kant and the Capacity to Judge* (1998 trans. by Charles T. Wolfe, Princeton University Press: Princeton, NJ)

Louden, Robert (1986) 'Kant's Virtue Ethics' *Philosophy* 61

Louden, Robert B. (2000) *Kant's Impure Ethics: From rational beings to human beings* (Oxford University Press: Oxford and New York)

Ludwig, Bernd (1990) 'The Right of A State in Immanuel Kant's *Doctrine of Right*' *Journal of the History of Philosophy* 27:3

Lyotard, J.F. (1983) *The Differend: Phrases In Dispute* (1988 trans. by Georges Van Den Abbeele, Manchester University Press: Manchester)

MacIntyre, Alasdair (1984) *After Virtue* (University of Notre Dame Press: Notre Dame)

Mauthner, Thomas (1981) 'Kant's Metaphysics of Morals: A Note on the Text' *Kant-Studien* 72

McCarthy, Michael (1979) 'Kant's Application of the Analytic/Synthetic Distinction to Imperatives' *Dialogue* 18

McCarthy, Michael (1982) 'Kant's Rejection of the Argument of *Groundwork* III' *Kant-Studien* 73:2

McCarthy, Michael (1985) 'The Objection of Circularity in *Groundwork* III' *Kant-Studien* 76:1

McFarland, John (1970) *Kant's Concept of Teleology* (University of Edinburgh Press: Edinburgh)

Michalson, Gordon E. Jr (1990) *Fallen Freedom: Kant on Radical Evil and Moral Regeneration* (Cambridge University Press: Cambridge)

Muirhead, J.H. (1892) *The Elements of Ethics* (John Murray: London)

Mulholland, Leslie (1990) *Kant's System of Rights* (Columbia University Press: New York)

Munzel, G. Felicitas (1999) *Kant's Conception of Moral Character: The 'Critical' Link of Morality, Anthropology and Reflective Judgment* (University of Chicago Press: Chicago and London)

Murphy, Jeffrie G. (1965) 'The Highest Good As Content For Kant's Formalism: Beck *versus* Silber' *Kant-Studien* 56

Nancy, Jean-Luc (1988) *The Experience of Freedom* (1993 trans. by B. McDonald, Stanford University Press: Stanford)

Nell, Onora (1975) *Acting on Principle: An Essay on Kantian Ethics* (Columbia University Press: New York)

Nietzsche, Friedrich (1872) *The Birth of Tragedy* (1967 trans. by Walter Kaufmann, Vintage Books: New York)

Nietzsche, Friedrich (1887) *On the Genealogy of Morals* (1967 trans. by Walter Kaufmann, Vintage Books: New York)

Nowell-Smith, P.H. (1954) *Ethics* (Penguin: Harmondsworth and Baltimore)

Nuyen, A.T. (1993) 'Counting the Formulas of the Categorical Imperative: One Plus Three Makes Four' *History of Philosophy Quarterly* 10

O'Neill, Onora (1989) *Constructions of Reason: Explorations of Kant's Practical Philosophy* (Cambridge University Press: Cambridge)

Oakley, Justin (1992) *Morality and the Emotions* (Routledge: London and New York)

Paton, H.J. (1947) *The Categorical Imperative: A Study In Kant's Moral Philosophy* (University of Pennsylvania Press: Philadelphia)

Pogge, Thomas (1997) 'Is Kant's *Rechtslehre* Comprehensive?' *Southern Journal of Philosophy* Volume XXXVI, Supplement

Pogge, Thomas W. (1988) 'Kant's Theory of Justice' *Kant-Studien* 79

Rawls, John (1989) 'Themes In Kant's Moral Philosophy' in Beiner and Booth (eds.) (1993)

Rawls, John (1993) *Political Liberalism* (Harvard University Press: Cambridge, Mass. and London)

Rawls, John (2000) *Lectures on the History of Moral Philosophy* (ed. by Barbara Herman, Harvard University Press: Cambridge, Mass. and London)

Riley, Patrick (1983) *Kant's Political Philosophy* (Rowman and Littlefield: Totona)

Rogozinski, Jacob (1996) 'It Makes Us Wrong: Kant and Radical Evil' in J. Copjec (ed.) (1996)

Rollin, Bernard (1976) 'There Is Only One Categorical Imperative' *Kant-Studien* 67

Ross, Sir David (1954) *Kant's Ethical Theory: A Commentary on the Groundwork of the Metaphysics of Morals* (Clarendon Press: Oxford)

Ross, W.D. (1930) *The Right and the Good* (Clarendon Press: Oxford)

Rousseau, Jean-Jacques (1762) *The Social Contract* (1974 trans. by Lowell Bair, Mentor and New American Library: New York and London)

Schaller, Walter E. (1987) 'Kant's Architectonic of Duties' *Philosophy and Phenomenological Research* Vol. XLVII, No 2.

Scheler, Max (1913–16) *Formalism in Ethics and Non-Formal Ethics of Values: A New Attempt toward the Foundation of an Ethical Personalism* (1973 trans. by M.S. Frings and R.L. Funk, Northwestern University Press: Evanston)

Schlipp, Paul Arthur (1938) *Kant's Pre-Critical Ethics* (Northwestern University Press: Evanston and Chicago)

Schneewind, J.B. (1998) *The Invention of Autonomy* (Cambridge University Press: Cambridge)

Schrader, George (1953–4) 'The Status of Teleological Judgments in the Critical Philosophy' *Kant-Studien* 45

Schwann, A. (ed.) *Denken in Schatten des Nihilismus* (Wissenschafliche Buchgesellschaft: Darmstadt)

Sedgwick, Sally (1990) 'Can Kant's Ethics Survive the Feminist Critique?' in Robin May Schott (ed.) (1997) *Feminist Interpretations of Immanuel Kant* (The Pennsylvania State University Press: University Park, Pennsylvania)

Sherman, Nancy (1997) *Making A Necessity of Virtue: Aristotle and Kant on Virtue* (Cambridge University Press: Cambridge)

Sidgwick, Henry (1874) *The Methods of Ethics* (Macmillan & Co: London)

Silber, John R. (1959) 'Kant's Conception of the Highest Good As Immanent and Transcendent' *Philosophical Review* 68

Silber, John (1963) 'The Importance of the Highest Good in Kant's Ethics' *Ethics* 73

Silber, John R. (1960) 'The Ethical Significance of Kant's *Religion*' in Greene and Hudson (eds. and trans.) (1960) *Religion within the Limits of Reason Alone* (Harper Torchbooks: New York)

Smith, Steven G. (1984) 'Worthiness to be Happy and Kant's Highest Concept of the Highest Good' *Kant-Studien* 75:2

Stratton-Lake, Philip (1993) 'Formulating Categorical Imperatives' *Kant-Studien* 84:3

Strauss, Leo (1932) 'Comments on Carl Schmitt's *Der Begriff Des Politischen*' in Carl Schmitt (1927) *The Concept of the Political* (1976 trans. by George Schwab, Rutgers University Press: New Brunswick and New Jersey)

Strauss, Leo (1953) *Natural Right and History* (University of Chicago Press: Chicago and London)

Velkley, Richard L. (1993) 'The Crisis of the End of Reason in Kant's Philosophy and the *Remarks* of 1764–65' in Ronald Beiner and William James Booth (eds.) (1993) *Kant & Political Philosophy* (Yale University Press: New Haven and London)

Ward, Keith (1972) *The Development of Kant's View of Ethics* (Basil Blackwell: Oxford)

Westphal, Kenneth R. (1997) 'Is Kant's Table of Contracts Complete?' *The Southern Journal of Philosophy* Volume XXVI, Supplement.

Westphal, Kenneth R. (2002) 'A Kantian Justification of Possession' in M. Timmons (ed.) (2002) *Kant's Metaphysics of Morals: Interpretative Essays* (Oxford University Press: Oxford and New York)

Williams, Bernard (1981) *Moral Luck: Philosophical Papers 1973–1980* (Cambridge University Press: Cambridge)

Williams, Howard (1983) *Kant's Political Philosophy* (Basil Blackwell: Oxford)

Williams, T.C. (1968) *The Concept of the Categorical Imperative: A Study of the Place of the Categorical Imperative in Kant's Ethical Theory* (Clarendon Press: Oxford)

Wood, Allen (1970) *Kant's Moral Religion* (Cornell University Press: Ithaca and London)

Wood, Allen (1995) 'Humanity as an End in Itself' in Paul Guyer (ed.) (1998)

Woolf, Robert Paul (1973) *The Autonomy of Reason: A Commentary on Kant's Groundwork of the Metaphysics of Morals* (Harper & Row: New York)

Yovel, Yirmiahu (1980) *Kant and the Philosophy of History* (Princeton University Press: Princeton)

Zupančič, Alenka (2000) *Ethics of the Real: Kant, Lacan* (Verso: London and New York)

Index

Aesthetic   101–3, 109, 110, 124,
   137, 203–5
transcendental   9, 14, 44
Allison, Henry   90–1, 93–4, 245
Ameriks, Karl   89–90, 245
Analogy/Analogies   71, 74, 115,
   117, 120, 122–3, 125, 130–1,
   141, 143–4, 146, 148–51, 169,
   205, 210, 216–19, 233
Second   39, 42, 46–8, 50–1,
   53–6
of Experience   45, 161
Analytic   38–9, 42, 53, 58, 60,
   66–7, 93–4, 96–9, 101, 103,
   104–5, 107, 109, 112–13
Animality   125, 183, 192
Anthropology   11, 14–15, 19–25,
   29, 33, 35, 65, 121, 124, 127,
   130, 155, 192, 195
transcendental   109, 117, 124–6,
   130, 185, 192, 247 *see also*
   Anthroponomy
*Anthropology From A Pragmatic Point
   of View*   8, 14, 20–5, 30, 242
Anthroponomy   185–6, 192–3, 195,
   198, 203–8, 216, 218–19, 231–2,
   235 *see also* Feeling
Antinomy   38–9, 41–5, 49, 59,
   107–9, 159, 164, 178
Third   3, 37–61, 69, 78, 83,
   89–92, 95–6, 100, 102,
   105–6, 108, 111, 142,
   155, 159, 244
of teleological judgment   37–8,
   49–50, 52–3, 55–6, 142, 244
Fourth   38, 40, 52, 57, 61–3, 243
Architectonic   181, 185–96, 233
Arendt, Hannah   6, 241, 248
Aristotle   2, 240
Arrogance   200
Autonomy   6, 73–4, 76–7, 79, 81,
   84, 98–9, 104, 106, 183, 192,
   199–200, 202, 207, 218–20,
   223–8, 230, 250, 258

Baumgarten, Alexander   8, 27–9,
   32, 35, 69
Beauty   12, 26
Beck, Lewis White   49–51, 53, 56,
   93, 105, 112–17, 242, 245–6, 251
Beneficence   198–201, 256
Benevolence   18, 195, 197–8, 217
Benjamin, Walter   133–4, 248–9
Bestiality   209

Canon of Pure Reason   48, 57–62, 78
Carnois, Bernard   57, 61, 243, 246
Casuistry   6, 196–203, 231–5
Categorical imperative   7, 67–73,
   77–8, 81, 84–7, 90–1, 95–6,
   98, 100, 154–8, 164, 178,
   182–5, 192–3, 196, 224,
   228–33, 244, 250–1
multiple formulations of   64,
   73–6, 183
Category/Categories   38–9, 49, 53,
   56, 74, 99, 101–2, 105, 162
Causality   39–42, 45–6, 48, 50, 52–3,
   55, 77, 96–7, 100–2, 105–6, 108,
   112, 115, 120, 161, 233
Caygill, Howard   240, 242, 246,
   248, 253
Character   16–17, 25, 48, 124,
   143, 145
empirical   37, 47–8, 80, 90
intelligible   37, 47–9, 80, 90, 145–6
Charles I   137, 236
Children   15–18, 25, 28, 33,
   161, 200, 254
Christian/Christianity   18–19,
   30, 111
Church   150
Civil Condition/Society   147, 152,
   159, 164–72, 179–80
Coercion   157–8, 165, 175
Concepts   4, 36, 38, 44, 52, 56, 70,
   72, 77–8, 95–6, 101, 103–4,
   106–7, 137, 157, 163, 169, 182,
   185, 217, 220, 225, 232–3

Condition/Conditioned 38–9, 61, 105–6
Conflict of the Faculties 13, 118, 128, 146–8, 205, 230, 236, 250
Conscience 34, 204
Consequentialism 26, 177, 244
Conservatism 173–4, 227
Contingency 39, 62, 97
Contract 152, 154, 168–70, 174, 177–80
Contractarian 152
Copjec, Joan 131–2, 134–5, 248
Cosmological 10, 38–40, 42–4, 55
Cosmopolitan 25, 213, 215, 257
Crimina Carnis 208–11
Critique 4–6, 8–9, 13, 63–6, 76–7, 79, 82, 85, 93–4, 98–9, 149, 211–13, 228–32, 235, 250
Critique of Aesthetic Judgment 12, 241
Critique of Judgment 5–6, 50, 104–5, 118–19, 121–3, 130, 133, 135, 153, 198, 200, 237, 241
Critique of Practical Reason 2–4, 24, 37, 65, 67, 83, 92–122, 125, 128, 156, 169, 203–4, 229–31, 233, 236, 245
Critique of Pure Reason 3, 13–14, 37–63, 66, 69, 77, 80, 92, 95–6, 98, 100–1, 110–12, 122, 160–1, 163, 165, 232–3, 244, 252
Critique of Teleological Judgment 10, 118, 136, 141, 241
Crusius, Christian August 9–10, 12–13, 38, 40

Deduction 3, 64–5, 77, 91, 94, 98–101, 106–7, 112, 145–6, 162, 165, 169, 232, 246
Demonology 119, 132–40, 239
Deontology 1, 6, 26, 185, 255
Determinism 9–10, 53, 56, 89
Dialectic 3, 24, 37–8, 49, 93, 105–17, 118
Dignity 17–18, 20, 176, 193, 195, 200, 218
Discipline 16
Doctrine/Doctrinal 4–6, 26, 29, 153, 156, 211–13, 228–32, 235, 238, 250

Dreams of A Spirit-Seer Elucidated by Dreams of Metaphysics 12–13, 44, 242
Duties 29, 36, 70, 76, 186, 188, 190–1, 193–6, 200–2, 205, 216, 219, 231
Duty 72, 76, 113, 116, 143, 156, 167, 182–3, 185, 188, 190, 193, 195, 197–9, 207, 209–10, 214, 217–20
imperfect 70, 72, 184, 186–203
perfect 184–5, 186–211
Dynamical 39, 42, 45, 53

Education 14–19, 34, 141, 228, 234, 254
Emotions 22–4, 122, 205, 256
Empiricism 43–4, 67, 96, 102
End(s) 7, 10, 71–4, 76, 78, 107, 122, 141, 151, 182–5, 188, 190–1, 193, 196, 205, 208–9, 215–17, 225–7, 230–1, 233
Enthusiasm 148
Equality 28, 158, 176, 201, 218
Eschatology 4, 118, 150, 177, 224–8, 235–8, 240
Ethics 1–2, 6–8, 11, 14–15, 25, 27, 118, 134, 153–4, 178, 182, 185–6, 188, 212, 217–19, 226, 238
Eudaimonism 68
Evil 124–40, 152, 204, 235, 247
Examples 67, 69, 76
Experience 42, 47, 53–4, 58–60, 99–100, 106–7

Faculty of desire 20–1
Faith 19, 150
Feeling 11–12, 14, 18, 24, 26, 28, 31, 80, 95, 102–3, 108–9, 123, 132, 136–7, 186, 195, 203–8, 216, 218, 235
moral 16, 26–8, 32, 103, 108, 125, 137, 203–4
Final End of All Things 235
Flikschuh, Katrin 154, 159, 164, 250–1, 253
Formalist 1, 7

Freedom 9, 18, 23, 37, 39–61, 77–9,
  81–9, 93, 95–9, 100–5, 107, 112,
  120–2, 124–5, 127, 130, 132–3,
  139, 155, 157–8, 161, 163,
  176, 180, 182, 185, 193, 202,
  219–24, 228–33, 246
  practical 37, 46–7, 48–9, 56–7,
    59, 64, 88
  transcendental 37, 41–2, 46–9,
    56–7, 59–60, 62, 64, 88, 90, 92
Friendship 206, 208, 218–19, 236

God 10, 14, 18–19, 26, 36, 40,
  58–60, 62, 67, 93, 95, 111–12,
  118–20, 123, 129–30, 133, 138,
  145, 150, 215–19, 235–6, 246
  Son of 141, 144
Goodness/Good 30, 35, 61,
  107, 113–15, 118, 125, 127,
  142, 144, 146, 148, 222–6,
  247, 250
Gratitude 198, 207
Gregor, Mary 158, 187–90, 193,
  196, 219, 226, 231, 240,
  251, 254–6
Grotius, Hugo 166, 252
*Groundwork for a Metaphysics of
  Morals* 2, 4, 6, 11, 28–9, 37,
  64–96, 98–102, 103–4, 108,
  122, 149, 155–6, 183, 186–7,
  191, 197, 224–5, 228–31, 233,
  236–7, 244–5, 257
Guyer, Paul 6, 75–6, 241–2,
  244–5, 256

Happiness 24, 35, 37, 60, 68,
  107–8, 111, 115, 121, 134–5,
  142, 183, 199–200, 216–19, 255
Hare, John E. 145–6, 149
Hegel, G.W.F. 116–17, 239, 246,
  257–8
Henrich, Dieter 88–91, 245
Herder, Johann 25–6, 28, 30
Heteronomy 80
Highest Good 24, 30, 35, 61, 106,
  110, 113, 121, 224 *and see
  Summum Bonum*
Highest Political Good 214
Hill, Thomas 199–200, 256

History 4, 6, 23, 118, 139–40,
  146, 148, 151, 177, 205, 215,
  217–19, 235–6, 238, 240
Hobbes, Thomas 26, 127
Holiness 110, 142
Holy Ghost 138, 143
Homosexuality 208–10
Honour 193, 205
Hope 36, 60, 138–9, 147–8, 237
Howard, Dick 5–6, 240
Humanity 20, 23–4, 71, 103, 125–6,
  129, 140–1, 145, 158–9, 169, 176,
  183, 186, 191–3, 195–6, 199, 201,
  207, 224–8, 251
  idea of 15, 18–19
Hume, David 95
Humiliation 18
Hutcheson, Francis 11

Idea(s) 25, 38–9, 46–7, 49, 62,
  78, 81–4, 91, 95, 106, 120,
  146, 148–9
*Idea for a Universal History
  From A Cosmopolitan Point
  of View* 236, 249
Ideal 34–6, 61–3, 72, 112, 116,
  148, 214, 236
  of pure reason 38
Immortality 58, 60, 93, 95,
  111–12, 115–16, 120
Innocence 18, 30, 128
Intellectualist 31–3
Interest 43, 46, 57–60, 84,
  109, 234
Intuition 52–4, 56, 98, 106, 123,
  142, 163, 232–3

Judgment 32, 34, 52–4, 83–4,
  88, 102, 123, 144, 162, 198,
  205, 233–4
  ethical 7
  reflective 6, 50, 52, 198–9
Justice 144, 171–2, 176, 196,
  216–17, 236

Kant and the Ends of Aesthetics 7,
  241–2, 246, 249, 258
Kingdom of ends 72, 74, 149, 178
Knowledge 151

Law   23, 34, 36, 69–70, 72, 74–7, 91,
   94, 97–100, 102, 104, 106–8, 110,
   112–14, 120, 122, 124, 128, 135–8,
   140, 142, 152, 156–7, 162, 167,
   173, 184, 186, 188, 191, 208, 226,
   229–31, 233–4, 255
   natural   152, 168, 171, 173,
      177–80, 253
Laws   40–2, 46, 59, 67–8, 81,
   105, 120, 125, 163, 176,
   214–15, 219, 234
Lectures on Ethics   25–37, 61, 65,
   69, 93, 186
*Lectures on the Philosophical Doctrine
   of Religion*   247
Legislation   150
Leibniz, Gottfried   9
Logic   35, 65, 136, 160–1
Louis XVI   137, 236
Love   28, 186, 195–6, 198, 202,
   205–6, 208, 216–18, 236
Lying   133, 137, 193
Lyotard, Jean-François   248

MacIntrye, Alasdair   257–8
Marriage   28, 169–71, 208, 252
Masturbation   208–11
Mathematical   39, 42, 45, 54
Maxims   16–18, 23, 25, 27, 31,
   36, 69, 72–3, 97, 107, 124–5,
   131, 133–6, 141, 144, 154–5,
   163, 182, 184–5, 188, 190,
   193–4, 196, 198–9, 202–3, 206,
   224, 226–7, 229
McCarthy, Michael   99, 245–6
Mechanism   51, 53, 56, 136
Mendelssohn, Moses   10, 242
*Metaphysical Foundations of Natural
   Science*   153
Metaphysics   9, 12–13, 35, 65–7,
   70, 96, 153, 155, 225, 251
   of morals   26, 64–73, 75–7,
      79, 83, 85, 89, 94, 98,
      155, 204, 228, 251
Metaphysics of Morals   4, 6, 17,
   29, 152–238
Method, Transcendental
   Doctrine of   37–8, 57
Modesty   18, 200, 208

Money   170, 215, 237
Morality   16, 29–31, 35, 43, 67, 79,
   86–7, 94, 105, 108, 114–17,
   149–50, 152, 154, 175, 182, 192,
   210–12, 219, 225, 229, 234–6
   supreme principle of   11, 32–3,
      64–92, 94, 109, 155, 192, 194,
      200–2, 224, 226, 228
Philosophy   5, 12, 64, 152–3, 158,
   178, 188, 190, 196, 223–4
Psychology   4–5, 204–5, 234–5,
   237
Mullholland, Leslie   178, 255
Mysticism   12–13, 21

Nancy, Jean-Luc   246, 248
Nature   38–42, 50, 58–9, 69–70,
   72, 74, 81–2, 99, 102, 118,
   120, 122, 124
Necessity   10, 37, 41, 47, 51, 61, 97
Nell, Onora (now O'Neill)   188–9,
   196–7, 245, 255
*New Elucidation of the First Principles of
   Metaphysical Cognition*   9–11, 38
Nietzsche, Friedrich   239, 247, 257
Nihilism   140, 249, 253
Noumenal   49, 91, 96

Object   24, 29, 53, 78, 101, 104–6,
   110, 134, 160–2
   Transcendental   46
Obligation   10–11, 18, 44, 65, 86,
   156, 184, 187, 195–6
*Observations on the Feeling of the
   Beautiful and the Sublime*   11–12,
   25, 28, 242
On Education   14–20, 25, 34, 242
*On the Form and Principles
   of the Sensible and Intelligible
   World*   13, 242
Opus Postumum   153, 250
Ought   35, 46–7, 60, 82, 229

Passion   21–4
Paton, H.J.   73–6, 83–90, 244–5
Peace   213–15, 236
Perfection   10, 18–19, 26–8, 30–2,
   35, 110, 113–17, 141, 183, 190,
   195–6, 202, 204–5

Perfectionist/Perfectionism   3, 10–11,
    14, 18–19, 25–6, 28, 31–2, 61–2,
    67, 117, 158, 181–6, 196
Perpetual Peace: A Philosophical Sketch
    139, 154, 215, 217, 236, 239,
    247, 250
Personality   16, 20, 33, 103, 125,
    139, 173, 235
Phenomenology of Spirit   116, 246, 258
Philanthropy   219
Philosophy   9, 13–14, 29, 65, 70,
    216
  practical   2–4, 6–10, 13–14,
    20–1, 26, 28, 30, 35, 37–8,
    43, 61, 63, 65–6, 78, 82, 84,
    91, 118, 122, 152, 154, 158,
    181, 185, 205, 212–13, 219,
    224, 228, 233–9, 257
  theoretical   1, 8, 21, 40, 63,
    89, 153, 232
Pleasure   26, 97, 108, 136, 210
Pluhar, Werner   51, 53, 56, 243
Pogge, Thomas   154, 180, 221,
    250, 253
Politics   118
Possession   154, 159–66, 168,
    170, 174, 178–9, 251
Possibility   47, 99–101
Postulates of practical reason
    110–12, 120, 153, 246
Principles   10, 12, 18, 21, 25,
    32–4, 36, 55, 70, 72, 76, 96–7,
    138, 141, 155, 175–6, 178, 181,
    186, 192, 217–18, 238
  formal   11, 71, 185
  material   11, 71, 191
  of application   7, 163, 180,
    253, 255
Progress   20, 39, 110, 115–16, 134–5,
    139–48, 177, 235–8
Property   152, 154, 159, 164,
    166–8, 170, 251–2
Providence   146, 215
Prudence   30, 34
Punishment   17, 33, 138, 144,
    176–7
Purposes/Purposiveness   7, 10,
    20, 22, 56, 68, 78, 95, 116,
    182, 200, 208

Quantity   39, 74, 176

Rational   71–2, 77
  beings   70–1, 78–9, 83, 87–8,
    90, 108, 216
Rationalism   27, 85, 102, 233
Rawls, John   7, 75–6, 241, 244,
    250, 254, 257
Reality   39, 47, 101
Reason   22, 31, 35, 38–41, 44–5, 52,
    57, 60, 62, 66–7, 72, 80–3, 97,
    101–2, 106, 109, 120, 145
  fact of   93–4, 98–9, 101, 106,
    109, 113
  practical   23, 61, 64–8, 76–9, 82–5,
    95–8, 101–3, 105–18, 132, 155,
    163, 180, 224–5, 230, 246
Redemption   140–9
Reformation   140–1, 150
Regulative principles   45, 49–50,
    53, 55
Religion   19, 29, 43, 118, 120, 122,
    137, 145, 215–18, 235
*Religion within the Limits of Reason
    Alone*   4–5, 13, 19, 29, 118,
    120–46, 149–51, 153, 185,
    192, 194, 203–4, 205, 208,
    216, 219, 224, 231, 234–5,
    237, 240, 248–9
Republican   147–8, 154, 173
Respect   18, 20, 83, 102, 108,
    123, 186, 195–6, 198, 200–1,
    205–8, 216, 218
Revolution   140–1, 147–50,
    174, 235
Right   137, 139, 148, 153–5, 157–9,
    162, 165–9, 170, 177–80, 182,
    210, 212–18, 220–4, 255
  doctrine of   137, 152–80, 182,
    211, 213–15, 220, 222–4, 231,
    236, 247, 250–1, 253
  private   152, 154, 158–9, 168,
    170–2
  public   152, 154, 158–60, 168,
    170–2
  supreme principle of   6, 157, 185,
    202, 223, 227–8
Rousseau, Jean-Jacques   12, 15, 27–8,
    30, 127, 172–4, 253

Satan/Satanic   133–6
Schaller, Walter   189, 255
Schematism   53–4, 102, 122–3, 125,
    131, 141, 143–4, 146, 148–51,
    205, 216–19, 231–5
Self-legislation   *see* Autonomy
Series   39
Sex   23
Sovereign/Sovereignty   138, 172–6,
    179, 215, 253
State   172–7
Stoic/Stoicism   17, 19, 30, 107–8,
    129, 191, 206–7
Stratton-Lake, Philip   75–6, 244
Strauss, Leo   247, 253
Sublime   12, 26, 237
Subreption   124, 134
Suicide   135, 137–9, 209–11
Summum Bonum   4, 30–1, 35–6,
    61, 93, 106–9, 111–15, 118–21,
    134, 142, 149–51, 183, 216,
    218, 236
Supersensible   120–3, 150
Supreme Being   39, 51–3, 61, 121
Swedenborg, Emanuel   12
Symbol   123, 169
Sympathy   198, 206, 208
Synthesis   38–9, 44, 58, 133–6, 142,
    165–6, 173, 249
System   31, 68, 76, 122, 152–5, 170,
    233, 236

Teleology/Teleological   51, 63, 76,
    118–22, 135, 137, 158, 178,
    181–6, 191, 198, 216, 225–6,
    231, 239–40, 244
Theology/Theological   119, 121, 137
Totality   38–9, 43, 45, 55, 67, 183
Transcendental Idealism   43, 52, 251
Transcendental Subject   47
Triebfeder   21, 71, 101–3, 125
Typic   102, 115, 122, 163–4, 169,
    205, 208, 210, 230–1, 233

Understanding   14, 27, 32–3,
    38, 43, 52, 58, 80–1, 101–2,
    183, 232
Universal/Universality   36–7, 40,
    67, 69, 73, 75–6, 98, 121,
    141, 157, 162–3, 165, 169,
    178–9, 184, 188, 200, 214,
    226, 229–31

Vice(s)   18, 24, 33–4, 125–7,
    132, 134, 136, 193, 199,
    201–2, 209, 211
Virtue   6, 12, 18, 24, 35, 107–8,
    114, 133–5, 149, 181–6, 193,
    201, 205, 211–13, 215–16,
    218–21, 227–8, 234, 240
    supreme principle of   6, 185,
        189–93, 196, 200, 202, 228
    doctrine of   18, 76, 133, 152,
        158, 177, 180–211, 215–18,
        220, 224, 231, 233–4, 236–7,
        253, 255–6
    duties of   184–5, 188, 191, 203,
        213, 215, 217, 226–8, 232

War   213, 237
Welfare   175
Westphal, Ken   159, 252
What Is Orientation in Thinking?   13
Will   32–3, 35–6, 65, 67, 69–70,
    72–3, 77–9, 82–4, 88, 94, 96–7,
    99–101, 106–7, 110, 164, 174,
    183, 193, 220, 224–6
Williams, Bernard   239, 257
Williams, Howard   221
Wolff, Christian   9–10, 12, 14,
    27–8, 38, 40, 65, 67
Wolffian   10, 28, 85
Women   12, 253
World/Worldhood   39, 163–4, 179

Zupančič, Alenka   131–2, 134–7,
    139–40, 248–9